SUPERCAT

Thanks

Best Wishes

SUPERCAT

the authorised biography of
CLIVE LLOYD

Simon Lister

FAIRFIELD BOOKS

This book is dedicated to the memory of our daughter
Ondine Mary Beatrice Lister
who knew Summer, Autumn and Winter, but not Spring.
A lily of a day.

Fairfield Books
17 George's Road, Fairfield Park, Bath BA1 6EY
Tel 01225-335813

First published 2007
ISBN 978 0 9544886 7 3

Jacket concept by Simon Lister, design by Niall Allsop
Page design by Niall Allsop

Printed and bound in Great Britain by Midway Colour Print, Wiltshire

CONTENTS

1 The greatest man in the world 7

2 I would have sat here all day for Lloydy 19

3 Crown Street was a cricketing street 24

4 Who is this bespectacled lanky guy? 44

5 You're looking swell, Hubert 59

6 The most important piece of news – and I hear it second hand 75

7 He brought the Prudential Cup to We 86

8 If people mistook this for black power, that was their problem 98

9 Don't call me a legend, an icon, a superstar, then pay me nothing 113

10 We failed, and then we succeeded 130

11 He has taken us to the mountain top. We salute him 143

12 The captain always has to be an hour ahead 161

13 If your country calls, you want to respond 176

14 To be happy, a man has to free his heart from hatred 184

15 We have to change the way we think about everything 188

16 I've never heard these guys say these sorts of things before 201

A brief statistical digest 207

Acknowledgements 210

The Cowdrey 'Spirit of Cricket' Lecture 212

Index 221

CHAPTER ONE

THE GREATEST MAN IN THE WORLD

Saturday 17 June 2006

Lord's on a sunny London Saturday. Salmon pink for the pavilion brick and egg and tomato for MCC members' ties. Served together, they are a famous dish.

Clive Lloyd's tie sports the blue and green stripes of the International Cricket Council. It is a work day; he is the match referee for the one-day international between England and Sri Lanka. One of his first duties is to witness the toss of the coin. He walks through the shady Long Room where his portrait hangs in the corner. He is painted wearing his maroon West Indies blazer while talking to the New Zealander Richard Hadlee and the South African Barry Richards.

Through the little gate he goes and onto the outfield. A walk he has made so many times with a bat in his hand. Before his 126 for Lancashire in the 1972 Gillette Cup final; before his 174 in the county championship two years later; before his best-remembered innings, his 102 against Australia in the first World Cup final in 1975. Nowadays the shoulders roll a little more but he still has that all-the-time-in-the-world gait that is possessed only by sportsmen with supreme self-confidence.

Out in the middle is Duncan Fletcher, the England coach. He is chatting to the commentator Mark Nicholas. While Fletcher talks, he flicks his fingers for an off break, leg break and doosra; maybe he is saying that the England batsmen have worked out a way of reading Muttiah Muralitharan. David Gower is there too, his broadcaster's microphone jammed in his trouser pocket like a pistol. He passes the time with the England captain Andrew Strauss. Next to the stumps at the Nursery End of the ground, Ian Botham stands alone, looking on.

A television technician is on his knees at the crease nearest the pavilion. He holds what looks like a white polystyrene coffee cup turned horizontally and he presses the rim against each stump in turn.

"That's fine," says the voice coming out of his radio. "Next one."

Clive makes straight for his old West Indian team-mate Michael Holding, now a TV broadcaster.

"Hello, Skipper," says the ex-bowler in his melted chocolate baritone.

Clive shakes his hand and bows, a gesture of affection and respect. They talk in a low whisper, easy in each other's company.

After a minute or two the Sri Lankan skipper Mahela Jayawardene arrives, and Andrew Strauss shakes his hand.

"Alright mate, how ya doin'?" says Strauss cheerily. The two players exchange team sheets and Strauss glances at the bottom of the page, perhaps hoping that by some chance it no longer reads M. Muralitharan at number eleven. But it does.

Clive ends his conversation with Holding, approaches the captains and takes the team sheets from them. A television director listens intently into his headphones. Everyone waits, then the director moves sharply towards the wicket.

"Yep. We can do it. Let's go."

Michael Holding fits an earpiece and stands facing the camera, relaxed and ready as if he is once again at the end of his run-up.

Strauss tosses the big brass coin and Clive has to chase it a little as it rolls on its edge in the direction of the Grand Stand. Jayawardene calls. Strauss wins. England will bowl.

. . .

In the umpires' room, on the first floor of the pavilion overlooking the Coronation Garden, the banter is flying. The big Australian umpire Darrell Hair is standing legs astride with his trousers at his knees. He is wearing a formidable pair of white underpants and is doing up the buttons on his light blue ICC shirt. Jokes are made, reputations rubbished and there is much laughter. The third umpire who will sit with Clive and make decisions with the help of a slow-motion replay is Ian 'Gunner' Gould, wicket-keeper, ex-Arsenal reserve goalkeeper and chatterbox. He sets the pace with jovial asides and dressing-room put-downs. He still has a stumper's busy hands, forever rolling up sleeves, reaching for a cigarette lighter, delving into a wash bag for a toothbrush, checking a yellow walkie-talkie, unscrewing the cap on a bottle of water.

For Darrell's partner Nigel Llong, it is a special day. It is his first time umpiring a limited-overs international. He is as lean as his experienced colleague is stout and calmly stretches his hamstrings while staring at the wall.

On a table by the window there are twenty brand new white cricket balls, individually boxed, and twenty old ones, scuffed and green as pond water. Clive unpacks one of the new balls and tosses it to Darrell.

"What's this?" asks the umpire, feigning ignorance.

"It's the match ball," replies Clive. "You might need it later on."

Clive is almost ready. He unbuttons his shirt a little and gives himself a dab of cologne.

"Gaw blimey, 'Oobert" complains Gunner Gould, fanning his hands around as if the room has suddenly filled with tear gas. "I've got to sit next to you all day, remember." He lights a cigarette in self-defence.

"Relax, Gunner," replies Clive. "I want to smell beautiful for the people. Shall we go?"

On the stairs down to the back door of the pavilion, MCC members say hello. Outside, as Clive turns right into the crowded walkway, people look up and realise who it was who just brushed past them.

Clive will oversee the game from a cramped and very warm L-shaped room at the furthest end of the Warner Stand. Already there in his own little booth is Johnny Dennis, the match announcer who has informed the crowds at England games since Clive led the West Indies here in 1976.

He is an actor by profession and is known by one and all as 'The Star'. He does all the home Test matches on behalf of the ECB. "It's my summer season," he quips. "Not Blackpool and Scarborough, but Headingley and Old Trafford."

"Morning, my loves," he says, half cockney, half repertory flourish.

"Johnny my boy," booms Clive. "And how's The Star?"

Gunner sits on Clive's left, in front of four television monitors. The first shows the Sky coverage, with the commentary on low. On top is another screen, an electronic scorecard that the TV commentators see. A third monitor is showing one of the two Lord's scoreboards, and a fourth records the game on videotape; a stopwatch is running in the top left-hand corner.

The ground is nearly full, the sun is shining and the two umpires are making their way towards the square.

"Darrell, Nigel, you can start when you like – and very good luck," says Gunner into his walkie-talkie. Mid-stride, Darrell Hair gives a thumbs up in the direction of the Warner Stand.

Four minutes later, at a quarter to eleven, Steve Harmison delivers the first ball.

"Did we start on time?" asks Clive.

"Bang on, guv'nor," says Gunner.

Do not be fooled by the Billingsgate porter accent and the 'my old man's a dustman' routine; Ian Gould is a clever bloke. And popular too. Last year the members of the Professional Cricketers' Association voted him their favourite umpire. He is fair, uses his authority lightly and, as a former player at Middlesex and Sussex, has seen all there is to see. In the referee's box he is sharp and no detail on the pitch escapes his attention. He is Clive's extra pair of eyes. The jokes are his way of retaining focus.

Gunner puts a piece of gum in his mouth and chews furiously.

"You alright in there, Johnny?" he calls out.

"On top of the world," replies The Star.

10:56:21. There is an injury to Sanath Jayasuriya, hit in the midriff by a fast ball from Steve Harmison. Gunner watches the replay.

"Oh, he's boxed him. Nasty."

Clive makes a note of the time, then asks Johnny and Gunner if they would like one of his mints.

11:05:38. An lbw shout. Not out. "Too high?" wonders Clive.

Gunner studies the TV replay. "Good decision, Nige," he says.

On his computer, Clive logs the unsuccessful appeal and the umpire's decision. As he is typing, Roger Knight knocks on the door and comes in. He is followed by a photographer. "Can we do some official snaps, Mr Lloyd?"

"Is this to prove I arrived?" jokes Clive.

Roger Knight is Secretary and Chief Executive of MCC. Not only does he have to make sure everything runs smoothly today, he also has to entertain guests. Gunner asks him who is in the Secretary's box in the Mound Stand, and Roger pulls out a piece of paper from his suit pocket. He reads from a list of names, each of which is followed by an instant reaction from Gunner.

"Blimey, not seen him for years … Strewth, he's hard work innee? … No, never 'eard of her … Is he still alive? Well, I never!"

The Secretary leaves with a smile on his face.

11:12:07. Jayasuriya is out. Caught behind, trying to steer a wide ball through square cover. Johnny clears his throat.

"The incoming batsman is Mahela Jayawardene," he announces.

Clive makes a note.

. . .

Today is Clive's 178th match as an ICC referee. His first was at Durban on 13 November 1992, the first match that South Africa had played at home since their readmission to the international game. For the first time South Africa fielded a non-white player in their side, Omar Henry, and for the first time a third umpire viewed television replays.

Clive likes technology in cricket.

"When the umpire gets it wrong, some people say, 'Well, it's the rub of the green.' But then the best team doesn't necessarily win. We want to have the best team winning, with the least amount of mistakes possible; that's what the game should be about. If the technology exists to get a close-up on a catch or to show what the ball's hit going down the leg side, we should use it. You can't tell me that the umpire is going to pick up every bat-pad with the naked eye. No man can do it. So sometimes he's going to end up looking stupid. All I would like to do is to stop guys getting exposed and looking bad.

"I like the idea of being able to check a decision with the TV umpire. But it should not be the players who are allowed the referrals, three appeals each innings or whatever, it should be the umpires themselves who get the opportunity. They should be allowed to speak to their colleague who's looking at the screen for these tricky decisions. That way you remove the issue of the umpire's authority being undermined. It's still in his hands."

Clive is tolerant of people making mistakes. He is less tolerant about players who stretch the laws. Technology should be used to expose and punish them. He gives the example of the Test player who scuffed up the pitch in the Faisalabad Test against England in 2005/06 when everybody's attention had been distracted by an explosion at a drinks stall.

"Here's a guy playing in a game, trying to get an unfair advantage. And yet he played on. Anyone who is punished during the game shouldn't be able to take any further part in it. When you get a red card in football, you don't keep tackling and passing, you're off. We should have sin bins at international games. Then we could do away with all this stuff of waiting until the end of the game and handing a guy a piece of paper. We should be able to say, 'Look, you've been reported for swearing, the microphones heard it, the cameras saw you, you're going to miss a session or half a day.' That would pull up a lot of players and captains."

He pauses.

"I think about what my duties are as a referee all the time. I'm a players' person. I don't want to take money off these fellows or ban them, but I'll do it if I have to. I've become a cricket administrator, and my role now is to try to improve the game."

. . .

The door opens silently, but Gunner senses someone behind him. He has a quick look, leans forward in his chair and says in an urgent stage whisper:

"Bloody 'ell, Lloydy, hide the betting slips. It's Arrie."

Standing in the doorway is Arrie de Beer, small but very broad and not to be messed with. Arrie is from the ICC's Anti-Corruption and Security Unit.

"Hello, Arrie. Everything alright?" asks Gunner in a fake-guilty falsetto.

"Hello, Gunner," says Arrie with a slight grin. "What have you been getting up to?"

"A South African with a sense of humour. What a relief," replies Gould.

Arrie smiles tolerantly, and his moustache does a little jump.

Arrie used to be a senior policeman in South Africa; nowadays he is a regional security manager. In official ICC language, he is here today to 'assist the ICC Code of Conduct Commission and the members of ICC in the eradication of conduct of a corrupt nature prejudicial to the interests of the game of cricket.'

In plain English, he is here to stop anybody nobbling the game. And that includes Clive and Gunner.

12:51:37. Paul Collingwood, at backward point, throws to the bowler Sajid Mahmood who runs out Kumar Sangakkara. Sri Lanka are 153 for three.

Arrie says his farewells with a firm double-handed pat on Gunner's shoulders.

When the door is shut, Clive recalls a Test match he played against India in Trinidad in 1982/83. The story goes like this. One supporter bet another that Sunil Gavaskar would score more runs than the West Indian batsmen Gordon Greenidge and Desmond Haynes put together. When India batted, Gavaskar was dismissed for a single and the distraught supporter, assuming his money was taken, paid up prematurely.

"But lo and behold," chuckles Clive, "when I came to the wicket, the score was one for three. Greenidge 0, Haynes 0. This fellow had won his bet after all. But was his friend there to pay out? No way! He'd cleared off to a different parish, taking the man's cash with him."

Out on the square, Upul Tharanga hits Liam Plunkett for another four.

Gunner is sitting with his head resting in his hands, a biro between his teeth like a dog with a bone. He removes the pen and drums his front teeth with it.

"Bloody 'ell, it's 'ot," he says.

Clive takes a sip of lemonade. The game has an orderly feel about it, although he knows from experience that incidents can appear from nowhere.

In January 2003 he was in charge of the one-day international between Australia and Sri Lanka at Brisbane when the Australian batsman Darren Lehmann was run out.

As he reached the dressing room, Lehmann shouted out an obscene curse about the Sri Lankans. The visitors complained to Clive, and he spoke in private to Lehmann. Then Malcolm Speed, the chief executive of the ICC, became involved, and some observers speculated that Speed was frustrated that Clive had not taken the appropriate disciplinary action.

"No," says Clive. "That's not right. The Sri Lankans called me in to say they were unhappy with what Lehmann had said, but they didn't want to make a charge. So I said to them, 'There's nothing significant I can do then.'

"Then Malcolm heard about it and, as chief executive, he can bring a charge if he wants. I couldn't do so after an unofficial complaint because I can't be the policeman and the magistrate. So he brought the charge. It wasn't a case of him intervening above my head.

"Mr Lehmann is someone who's played cricket for so long throughout the world. He's been a state captain and shouldn't indulge in such language. People abhor this kind of behaviour. Cricketers and other sportspeople have a duty to inculcate the right attitude in young people. I believe you don't see colour; I believe you just see other human beings. Provocation is not an excuse. Honesty, integrity and fair play, that's what cricket is all about. Respect yourself, your family, your team and your country."

Out on the square, Tharanga hoists Harmison towards the Mound Stand for another four.

• • •

The hampers in the Coronation Garden have been opened. Men and women sit on car blankets and stand around the big trees, glass in one hand, Marks and Spencer samosa in the other. The Sri Lankan innings is over. England bowled too wide and without direction, and Tharanga scored a hundred. Clive hurries past the picnickers for a word with the umpires and a few quick forkfuls of lamb curry. Soon he is back in his seat.

The Sri Lankans run onto the outfield. Gunner, who misses nothing, calls out, "Johnny?"

"Yes, my old cock?"

"Tharanga's not on the field."

"Right you are, luv."

A few seconds later the Lord's crowd is caressed by Johnny's velvet larynx. Upul Tharanga has been replaced by a substitute fielder.

Apparently he has cramp.

"Looked alright to me when he was hitting the cover off it," muses Clive.

England need 258 runs to win but do not start well. The new captain Andrew Strauss is soon caught behind. Not long after, Ian Bell under-edges a ball onto his stumps. The Sri Lankan fielders stop almost everything that is hit near them. Only Marcus Trescothick looks happy.

"Shot," says Clive as Trescothick slashes square for four to the Grand Stand. "I'd have been proud of that."

16:20:45. The Sri Lankan captain Jayawardene leaps brilliantly to catch Kevin Pietersen at mid-wicket. England are 65 for three.

Straight away, a breathless young television producer from Sky runs in, wearing sunglasses, headphones and a radio bouncing off her hip.

"Is it drinks?" she asks.

"It should be," says Clive.

She radios the director.

The drinks arrive. Clive takes the opportunity to nip to the nearby lavatory.

"I hope I can get this belt undone in time," he says as he pushes past Gunner's chair.

In the hotel that morning, Clive had realised as he unzipped the bag containing his suit, tie and shirt, that he had left his belt in another pair of trousers at his daughter's house the previous evening. Today he has been forced to borrow an ill-fitting replacement from a friend. This has caused his colleagues in the umpires' room much enjoyment, especially Gunner, to whom Clive confessed that he had given his driver, a stranger, £50 to buy him a new belt which he asked to be delivered when the match finished.

"Fifty quid?" hoots Gould. "That'd get me four pairs of trousers. I'll tell you what, 'Oobert, we'll never see that driver again. He'll be legless in a boozer in St John's Wood Road by now."

"Hmm," is all Clive says as he leaves the room.

Gunner pops another piece of chewing gum in his mouth.

"The thing about Lloydy," he says, "and I'm being honest now, is that he is so generous, so trusting, that he would lend you his last tenner. He is the greatest man in the world."

. . .

Gunner is strangely quiet. He has been watching Muralitharan bowl.

The Sri Lankan spinner runs in and, as he delivers another ball, Gunner speaks for the first time in a while.

"Offy."

 Next delivery. "Offy."

The next ball. "Doosra."

He turns to Clive. "You know what," he says excitedly. "I can only bloody read him! Look, he's giving a sign to the keeper!"

Gunner stands up quickly, and his chair squirts away on its wheels behind him.

"It's all in the left elbow," he continues as he demonstrates Murali's run-up in the tiny office.

"What he does is he pops his left elbow out for the doosra as he sets off!"

Clive studies Gunner over the top of the glasses with some scepticism and sucks loudly on his mint.

"Yep," says Gunner sitting down. "I've cracked it. Shall I ring Fletch in the dressing room? Off break!" he predicts triumphantly.

Dalrymple pushes at a Murali doosra that he misreads completely and is nearly stumped.

"Then again, it could be absolute bloody rubbish," reflects Gunner.

Clive fills in his overs sheet, nodding slowly.

It is still very hot in the office and the fans are spinning the warm air around the room. England are batting in laboured fashion and, for a one-day game, the scoreboard hardly seems to be moving. The game is slipping away.

"Oh dear," says Clive to no-one in particular. He studies the field.

Perhaps he sees himself in the middle. Perhaps he is thinking about how thirty-five minutes from Clive Hubert Lloyd in his prime might change the game.

He has left many such innings in people's memories, one-day games that he turned upside down – such as the one in the Sunday League at Old Trafford in July 1981. Middlesex, having scored 218 in their 39 overs, had Lancashire 87 for five. Game over. At least that was the view of Clive's team-mate Jack Simmons when he came out to join Clive at the wicket.

"He said, 'We can win this,'" Jack remembers, "and I replied, 'If you think so, Clive.' In my head I was thinking, 'Can he not read the bloody scoreboard?' It wasn't like he'd got fifty and was in good nick. He only had a dozen.

"'If you think so, pal, I'm with you,' I told him. We needed another 130-odd from 18 overs. 'Tell you what, you get the hundred, I'll get the 30-odd.' And he did. Mike Brearley – you know, England captain, tactical genius, nothing he couldn't work out – was stumped. There were no fielding restrictions and nine men were halfway to the boundary. The ball just kept flying past them."

Among the Middlesex bowlers that day was Simon Hughes, and he was on the receiving end again a fortnight later in a championship match at

Southport, a game that coincided with the wedding of Prince Charles and Lady Diana Spencer:

> Between the time Charles entered St Paul's as a bachelor and emerged as Diana's husband, Clive Lloyd progressed from 0 to 91. I was bowling at him for most of that time, slightly apprehensively at first, until he'd blocked four successive maidens. Just as I was starting to feel I'd got him cornered, he swayed on the back foot and pulled a perfectly respectable ball into some distant allotments. It was as if he were swatting a pesky fly that had suddenly woken him from a mid-morning nap. After that he went berserk.
>
> Being toyed with by someone who looks such a misfit is very humiliating. The loping gait, the round shoulders, the thick-rimmed glasses and the sunhat like a German helmet totally belied Lloyd's awesome power. When he suspended the carnage temporarily to have a drink, I picked up his bat. The handle had six rubbers, the edges were two inches thick and it weighed a ton. It was like wielding a railway sleeper, and from the bowler's point of view, that's what it looked like.

"I liked a nice bat," says Clive, "but it probably wasn't as big or as heavy as people thought it was. The extra rubbers I needed because I have very large hands and without them I used to find that the handle would spin around in my palms when I played a shot."

The bat-maker Duncan Fearnley keeps one of Clive's bats in his house to this day. It is the bat that Clive used to score his century in the 1975 World Cup final. It has four rubbers on it; without them the bat weighs 2 pounds 12 ounces. The rubbers, and the extra inch that was especially built into the handle, completed the balance. It is a thick bat with a lot of wood in it, but for Clive it always picked up beautifully.

"I borrowed his bat once," remembers Jack Simmons. "I played this forward defensive push, and the ball went past mid-off like a bullet. I said to myself, 'No wonder he gets so many bloody runs.' But you had to be able to handle the power. The next over I played back defensively and was caught and bowled. When Clive used it, the bat was like a wand."

• • •

Sri Lanka appeal for a run out. It is close and Nigel Llong draws the shape of a box in the air with his hands. Gunner sits up in his chair.

"Standby B. Mix B," says the black box containing the voice of the television director who is giving instructions to the cameraman.

Gunner studies the slow-motion, side-on pictures from camera B. Once. Then again.

After a moment he presses a switch and speaks into the microphone in front of him.

"That's not out, Mark," he says to the director in the TV truck.

"Load not out," says the director.

A cheer goes up around the ground as the huge screen at the top of the Edrich Stand shows the umpire's decision.

• • •

17:50:17. A rare success for England. Jamie Dalrymple has made 50. But the score is 174 for six and England are some way off the pace.

The producer from Sky bounces back in to the room. Is it OK for them to film the white ball that has been changed? The ball is back in the pavilion with the reserve umpire, Peter Hartley. Clive decides it is OK and off she goes.

Dalrymple hits Dilhara Fernando for four. "Shot, boy," says Clive. "Now if they can get to 210 in the next three overs, they'll be back in the game."

But, soon after, Dalrymple is bowled by Muralitharan. England's last faint chance is all but over. Forty-four needed from 21 deliveries and just the tail in.

"The thing is," says Gunner, "I brought this lad on when I was coach at Middlesex. He's very bright but the problem is this" – he taps Dalrymple's helmet on the TV screen with the end of his biro – "he thinks about what he's doing too much. Me, I never had that problem."

In the next couple of overs England hit just a single boundary. The crowd know that the game cannot be won from here.

Soon there is only one ball left. England need 22 to win. Gunner puts the top back on his biro.

• • •

Clive sits sideways on a chair in the umpires' room. He has a big white towel draped over his shoulder and looks like a Roman emperor. He has seen the scorer – everything tallies – and is in good spirits. Before he has a shower, he uncorks a bottle of wine provided by the Lord's staff.

"MCC claret?" he says out loud to himself, looking at the label and raising the open bottle to his nose. "I think this must be one that Donald Carr left behind."

Lasith Malinga, the bushy-haired fast bowler passes the open door with a towel round his waist.

"Malinga, my man," calls out Clive.

The bowler stops and comes into the room to shake Clive's hand. His other hand takes a firm grip around the towel.

"Hello, Mr Lloyd," he says shyly.

Across the corridor there is a high-pitched yelp as the Sri Lankan wicket-keeper Kumar Sangakkara sits down in a bath full of ice and cold water.

"At least 45 seconds," says one of the backroom staff looking over him.

Murali walks past naked, grinning as usual.

The talk is of the day's events: decisions, right and wrong, taken in an instant and now viewed with that beautiful thing, hindsight. Gunner lights a cigarette before changing into a tracksuit for the drive home. Darrell says he is looking forward to going to the races at Windsor later in the week. Bodies are patted dry. Hair is combed in the mirror. Coat hangers are relieved of their burdens.

On the way to the car park, in one of the less-trodden upstairs corridors of the pavilion, an MCC member in his seventies – blazer, tie and grey slacks – walks towards Clive with a 1971 copy of the *Wisden Cricketers' Almanack*, featuring Clive as one of its five cricketers of the year. Clive signs it, then sets off down the stairs where at eye-level, as the stairs turn, hangs a large framed picture of the 1984 West Indies team. Clive sitting in the middle of the front row. Captain of the only touring team to win a Test series 5-0 in England. A captain who lost just two Test series in more than ten years. Clive heads straight down without a glance.

• • •

In the car park the day's officials, all except Gunner, are clambering into the back of a black people-carrier: Darrell Hair, Nigel Llong and Peter Hartley. Clive is last in and pauses, one foot in, one foot out.

"Oh yes," he says, holding up his grey slacks. "Mr Driver! Do you have my belt?"

"I do, Mr Lloyd," replies the driver, handing over a carrier bag. "Your new belt, your change and the receipt."

"Thank you," says the referee.

"It was a pleasure," says the driver.

CHAPTER TWO

I WOULD HAVE SAT HERE
ALL DAY FOR LLOYDY

Clive Lloyd and I go back a long way – to 1976. I was seven, he was 31. I
was a schoolboy squirt from Shropshire; he was captain of the West Indies.
It was at The Oval on 16 August that our paths converged: my first Test
match and Clive's 58th. I had come to see Alan Knott, Dennis Amiss and
David Steele, but the West Indians – their players and supporters – utterly
threw me off course. In the 1970s rural Shropshire did not really do black
people. The little town I lived in had an Old Times fair in the summer, a
pair of swans on the mere in the next field but definitely no black people.
Yet here they were next to me in the stand, radios on, shirts off, cans open.
They had come to see Roy, Viv and Mikey.

I decided in an instant to defect from England. I went straight to the top
and kept my eye on Clive. He looked as if he was the tallest and, through
my grandfather's binoculars, I could make out his hat, his big glasses and
his big moustache. He was in charge.

Watching the game was a thrilling sensation and gave me perhaps my
strongest childhood memory. That evening, in the back garden of my
grandparents' house in Streatham, I skipped around not with a bat in my
hand but with a drained beer-can full of pebbles collected from the flower
beds. I shook it to the newly-discovered beat.

And that was that. I did not see Clive in the flesh for another thirty
years. When we met, in a hotel off the Shepherd's Bush roundabout, it was
because he had agreed to let me write this book about his life.

"What do you want to say?" I asked him.

"I want to tell people who I am, where I came from and what I believe."

By the time of that meeting in January 2006, Clive had been immersed,
saturated, marinated in West Indian cricket for more than forty years. The
emergency fielder at Bourda against Bobby Simpson's Australians in 1965
had become player, captain, coach, manager, committee man, then – a year

on from our first meeting – he would be brought back once more as team advisor during the World Cup. In times of difficulty he is still the embodiment of what West Indian cricket once was – and what it would like to be again.

This book is Clive's book. It is not so much a record of the cricket matches that he played in; it is more about the man who played in those matches. As Clive says, "If people want to see my scores, my hundreds and my noughts, they can easily look them up on the internet."

• • •

Clive Lloyd had just become a West Indian Test cricketer when he went to Haslingden in the Lancashire league for the 1967 and 1968 seasons, and his eyes were opened to seaming green wickets and the virtues of playing the ball late. Clive became a better cricketer and was all but blown over by the westerlies from the Irish Sea and the warmth of the Lancashire people.

Forty years on, his home is still a few miles from Old Trafford. In one of Clive's sitting-room windows there is a red rose in stained glass. He loves Lancashire, and it is a two-way thing. In 1988, Clive was voted Mancunian of the year, an award which has also been given to Sir Matt Busby and Sir Bobby Charlton. In 2002, all four of the Manchester universities awarded him an honorary doctorate. When the IRA bombed the city's Arndale shopping centre in 1996, one of the huge murals commissioned to cover the damaged shops, and to cheer people up, was a painting of Clive.

"I've admired a lot of people," says Jack Simmons, "but I haven't admired anybody more than Clive Lloyd. He was a delight to play with, and it's a delight to have him as a friend."

Under another Jack, the Lancashire captain Jack Bond, Clive helped to transform the way the county played cricket. Would they have won five one-day titles in four years without the withering power of his middle-order innings? How many lost causes were turned into thrilling victories thanks to Clive's brutal, but almost always orthodox, hitting?

Orthodox and self-taught. No-one coached Clive, and he always played the same way. His World Cup final hundred surprised none of his childhood friends watching in Guyana. "He played exactly like that with us when he was a kid," they say now.

At cover-point, say some who fielded alongside him, he was better than the great South African Colin Bland. His example, they say, changed the way people fielded, not just at Lancashire but throughout the country.

Yet the contribution he will be remembered for above all others, the one that will one day be chiselled on a block of stone somewhere, is that he was the greatest leader the West Indies have known. By the time he retired from Test matches at the beginning of 1985, Clive had been captain of the

West Indies for more than ten years, and he had turned them from losers into world champions. From March 1980 to January 1985 the side lost once. There were 11 straight victories and a record 26 consecutive Test matches played without defeat.

The triumph of his leadership was not primarily a tactical one. With his beautiful fast bowlers and his beautifully fast batsmen, there was rarely any need to out-fox the opposition. His was a captaincy characterised by a profound emotional intelligence. Through his example, his own authority and his inspiration he shepherded his men, who were drawn from territories scattered across the Caribbean Sea; he banished their prejudices and showed them how they could be peerless.

"It was Clive who let us give our best," says Vivian Richards. "He is the calmest man I know. Never bewildered, always in control. He built us into a great team. We always knew he had the ability to lead us and so we trusted him. Because we respected him so much, we were ready to follow this man. It was a complicated thing to bring a West Indies dressing room together. Clive sent a message to the whole region, 'Hey, West Indians can be happy together.'"

Clive's own responsibilities started young with the death of his father in 1959, when he was forced to become his family's provider. The leadership skills were born in those years in Georgetown and, along the way, four people in Clive's life helped those skills to grow.

The first was his mother, Sylvia. She came to Guyana from Black Rock in Barbados when she was six years old. For a time, after the death of her husband, she was bringing up six of her own children alone, as well as several more of her sister's. She was a strong woman – and her roots mean that Clive is half-Barbadian. "Of course he has Bajan blood!" they say in Bridgetown today. "It's obvious! Have you not seen how he drove through mid-on off the back foot!?!!?!"

The second great influence was Fred Wills, the lawyer who was captain of Demerara Cricket Club in Georgetown; he recognised something special in Clive and in his cricket. The third was Berkeley Gaskin, the Guyanese selector who championed Clive in his early hesitant days in the first-class game.

And there was Frank Worrell.

Clive says in a matter-of-fact way, and without any flourish, that his life's work is dedicated to trying to make the West Indies a great cricket team once again. He is a man with a providential streak and believes that he is here for a purpose. And this is it: to continue the work Worrell began.

"I want to do whatever I can to help," he says. "And that's why, whenever the West Indies ask me to come back, I do."

It is an uncomplicated statement of faith, but it would be a mistake to see it as naive. The easy authority and the charm are the soft casing around a tough core of self-belief. "You don't get to the top of the game by being a pussycat," he says.

"Clive had to fight for everything," reflects his old friend Ronald Austin. "I don't think that many people know, even in the West Indies, that though he has a very calm exterior, he has a lot of steel inside. He knew what it was to be near the bottom of a society. If he hadn't made his way in cricket, one wonders what would have happened. His family certainly didn't have the money to send him to university."

Ronald thinks for a moment. "You know, in all the years I've known him, I've never seen Clive Lloyd in a brawl. I can't remember any sort of major misbehaviour, not when he played for DCC, not when he played for Guyana. Now, if you get to your sixties like that, it says something about the way you were brought up. One thing I do remember from the days when I watched him: he was a very quiet young man when the game was on; no noise, very studious, good powers of observation. What became clear later on was that he was able to grasp quickly the implications of certain types of human behaviour. He doesn't miss very much. A lot of people don't understand that. They think that, because he's quiet, he's not seeing or hearing."

Ronald still lives in Georgetown. He is one of the pals that Clive seeks out whenever he returns to Guyana. Clive does not hold court from a suite at the Pegasus Hotel; he natters while snacking from a plastic basket of fried fish and cassava chips at the back of one of the city's little bars. Over a beer, or a rum and coke, or maybe a brandy and coconut water, he will laugh with the men he has known for forty, fifty, sixty years and ask about others who aren't there. The club cricketers, the school mates, the neighbours, the children of the friends of his mother.

The camaraderie is not difficult to understand. Clive Lloyd and his friends are the product of a particular environment, and they grew up in a particular time. Clive was born into the black lower-middle class in the last years of colonial British Guiana in 1944. He came to absorb what they call in Georgetown, for the want of a better term, British Christian values. He gives respect where it is due; he has a fondness for education and the tradition of the teacher. He believes in the commitment to excellence. He doesn't get involved in things that don't concern him, and he observes the requirements of different social circles. The foundation of all this was laid by his schooling and, before that, by his mother.

Clive benefited from the sudden surge of talent in British Guianese cricket. Before the mid-1950s the colony had produced few outstanding West Indian cricketers. Then in a rush came Rohan Kanhai, Joe Solomon and Basil Butcher.

Lance Gibbs, Ivan Madray and Ivor Mendonca. All made their debuts for British Guiana between 1953 and 1958, and all went on to play for the West Indies. That they did so was largely down to Clyde Walcott. Accepting a job with the country's Sugar Producers' Association, he nurtured and developed the cricketing talent on the plantations and in the towns. The teenaged Clive noticed these names and was encouraged to excel in his own game.

One of the Georgetown spectators who watched Clive make his way in local cricket is the academic and cricket writer Clem Seecharan. "He would always entertain you. Sooner or later the short ball would go out of the ground, but there was no ostentation to him at all. He had a great humility which I think was a great strength."

That humility still exists today but is accompanied by a quiet certainty. Clive dislikes dogma and is happy to mix with all types. He has drunk champagne in the riverbank apartment of Jeffrey Archer, and he has prayed in the funeral congregation of the left-wing Labour MP Bernie Grant.

He has been a businessman and a freemason, and at the same time he is preoccupied with social justice. His first job after cricket was with a government-run scheme called Project Full Employ, which taught people skills to find work. There are two buildings called Clive Lloyd House, one in North London, one near Manchester; they are council developments which offer sheltered living for the disabled and for elderly people from the West Indian and African communities.

It is rare to find a photograph of Clive which includes a smile, yet the next guffaw is never much more than a sentence away. He is sensible with money, yet he can be abundantly generous. When he heard of the death of the old retainer, who for years had tended the dressing rooms at the Test ground in Guyana, it was Clive who sent the money that was needed for the funeral.

It is easy to see why people have been drawn towards Clive Lloyd; why he has made friendships from cricket that have lasted decades, why he has been able to tease the best out of men. Discipline and decency informed his captaincy. His lightness of touch freed him to manoeuvre around the big personalities of the West Indies dressing room.

His reward was loyalty: ten years of it from professional men who brought thousands of Test runs and hundreds of wickets and laid them at the feet of the West Indian people. It was a loyalty that made his side the best in the world, the best cricket team there had been. And that loyalty remains to this day.

Last autumn, inexcusably late for an appointment with Desmond Haynes that Clive had arranged, I apologised. "It doesn't matter," smiled Desmond. "I would have sat here all day for Lloydy."

CHAPTER THREE

CROWN STREET WAS A CRICKETING STREET

Friday 17 November 2006

Below the 'Welcome' banner over the front door of the wooden pavilion at Demerara Cricket Club is a sign which says, 'All hats off please'. To the left is another reminder for visitors and members: 'No indecent language'. On the outfield, half a dozen boys bowl at half a dozen batsmen. The wicket-keeper is the whitewashed wall that runs around three sides of the ground.

Inside the pavilion Billy, one of the older, well-respected players, is at the bar. He wants to show off a couple of the youngsters of whom the club is proud.

"Christopher, Richard, get yourselves over here! This one," says Billy, "a very good all-rounder. But he's clever, so he'll probably end up at university. This one," he goes on, pointing his finger, "great opening batsman and leg spinner. Would have been another Clive Lloyd but he's dropped down now, womanising. He's lost his strength."

Everyone at the bar laughs.

Behind them on the back wall is a framed poster of the club's great hero.

"Clive Hubert Lloyd. DCC, Guyana, West Indies and Lancashire. The Supercat."

· · ·

Georgetown, British Guiana. Some time in the early 1950s

On a Sunday there would be no cricket until the afternoon at the earliest. Sunday meant church, then religious instruction, then lunch. On a Sunday Clive knew it was important to be well behaved because a transgression could mean being sent back to church for the evening service.

The Lloyds were an Anglican family, and their parish was Christ Church. Clive's mother Sylvia and his aunt, Marjorie Gibbs, would lead the children from 150 Crown Street, down the road and through Georgetown for the early-morning six o'clock service. Clive, with his stomach rumbling, would follow with his older brother Teddy and his sisters Jean, June, Jacklyn and Elizabeth. Several cousins – Marjorie Gibbs' children – would be there too including Lance, ten years older than Clive and a very promising bowler.

Clive's father would not be with them. "The Lord knows I love him," Arthur would say. "I pray. I don't have to go to church to prove that."

The children and the women would be in their best clothes. Suits for the boys and hats and dresses for the girls. They could have been going to a wedding.

"You know that phrase, 'Render your heart and not your garments to the Lord your God,'" smiles Clive. "Well, Mum made sure we did both."

> *Brightest and best of the sons of the morning,*
> *Dawn on our darkness, and lend us thine aid,*

sang the congregation as the muggy sun warmed up and the first glistening brows of the day were dabbed with a scented hanky.

> *Star of the east, the horizon adorning,*
> *Guide where our infant Redeemer is laid.*

In the pew, Clive would try not to think of the breakfast waiting for him back at Crown Street. He had not eaten because the fast could not be broken before communion. A gulp of water was all he had taken since he woke up. Instead he would look beyond the vicar to the stained-glass window. Christ the Good Shepherd in one panel; in another, Christ with the children.

"The smell of an old woman's cheap perfume on an empty stomach was almost too much," Clive remembers. "I was there trying to be prayerful, but I often thought that I was about to pass out. Oh, that wine and that wafer at communion couldn't come soon enough."

Sylvia would hand her children ten cents in coins for the offertory collection. By the time Clive's donation had reached the basket it may well have diminished to seven or eight cents. That way he would have enough money to buy a coconut biscuit on the way to Sunday school.

"I would break them up and put them in my pocket to nibble in the class. I don't think The Lord minded. I used to think he'd be glad that the church was getting something. After all, eight cents was better than nothing."

With the coconut biscuits and Sunday school finished, only lunch stood between Clive and a game of cricket. On the way home from hearing the stories about David and Goliath or Jonah and the whale, he would look at the house where the Christiani family lived. Ernest, Robert and Harry were the three sons, and all of them had played for British Guiana. Robert had batted for the West Indies against England at Lord's.

Crown Street was a cricketing street and many of the local boys played, usually in the Lloyds' yard. The fence dividing the house from the next-door neighbours had been gradually dismantled by the boys to double the size of the playing area. A pitch was always prepared in between the banana trees and the mango trees, the rubbish had been removed and any weeds that interfered with the path of the ball were dug up.

At 150 Crown Street there were two houses, one behind the other. The family had inherited them from relatives who had moved to America. The Lloyds had more space than most, and some of the property was rented out. Aunt Marjorie's family lived there too.

Clive loved batting in his yard. And he was good too, even against bigger boys such as Richard Hector, who would one day get Len Hutton out for a duck, and another neighbour, Colin Wiltshire. Both would soon play for British Guiana. Clive would be at the crease when his mother came out to sweep around the door, and he would be there when she called him in for tea. "Clive? You still batting?" Sylvia would ask with half a smile.

If he was going well, the only other interruption to his innings would come when Marjorie needed to rest in the afternoon. "You boys, get out of the garden and go home. You're making too much noise. I need to sleep," she would shout from the window. Marjorie worked as a nurse, sometimes through the night, at The Palms, a local old people's home.

Within a couple of years, she would move to America by herself to continue her nursing. She was employed in Brooklyn and would contribute to the income at Crown Street from her salary. Sylvia remained there, acting as guardian to those of Marjorie's seven children who still needed looking after.

"Marjorie was a hard lady who instilled in us that fighting spirit," says Lance Gibbs. "I think I had the same sort of spirit in my cricket. She was the main person behind all that we have achieved."

If Lance's mother needed to sleep and there could be no cricket, Clive might instead help his father polish the big black Buick that sometimes sat on the street outside the house. The car did not belong to the Lloyds; it was owned by Doctor Singh who lived nearby. Arthur was his chauffeur. He was paid to drive the doctor around Georgetown and its outskirts to see patients.

At the weekend Arthur would take Clive in the car and together they would drive to Durban Park, the racecourse in Georgetown. Arthur was friends with some of the jockeys and would take a look at the horses before putting a little money on one of them.

Clive liked the jockeys. In the evening, a couple would often come to the house to sit with Arthur. Lying in bed before he fell asleep, Clive would sometimes hear laughter and the chink of a glass. Once, one of the jockey's gave Clive a present, a horse whip made from balata rubber. It was a kind gift but cricket, not racing, was on Clive's mind.

"We were an inventive bunch of kids," he says. "We couldn't afford proper cricket balls; we had these cork balls but they'd soon go out of shape. So I melted this whip in a pan on the kitchen stove and poured the balata into the concave base of an up-ended brandy bottle and let it cool. When we had two halves we fused them together and had a rubber cricket ball. We'd play with it until it split."

Yard cricket was complemented by coverage of big matches on the Lloyd family radio. The set was rarely turned off and provided entertainment, not always shared, for both the male and female members of the house. Radio Demerara would broadcast hours of programmes from the BBC as well as rather dry colonial government output. Other offerings were more welcome. Sylvia enjoyed *A Second Spring*, the long-running soap opera about Christine and Wade, two lovers whose chaste kisses were regularly interrupted by unlikely calamities that confronted them at every turn.

'Can a woman who has once loved completely ever find true love again?' asked the radio every weekday evening while background crooners sang *Beautiful Dreamer*. 'Can she find … a Second Spring?'

When Christine was not searching for her second spring, there might be a Test match to listen to. Clive would hear the crackle of Christiani and Ramadhin several thousand miles away as the West Indies took on England, New Zealand or Australia. When there was Test cricket in the West Indies, the radio in Crown Street was always hot. The names of the players were well known to Clive, and he had his favourites.

Garry Sobers and the Three Ws: Worrell, Weekes and Walcott. Lance Gibbs. Denis Compton, Colin Cowdrey and Tom Graveney.

The grounds across the islands were also familiar to Clive's ear. The Kensington Oval was in Bridgetown in Barbados. The Queen's Park Oval was in Port-of-Spain in Trinidad. In Jamaica the ground was called Sabina Park and was in the capital, Kingston.

Best of all, there was a Test cricket ground in Georgetown. Bourda.

"We'd get a half day away from school and head there when the West Indies were playing," remembers Clive. "None of us had tickets when we were young but, if you were very quick, it was possible to get what we used to call a 'bird ticket'. By that, I mean we watched the game from the branches of a tree."

The keenest young cricket-watchers, including Clive, took up their spots in one of the saman trees planted outside the walls of Bourda. Rope pulleys were slung up to allow an all-day stay, and food and drinks were hauled up by assistants.

"You didn't want to lose your seat," says Clive. "We would perch up there for hours. As I got older, I was more fortunate because of two things.

My cousin Lance may have been playing himself, and he usually had a couple of tickets to give away. If not, the father of a friend of mine would get us in. He was a gateman and worked the turnstiles. He would make a couple of strategic adjustments to the attendance figures, and then – *click, click* – through the gates and we were watching a Test match for free."

Once inside the ground Clive would often meet a boy he had got to know called Steve Camacho, who was a year younger. During the lunch interval the two of them would take a bat and ball onto the concrete strip on the other side of the outfield and re-enact the morning's play: Everton Weekes heroically defying the snort of Lindwall or of Miller, Sobers taking three quick wickets as the Australian middle order collapsed.

Within a decade or so, the pair would become Test team-mates and, on the concrete wicket of Bourda, a new generation of boys would be hitting tennis-ball drives, this time in the style of Clive Lloyd.

· · ·

When Clive was born on 31 August 1944, he became one of the hundreds of millions of subjects of the British Empire. British Guiana was not a Caribbean island like Jamaica or Barbados, it was on the north coast of South America. To the west was Venezuela, to the east Suriname, then French Guiana. The four northern countries acted as the windbreak for the vastness of Brazil and took the first breezes from the Atlantic Ocean.

Clive Lloyd speaks English because the British finally took control of Guiana during the Napoleonic Wars in the first dozen years of the nineteenth century. Had history been played out slightly differently, he could instead have spoken Dutch, or possibly French or Spanish. These European powers had squabbled over Guiana, a country of great forests, wide rivers and the mythical wealth of *El Dorado,* for two hundred years. It was the Dutch, in the 18th century, who used their ingenuity and experience to become the first Europeans to get something back from the land. They saw potential in the soil of the country's coastal strip for growing the cash crops of the day: coffee, cotton and sugar. They were the overseers, though, not the workers. The work was done by black slaves, kidnapped from West Africa, then sailed across the Atlantic.

Clive's ancestors.

Two million slaves were brought to the Caribbean by the British from the 17th to the 19th century. The French brought another million and a half; a further million were brought by the Dutch. By 1820, slaves made up about 96 per cent of the population in the colony of Demerara in Guiana. Their lives consisted almost entirely of work. Twelve hour days, six days a week. Cutting, digging, stoking the furnaces that heated the juice from the cane. Violent punishments such as floggings, beatings and imprisonment in stocks or the treadmill were commonplace.

"When I was growing up," says Clive, "we read very little about all this in the text books. We did English history. Trafalgar. The Hundred Years' War. The Battle of Hastings. I think we were starved of a lot of information.

"When I think of slavery, I don't particularly think of these big guys like William Wilberforce, or even the wonderful people like Toussaint L'Ouverture or William Dubois. My mind always returns to the slaves themselves, who suffered so much and fought so hard before they got anything like freedom. Imagine what they saw. The daily sights of people beaten, raped, mutilated, hanged, burned. The traumas the children must have witnessed. People must know that the black person has suffered. Just as I am grateful to the past cricketers, I feel gratitude for my ancestors who endured so much when they arrived in the West Indies.

"Today things have changed a lot, of course. We have black MPs, black senators, and we have Barack Obama, who has the credentials to be the first black president of the United States. But a lot has happened to us over the years. When I was born, my culture had already been taken away. I should be sitting here speaking some West African dialect or something, but what language do we have? We don't have the language of our ancestors. Slavery happened, and I've lost my culture. I shouldn't have a British name; it should be African.

"Now in Guyana the Indians and the Chinese, who were the immigrants of the 19th century after the abolition of the slave trade, were able to retain some of their past, they brought their culture with them, but we lost everything. We suffered a lot. So it's unsurprising that, even now, there are people who are still bitter."

When Clive was growing up in the Georgetown of the 1950s he had few role models to inspire him. The black actors he saw in films were maids and chauffeurs. There were was one exception though.

"I was a teenager when I saw *The Defiant Ones* with Tony Curtis and Sidney Poitier. I loved the way Poitier strutted when he walked; in the same way that I loved the way Garry Sobers walked to the wicket, the way Wes Hall marked out his run-up. These things influenced me because these men were saying, 'We're on our way up'. Seeing those things was as important to me, as influential and memorable as seeing our flag go up for the first time or seeing a black prime minister in the Caribbean. They showed that we were moving somewhere. My ancestors, Garry's ancestors, Wes's ancestors, they all came from Africa. My great hope is that the countries where these people were taken from will one day become great cricketing countries.

"What has the fact of slavery done to me? It has made me a giver, a helper. It's a fact that I am the consequence of a great struggle and the end result is that I have a soft spot for those people who are less fortunate. You cannot just go through life taking. My life and my experiences have been overwhelmingly positive, but things have still happened which make you wonder what other people think of you because of your colour. When I retired from cricket and set up a business I had almost all of the capital and it was a very healthy proposition, but I had to go to four banks before I was able to arrange the finances. Now, this is a small example, but if I had these problems when I was fairly well known and well established, what do other guys have to cope with who haven't had the advantages I've experienced?"

He offers a resigned smile.

"I was coaching cricket in the townships in South Africa one time and the boys I was teaching started giggling. I said to the other coach, 'What's the joke?' and he replied, 'They want to know how come you're their colour but you can't speak the language.' I said, 'Tell them that if they have a day to spare, I'll be able to explain it.'"

* * *

The plantation owners were still kings in the twentieth century, controlling most of the industry – including the tobacco plant in Georgetown where Clive's mother worked as a young woman. She left her job to get married, and she stayed at home to bring up her family.

By the time Clive was seven, he had left his first school, Saint Ambrose, and was a pupil at Fountain, which was run by the African Methodist Episcopal Church. One of the school's greatest attributes was that it stood on the street at the back of Demerara Cricket Club. DCC was not the biggest club in British Guiana – that was the Georgetown Cricket Club which played at Bourda – but it was one of the oldest. This was where Lance bowled his off breaks with such promise. It was also the club of Maurice Fernandes who, at Bourda in February 1930, had captained the West Indies to their first victory over England.

DCC was the cricket club of Georgetown's black lower-middle class. Just as GCC was the preserve of people with lighter complexions, mostly whites and Portuguese, whose genes – and authority – had been handed down by their plantation-owning ancestors. Cricket in British Guiana in the 1950s reflected the rest of Guianese society. The lines between different social groups were firmly scored and rarely merged. East Indians played for EICC; the Chinese played for the Chinese Sports Club. These divisions added intensity to the interest of the cricket-watchers of Georgetown. It was not unusual for weekend matches to draw a crowd of a thousand. People would cycle from twenty miles away to sit on the boundary edge to watch club cricket. The standard was high, and Test players were often in the teams.

"I was an associate member at DCC," says Clive. "I couldn't join as a full member because I was under 16. I got my little membership card for a dollar or something. We weren't allowed to bat in the nets, of course. Batting was for men, but we occasionally bowled a bit."

What was allowed all afternoon was fielding. "I was desperate to stop the ball and be noticed by the senior players," says Clive. "I think that is where my love of fielding came from."

Other duties included working the scoreboard on match days, helping out with the teas and running on with drinks. But occasionally, in front of the pavilion, he would hold a bat and be thrown a few balls by one of the players. And gradually he began to absorb the rhythms of good club cricket. He noticed field placings, he saw how a bowler gripped the ball, and he looked on and noticed the camaraderie of the dressing room. He wanted one day to share in it.

He grew taller and started making runs in school cricket. He batted left-handed and bowled with his right. "I really don't know how it happened like that, it just felt right." He thinks he was about ten when he first noticed that he had some talent for the game.

There were other sporting distractions. He played football, an all-knees-and-elbows inside-right, and brought athletics trophies home to Crown Street. The 100 yards. The 440. The hurdles were no obstacle.

Clive also took a passing interest in weightlifting. Mr James, who was of Chinese origin, lived a few doors away and his son was a friend. In one of the rooms there were dumb-bells, benches and the odour of hard graft. "Mr James was a big guy and he was pretty fit," says Clive. "Fellows used to come to his house from the Guiana Weightlifting Association, and his son and I took it upon ourselves to become their junior section."

Perhaps it was the confidence brought on by developing his muscles that led Clive to try to break up a fight between two boys on the way home from school one day. He took a blow to the right eye with a ruler, and his vision never recovered. He could no longer pick up important details on the blackboard or the scoreboard. Eye-drops from the optician did not work, and Clive was told that he would need to wear glasses. He was determined that it would not stop him playing cricket.

"I knew my eyesight was not as good as other people's. But in some ways it worked for me. I was never going to have twenty-twenty vision. Other players used to say, 'Who's this fellow coming in with glasses who can't see?' They thought they were funny until I exploded with a few cuts and drives. I think I did a lot for spectacled people! I never let it worry me. I knew that once I stayed at the crease a while I was good enough to conquer anything that came to me."

At school, on the outfield of DCC, in the yard he took on anything that came to him. But when Clive was twelve, playing his favourite sport almost cost him his life.

• • •

It was during a game in the garden that Clive climbed over a fence made of greenheart wood to fetch the ball. The fence snapped and a splinter lodged in his right shin. His mother disinfected the wound, and Clive ran back outside to carry on with the cricket. All seemed to be well until he woke one morning later that week.

"I was hazy and grey, and everything looked different. My mother took me to the doctor and they admitted me to hospital right away because my jaw was beginning to lock."

Clive had been infected by the bacterial disease tetanus, and became seriously ill. He fell into a coma.

"They just caught it in time. Boy, it was traumatic. My skin started peeling away. I became much taller and thinner over the weeks. Even now I still have this involuntary shudder sometimes because the tetanus gave me spasms."

"In the ward," remembers Clive, "there was this clock, and anybody that was put under the clock died. I was in that bed, and my mother said, 'Uh-uh. Move him away from there!' She didn't sleep for weeks until I was out of danger. I was close to death and couldn't eat. They used to feed me through a tube, but the doctor said I was a strong fellow – and I pulled through. Another couple of days, though, and I could have been out of it."

Clive spent about six weeks in Georgetown Hospital. By the time he went back home, he had grown several inches and his shoes no longer fitted. He had also lost a lot of weight.

The illness had, for the first time, revealed in Clive a fighting spirit – and a determination to overcome setbacks. Despite missing several months of school, he passed his leaving exams. In the pew at Christ Church, Sylvia offered a prayer of thanks for her son's safe return. She was unaware that, before long, tragedy would engulf the whole family.

• • •

Clive had witnessed the decline of his father's health since he was a young boy. From time to time he would be frightened by the sight of Arthur leaning over a basin with blood pouring from his nose. The doctor warned that Arthur's condition was not helped by the amount he drank.

"I was very traumatised. I mean, it happened often and every time he would be admonished about the alcohol. He used to go at it pretty heavily with his brothers, but in Georgetown in the 1950s a man's options were limited. You could go to a dance or to the cinema, but there was not a lot to do."

Late one night in 1959 Arthur got out of bed to shout at the family dog howling in the yard. It was the last thing he did. Clive was woken to be told that his father had died. In the middle of a storm, he had to cycle through the Georgetown dark and rain to tell the extended family.

"I was 14, and it hit me that there was nobody else. My mother was there, of course, but there was no man."

The death of his father forced Clive to be a man while he was still a boy. Back-yard cricket would now have to come second to looking after his family. His elder brother Teddy was living in England, and Sylvia didn't work. Arthur's job had brought in the family money; now that would have to come from a new source. Although he was a scholarship boy at Chatham High School, Clive would have to leave for work when he was 17.

"It was a rough, rough scene," he recalls. "My life then was not easy. After my father died I knew that I had to be somebody. I had to make sure that my mother was okay and my sisters got a good living and they were brought up right and always had food and school clothes and education – which I did with all of them. I saw that as my role, the father role. I suppose later on that came out in cricket, in leading people. I wasn't used to making any real decisions, and most of the decisions I made, I made on my own because I only had my mother. I didn't have a father to say, 'Clive, do this, do that.' I'd have loved that guidance, but Dad was no longer there."

The job Clive found was as a clerk working for the Department of Health at Georgetown Hospital. For 80 Guianese dollars a month, Clive administered the paying of the nurses' salaries and worked for the out-patients' department.

"I learned a lot about illnesses and what caused them. No computers, of course, so we had all the information on charts, which we read all the time, to keep track of the patients who had on-going treatment. I was forever going into this dungeon of a room to look for a particular set of patient records, only to find that the guy on the desk had spelt their name wrongly. You could spend hours down there for nothing.

"Once I did a stint as the stores clerk, responsible for all the hospital food. I hadn't been there long when a team of auditors came in. After they'd done all their sums they approached me and said with great solemnity, 'Lloyd, you're 900 eggs short.' I was horrified and was left fearing that I'd have to make up the difference out of my pay packet at ten cents an egg. I think in the end one of the managers took pity on me and sorted it all out."

With his school years foreshortened and a wage helping at home, Clive could at least spend some of his free time playing cricket with a clear conscience. In many ways he was still a boy but, as in other areas of his life, he played cricket with a touch that was beyond his years.

Gordon Rohlehr, now a professor at the University of West Indies in Trinidad, was a friend and a teenaged opponent.

"Rupert Roopnarine, who is now a politician and poet in Guyana, had a concrete strip in his yard. Rupert's place was close to DCC. Clive bowled very high, looping leg spin with bounce and turn. He was already a superb fielder and was known for hitting the ball a long way. But it is the bowling that I remember most. At the time I don't think anybody believed that he would play for the West Indies, except perhaps Clive himself. He was seen as having the potential for being a very good club cricketer – perhaps a player for British Guiana."

Even while he had been at school, Clive had been to a trial for the Guianese colts side. He recalls how a teacher, when she heard about the game, scoffed, 'You'll never make a living from cricket.'

If Clive received little encouragement from his teachers, the support he received from the captain of DCC more than made up for it. Fred Wills would one day become Guyana's Foreign Minister and twice address the General Assembly of the United Nations. In the late 1950s he was a solicitor working in Georgetown, but was already highly regarded by his fellow club cricketers.

His official government portrait still hangs behind the bar at DCC today. In a pin-striped suit and a cravat, he holds a cigarette high in his right hand, looking like a man who knows his own worth.

Fred was DCC. Being a member of the club meant subscribing almost to a state of mind, a condition. The club was like a family, and cricket was played the DCC way. Fred's arms stretched wide enough to embrace all the players.

When his side played cricket, Fred loved to attack. At the start of every game the first-eleven scorer, a man called Monty, would go to the score box or the table with his counterpart. As the first ball was being bowled, Monty would shout out, "Attack! Attack! Attack!" From this tradition Clive's own batting style grew.

Fred Wills became an important influence in Clive's life. From him, Clive learned to be professional, disciplined, to persevere for what was worth having. He would spend a lot of time in the public gallery of the city's court, watching Wills at work. And of course the skipper-solicitor filled another role too.

"I had no father, so I held on to other people. When I was still at school, Fred would sit down and chat with me or give me extra lessons free of charge when I was doing my homework. I was very grateful for that. This man had one of the best brains in Guiana. Later, when we played at DCC, Fred would say, 'Whoever makes a hundred today will get 30 dollars.' Now, when I was a kid, that would pay my school fees for quite a while. Fred was the kind of guy that, even if you got near and got out, he'd still pay the money. He looked after me.

"I remember an instance when I was slightly older," continues Clive. "I was planning to go to a night club with the rest of the fellows and he said to me, 'No way, you've got more ability than them. Here's 20 dollars; take your girlfriend to the cinema instead.' He was a very good man."

Clive had played just one second division game for DCC, in a competition called the Wight Cup, when Fred Wills picked him for the first eleven. It was a Case Cup tie against Georgetown Cricket Club, and it was to be played at Bourda. There would be no need to rely on the sleight of hand of a friend's father at the turnstile to get the young Lloyd into the Test ground this time. Clive walked in through the main entrance with his bat under his arm. In his bag was a pair of proper cricket boots, borrowed from cousin Lance, that were probably a little too big. It would be the first time in his life that Clive had not walked on to a cricket pitch in a pair of plimsolls.

He made little real contribution to the match and was bowled for 12 by the British Guiana off-spinner Norman Wight, who had three brothers and two cousins who had all played either first-class or Test cricket. Clive played for a bit of turn when Wight came round the wicket but was done through the gate. His memory of the day is that he felt out of his depth, but that it was incredible to play at Bourda.

Clive had barely established himself in the DCC first team when, in August 1961, just before his 17th birthday, he was picked to play in a trial game, from which the district of Demerara would select a side for the inter-county series of matches. 'He contributed a sound 30,' the *Daily Chronicle* reported, and the following March he made his first appearance for Demerara, scoring 50 against Berbice. He was starting to make his mark, and within weeks he had hit his maiden century, in just over three hours, for DCC against the East Indian club. Yet he was still a long way from attracting the interest of the British Guiana selectors. Even the next year, 1963, when he was always near the top of the Case Cup averages, his name attracted little positive comment in the *Chronicle*.

A commonly held local view was that the best cricketers did not come from the black Georgetown clubs such as DCC and British Guiana Cricket Club. They came from GCC or from eighty miles or so down the coast in Berbice, where Basil Butcher, Joe Solomon and Rohan Kanhai all played. When the district of Demerara beat Berbice by an innings in November 1963, the *Chronicle*'s cricket correspondent – ignoring Clive's season of heavy scoring – felt able to write that 'Berbice still has the best potential'.

"People thought that anybody coming from my club, with the odd exception such as Lance Gibbs," says Clive, "did very little. For example, 'Bruiser' Thomas used to make a lot of runs, but he was known as a 'Saturday-afternoon batsman'.

"So I came up in that same mould and was viewed with similar expectations. I suspect that the *Chronicle* writer was one of those who thought that only Berbice players were going to make it. There was probably a bit of bias running through his column. But, as a young man, I didn't recognise that. Whenever you made runs you wanted to read what the *Chronicle* said about you. As I got older, I got smarter."

In Georgetown, however, Clive already had a reputation. His friend Ronald Austin remembers a rival of Clive's who was certain that he would get the better of him with his leg spinners one weekend.

"This fellow rode around on his bicycle all week before the game," says Ronald, "telling anyone who would listen, 'I'm gonna get Lloydy, I'm gonna get him!' Sure enough on the Saturday Clive came yards down to him and was beaten in the flight. The wicket-keeper should have stumped him but he messed it up." Ronald is now laughing loudly. "After that it was sheer murder. Clive destroyed this guy. If you didn't get Lloydy when you should have, forget it."

Clive's power also earned him his first nickname: Slogger. It originated as an insult and no-one said it to his face. "There you have it!" barracked a man from the boundary edge one Saturday as he watched Fred Wills lead DCC onto the field. "A lawyer, a slogger and nine hooligans!!"

He may have been a wit, but he was wrong. Clive was not an unrefined heaver of the ball, but he was a very forceful hitter. Across the road from DCC, near the main gate, was a clinic. It was often the first solid fixture to put up resistance to a Clive Lloyd straight six. Spectators and small boys regularly spent part of their Saturday afternoon searching for cricket balls in its grounds. People who watched Clive in those early years say now that he drove exceptionally straight, right down the ground. Long-on and long-off may as well have not been there.

• • •

In the years that Clive was establishing himself as a club cricketer of some promise, his country was experiencing substantial difficulties as it sought to move away from its colonial past. As early as 1953, the British had suspended the constitution and sent in troops because they feared that Guiana's elected administration was too sympathetic to communism. A decade later, the split in Guianese politics – with two parties broadly representing the differing interests of the black and Indian communities – had created extreme racial tensions. In 1964 a strike by mainly Indian sugar-cane cutters, who were replaced by mostly black labourers, set off a savage outbreak of murders, reprisals and yet more murders between the two racial groups.

Soldiers patrolled throughout Georgetown, including Crown Street. Clive woke up one morning to see through the window that the next-door neighbour's house was surrounded by military vehicles.

"Nobody went to school," remembers Clive. "It was quite frightening. People got shot."

When Arthur had been alive, he would often lean on the fence to the left of his front door, passing the time with his Indian neighbour. He never saw colour and neither did Clive. The trouble made no sense to him.

"In Georgetown I was surrounded by Indians. I went to school with them, played cricket with them. I don't believe that the Guyanese are racist. Not even during those riots. I think it was more about people wanting to find themselves a little better off than the others. We didn't know anything about race; it was not something we were worried about. If you had an Indian friend, you had an Indian friend and that was that. When I worked at the Department of Health, many of the doctors were Indian and others were Chinese. It wasn't a problem."

• • •

Early in 1964, when he was 19, Clive was asked to play in a trial for the British Guiana side, a game that was part of a complicated selection process. It was important to do well at the national trials, but even if a player put in an outstanding performance, he could lose out during the round of lobbying by club officials that was riddled with political scheming. It was barely different on the pitch.

"A team-mate of mine, Leslie Amsterdam, offered me some advice at the trials," says Clive. "He said, 'Look, get a hundred, but whatever you do, don't run until the ball passes the in-fielders.' The competition was so fierce that the guy batting at the other end could easily be trying to run you out. I've heard a saying which goes, 'The batsman's your friend, so run like a deer.' Well, at the trials you needed the opposite philosophy."

Clive passed the test on the field. Now he waited.

"We would all stand around outside," remembers Clive, "and the selectors would make their decisions. Eventually, when they had their team, they would come and read it to us. It was just like waiting for the results of an exam. Had I passed or had I failed?"

He had passed. Clive was about to play first-class cricket for his country.

The regional tournament of the day was made up of only four teams: British Guiana, Trinidad and Tobago, Barbados, Jamaica. Guiana's first fixture was against Barbados in Bridgetown, and Clive was not selected for the final XI. The side was built around the middle order of three experienced Test players, Kanhai, Butcher and Solomon, as well as the off spin of the fourth international, Lance Gibbs. The match ended in a draw. It was not until three weeks later that Guiana played their next game in the competition, against Jamaica at Bourda. Rohan Kanhai had flown to Bombay to play an exhibition match, and Clive was picked in his place; he was to bat at five. His confidant from the trials, Leslie Amsterdam, opened the innings, partnered by another batsman making his first-class debut, Roy Fredericks. Joe Solomon and Basil Butcher were at three and four, and the captain Clyde Walcott came in at six.

Then there was the medium pacer, Carlyle Miller, followed by three spinners. Indal Persaud to bowl off breaks, Lance Gibbs and the slow left-armer Rex Collymore. The wicket-keeper Geoff Murray batted at eleven.

'The weather was ideal for cricket and the ground, which was fairly scant before lunch, picked up considerably and towards the end the crowd was reasonably handsome,' reported the *Daily Chronicle*. Its correspondent watched British Guiana score 346 and then bowl out Jamaica for 142 and 143 to win by an innings. Clive's contribution was just 11, caught by Teddy Griffith off Lester King.

'Persaud and Collymore, two of the newcomers, played a great role in the hosts' victory,' was the verdict. 'But the same cannot be said for Clive Lloyd who had a bad match. He only got eleven runs, put down two catches at silly mid-off – both pretty scorching, yet offerings he would normally have accepted – and a possible one in the slips which would have gone to hand had he dived forward instead of sideways.'

For the final game of the season against Trinidad and Tobago, Rohan Kanhai returned and Clive was dropped. He had played first-class cricket, a great advance in his career, but the season had a frustrating feel to it. Those three Guianese Test batsmen – Kanhai, Butcher and Solomon – were such an obstacle. If they kept batting well, how could Clive hope to replace one of them? Would he too be remembered only as a 'Saturday-afternoon player'?

"I knew I had a long way to go," says Clive, "but the opinion of people such as Fred Wills was so important to me. Even if I had trouble convincing myself sometimes, Fred kept telling me I had a future."

The season ended and all Clive could do was to keep scoring Saturday-afternoon runs for DCC, especially as there would be no regional first-class cricket in the 1964/65 season because the Australians were visiting to play a Test series.

Everyone knew that these matches were being contested for the title of unofficial world champions. Australia had kept the Ashes since defeating Peter May's England side in 1958/59; the West Indies, under Frank

Worrell, had beaten England in 1963. Now they had a new captain, Garry Sobers.

The series began well for the West Indies with a victory in Jamaica. The second Test in Trinidad was drawn and the sides flew to British Guiana, where Australia would play the national colts, then the full British Guiana side before the third Test.

Clive was in the Guiana side. It would be another chance for him to show his talent as a young batsman but, playing alongside his friend Steve Camacho, he scored only 2 and 17 – although there was a hint of the attacking play for which he had already become known:

'Lloyd's first scoring stroke was a six, smack in the pavilion off a rank long hop from Philpott,' noted the *Daily Chronicle* in the second innings. 'It was a hook stroke that had everything in it.'

It was at this game that Clive experienced a brief taste of cricket at all but the highest level, but he also experienced the rigid reality of Guianese society.

"Rex Collymore and myself were in the clubhouse," remembers Clive. "We were standing in there and this fellow, Ken Wishart, made us leave because we didn't have seats. Can you believe it?"

Ken Wishart was the President of Georgetown Cricket Club. He was a man of considerable influence in both Georgetown society and Georgetown cricket. The local joke went like this: 'Our Father, Wishart in Heaven …'

Collymore and Lloyd were sent on their way, but very soon Clive had engineered a pleasing postscript to the incident.

Within a week he was at Bourda again, running out in his whites during the Test match. Not to play, just to deliver a message from the dressing room to the field. He had been chosen as the emergency fielder; it was nothing of consequence but Clive was hoping that the West Indies selectors saw him as a cricketer with a future after all.

"I saw Ken Wishart in the pavilion. I caught his eye and said with a smile, 'Can't move me now!'"

It was a satisfying moment, but nothing compared to the feeling he got from being in the West Indies dressing room.

"It was an incredible experience. Frank Worrell was there as the manager. Garry was there. I got a glass of water for Rohan Kanhai. You know, a couple of years previously I'd been watching these guys play here from a nearby tree."

• • •

The experience of being so close to Test cricketers made Clive even more certain that this was the life he wanted. The answer to living it was runs, runs and more runs. He did not own a copy of the 1966 *Wisden Cricketers'*

Almanack but, if he had, his attention could well have been caught by the preview of the new Caribbean season.

The regional tournament was due to be revised in the early months of 1966; ten matches were to be played in Barbados, Trinidad, Jamaica and the Windward and Leeward Islands for the Shell Shield. 'If any surprising choices were made for the tour of England it was expected that the selectors would find the talent in this tournament.'

Some good performances from Clive for British Guiana in this new competition could give him a chance of being one of those 'surprising choices'.

There was no place for him in the team for the first game against Trinidad but he was told at the hotel, the night before the match in Barbados, that he would be in the side.

He was number six in the order. Steve Camacho and the other opener, Vince Mayers, both got out quickly to Charlie Griffith but Kanhai, Butcher and Solomon took the total on. It was 183 for four when Clive walked out.

He faced Garry Sobers and played forward and across to a ball that cut back. There was a cry from wicket-keeper and bowler. The ball had hit Clive on the pad. He looked up to see the umpire's finger high in the air. He was lbw for a duck.

"Fred Wills told me later that he was in Georgetown," says Clive, "and he bumped into this fellow that everyone knew called Waterloo. He was an after-school teacher but was just as well known as a sort of local critic. He said to Fred about my dismissal, 'Your boy Lloyd shuffled, shuffled like a pack of cards.'"

Elsewhere in Georgetown, Ronald Austin was greatly depressed by Clive's first-innings failure. After reading about it, he had gone round to Crown Street to see Sylvia who told him that some malicious folk had already let it be known to her that her son's opportunity was now gone, telling her that Clive was not good enough and would never make it after this failure.

A different conversation was overheard by Clive in the dressing room at the Kensington Oval, where Sobers was sitting with the British Guiana manager, Berkeley Gaskin.

"Oh Berkeley, I noticed your boy didn't make any runs today."

"Yes, I know. But let me tell you two things, Garfield. First, he's not my boy, but a boy that I like. And secondly, this match has another innings."

Like Fred Wills, Berkeley Gaskin had looked out for Clive when he was forced to grow up so quickly after his father's death. He too was from DCC. He had played two Tests for the West Indies, then managed the side on the 1958/59 tour of India and Pakistan as well as on the 1963 tour of England. His wife Winifred was a government minister and once saved Clive from being sent into the Guianese interior to work for the Department of Health. Berkeley thought it would never do, especially as DCC would have lost one of their best batsmen. A word in his wife's ear meant that the transfer was quietly forgotten, and Clive remained both at his desk and at the crease in Georgetown.

"Berkeley was a special guy," remembers Clive. "I always thought he was very sophisticated. He had this aristocratic laugh – *ho, ho, ho!* – and the words flowed. Berkeley loved the English language and, when he spoke, you were just waiting for the fine phrasing. 'It would be remiss of me,' was one of his sayings. Lovely phrasing."

In the face of Clive's meagre first-class batting record – 11, 2, 17, 0 – Gaskin still had faith in him and had told Sobers so. That commitment made Clive determined to give his mentor something to be pleased about before the game ended.

All British Guiana could hope to do was to save the game. Sobers had taken six wickets in dismissing them for 227, and he had scored 204 in Barbados' reply of 559. The openers were again dismissed promptly in the Guianese second innings, then Basil Butcher was out for nought. Joe Solomon and Rohan Kanhai put on 54 but, when Kanhai was bowled, the score was 86 for four. It was Clive's turn to bat.

"As I walked out, I was thinking that this may be the last time I batted for British Guiana, so I just tried to play as professionally as I could."

Against the express pace of Charlie Griffith and the nous of Garry Sobers, Clive dug in. First defence, then consolidation, then attack. With Berkeley Gaskin beaming in the dressing room, Clive made his first first-class century. It was 22 February 1966.

"I was mentally drained," says Clive. "Most of the runs had come against a couple of bowlers that had demolished England in 1963. At the time it was the most important innings of my life, and the actual hundredth run did come as a welcome and unexpected surprise – overthrows from Conrad Hunte."

Clive raised his bat to acknowledge the crowd's appreciation. The century had, at the very least, assured his selection for the rest of the tournament and, with a fair portion of his runs coming off the captain of the West Indies, the innings might help him when they chose the side to tour England. Clive was delighted for himself but also for Berkeley Gaskin.

"He was cock-a-hoop because, when I was a youngster, he always thought I had the qualities to be a good player. He was one of those inspirational people. I have a great respect for him because when I overheard his line about there being a second innings, I said to myself, 'This person thinks that I'm good.' It gave me that little extra when I needed it and helped me believe that I was a good player. I will always be grateful to him."

There was better to come for Clive. Later that month in Jamaica he made 194, the highest score he had hit in any form of cricket. He finished the season with 40 and 3 not out in the victory over the Combined Islands on St Kitts. He was the leading batsman from British Guiana with an average of 86.

There had even been a change in tone by the *Chronicle* during that last game. In its Sunday edition on 6 March, the headline read, 'Lloyd is a cert for W.I. Team'. Inside, the two cricket correspondents, Cedric Wiltshire and Charles Chichester, wrote a piece about those players whom they thought would play in England in a couple of months. It took the form of a conversation:

WILTSHIRE: *Well Chuck, if Clive Lloyd is not among the West Indies selectees to tour, I'll want to know why.*

CHICHESTER: *Clive Lloyd must be considered the find of the Shell Shield Series. So fine a player had to get going sometime.*

Within two days, the *Chronicle*'s confident headline was utterly out of date. Clive had been left out. He would not be going on the West Indies tour of England in 1966.

"Oh boy, I was bitterly disappointed," he says. "I think a lot of people that season, fellow players, expected me to get in. It was quite a shock."

Clive did not know it, but his omission had very little to do with cricketing talent. He had just become the latest victim of the West Indies' unique selection procedure.

The often self-defeating system had a habit of choosing players with only one eye on individual skill; the other was fixed on the selectors' own territorial loyalties. Except for the cricket team, there was no such thing as the West Indies, so each territory wanted its own players in the side as a symbol of well-being and pride. When the West Indies were losing, the parochial squabbling became worse. When they were winning, nobody cared which island or territory the stars came from.

The men who chose the 1966 side were the former captain John Goddard, the chairman of selectors Jeffrey Stollmeyer, Gerry Gomez, Garry Sobers, Frank Worrell and Berkeley Gaskin.

According to Sobers, Worrell did not want the Barbadian opener Robin Bynoe included in the party. He wanted the Jamaican, Easton McMorris.

'Berkeley Gaskin agreed with him. Jeffrey, being a Trinidadian, voted with him and suddenly Bynoe was out of the tour.

'It was absurd. I smelled a rat,' Sobers would write years later. 'I kept my mouth shut and waited to see what other surprise was lurking for me around that table. Sure enough, it was waiting in the shape of the promising young batsman Clive Lloyd. Gaskin had voted yes for a youngster who had done well and clearly had a good future. But when it came to me, I dug my toes in and said no.

'I said outright that I was not going for Clive Lloyd; I said that I preferred to go for Rawle Brancker. I backed it up by telling them to look at Brancker's record batting for Barbados ... An all-rounder of that quality had to take precedence over an inexperienced batsman. John Goddard agreed with me, as did Frank. Now Berkeley Gaskin was left out on a limb with no chance of getting his man in the side.

'That is how political it was. It was disgraceful. But I had guessed what was going on. Frank was clever. He manoeuvred Gaskin on to his side but he knew that I was going to get one in somewhere. That's the way it was.'

• • •

At 150 Crown Street the radio was on and the Test match commentary from England filled the room. Clive looked at the clock on the wall. He needed to leave for work at the hospital.

Hunte and Kanhai. Butcher, Nurse and Sobers.
Boycott, Milburn, D'Oliveira.

These were not lines from the sweet cricketing poems that Clive had heard coming out of the set when he was a boy. This was harsh prose. There was a name missing.

CHAPTER FOUR

WHO IS THIS BESPECTACLED LANKY GUY?

The 1966 tour of England was a successful one for the West Indies. They won the series by three Tests to one and Sobers, the captain, played some of his best cricket. He scored more than 700 runs and made three centuries. He took twenty wickets and ten catches. Even if Clive deserved to be there, he was not missed.

"Clive suffered from the way the team was chosen and it was very unfortunate," says Sobers today. "It was one of those times when the process didn't work properly, but the side still did pretty well. I suppose you could say the selectors didn't get it so wrong."

The tour ended in September. Back in Georgetown, Clive knew there would be no first-class cricket in the Caribbean before a side was chosen to tour India and Ceylon at the end of the year. Without batting, he had little hope of getting into the middle order of a winning side.

• • •

When his day at the hospital ended, Clive would pick up his sister Jacklyn from school and give her a lift home on his bicycle. She was good at languages and was learning French, Spanish and Latin. Clive would help her with her homework.

One afternoon they came home to Crown Street, and Clive saw a letter addressed to himself propped up against the radio. It was written on the paper of the Guyana Cricket Board. What Clive read left him feeling a little dizzy. The President of the Board was informing him that he had been chosen to play for the West Indies.

"Oh, how I was elated!" he recalls. "There it was, this letter, with the news that I had succeeded in my ambition. It was so well written, with such enthusiasm, exhorting me to achieve great things, that I had no option but to take up the challenge and do my best."

It was Joe Solomon from Port Mourant along the coast in Berbice who had changed the course of Clive's cricket career. The man who had thrown down the stumps for the most famous run-out in cricket's history, the direct hit that tied the Brisbane Test against Australia in 1960, had turned 36 on the tour of England. He had played in plenty of the first-class games there, but he had not been picked for any of the Test matches. He had decided to retire from international cricket, and a place in the middle order became free.

What a difference the letter had made. Clive's disappointment earlier in the year had been immense. Other players had told him he was certain to go to England, and Clive had allowed himself to daydream about the trip. Now he had a chance to prove to people that he was a player of the highest quality.

"At the time there were those who didn't think I had the skill to be an international cricketer," says Clive. "One thing in particular stays with me. The Guyanese Test player Robert Christiani, who of course lived on Crown Street himself, was asked his opinion of me. And he said, 'Oh, he'll never become a Test batsman.' I heard this and, soon after, I got a big score at Bourda and he was sitting there as I walked off the field. 'There's more to come,' I told him as I passed. You see, people didn't realise that when they said cruel things, they tended to galvanise me into doing well."

• • •

The memories of that first trip outside of the Caribbean are still strong today.

"I went to places that I had only read about: Calcutta, Bombay. I saw Sikhs, Hindus at their temples; I was taking in the way these people lived. This was the real thing. My mother used to make me a curry; now I was getting one from the original country! Rotis and paratha from the place where all these dishes came from. To hear the languages, it was so exciting. But it was startling too. The poverty. I mean that was a real education. There were poor people in Guyana, but this was something else. The tour presented me with my first real opportunity to look at life differently.

"I was overwhelmed too by the Indians' fanatical following of cricket. People I met loved the game. They knew a lot about it, and some of them seemed to have heard of me. I was signing autographs for the first time in my life."

Even though the locals knew who Clive was, the young player thought it most unlikely that they would see him on the pitch during the first Test in Bombay. The middle order of the West Indies side was well known and all but picked itself. At six was Sobers, the captain and great all-rounder, and at five was Seymour Nurse, whom the 1967 *Wisden* called 'a stroke-maker fit to line up with credit beside the likes of George Headley, Frank Worrell and Everton Weekes'. At three and four were two of Clive's senior

Guyanese team-mates, Rohan Kanhai and Basil Butcher, who between them had scored 5,700 Test runs.

On the morning of the game Clive had left his room, which was in the Brabourne Stadium itself, and was taking in the atmosphere. Tens of thousands of people were in the stands, more spectators than he had ever seen at a cricket match. He was expecting to bring on drinks for the players and perhaps do a spot of emergency fielding if needed. The selected eleven had been at the nets, and it was from there that Captain Sobers went to find Clive. He had some extraordinary news.

"Lloydy," he said. "You're playing."

Sobers explained that Seymour Nurse had hurt a finger. Clive would replace him in the middle order.

"I was so excited and the adrenalin was certainly pumping," he says. "First, I was playing alongside some of the guys I had idolised as a youngster, hoping that one day I'd be there and now very suddenly I was. Secondly, these eleven men were known as the world champions."

The boy from Crown Street was playing in a Test match.

• • •

By the afternoon of the second day, Clive was padded up and next in, watching Bhagwat Chandrasekhar bowl. The leg breaks and googlies were fired quickly from a right arm wrenched by polio when Chandrasekhar was a child. The Indians had three other spinners in the side: Venkataraghavan, Durani and Nadkarni.

When Basil Butcher was bowled with the score on 82, Clive picked up his bat and set off for the middle.

"I was terribly nervous to begin with," he remembers. "At first I couldn't read Chandrasekhar. He fizzed that ball and actually bowled at quite a pace for a spinner and so got a lot of bounce."

Clive was uncertain whether to play forward or back and before long had edged a ball to slip – but to his great relief he was dropped.

His second chance gave him heart.

"I decided to get forward to as much as I could and sweep whenever possible."

His strategy worked, his timing improved and, as the afternoon session went on, Clive's score grew. With Conrad Hunte as his partner, the West Indies steadied themselves and looked towards the Indian total of 296.

"Conrad was such a lovely man," says Clive, "and a great cricketer."

Hunte was on his way to making his eighth and final Test century for the West Indies. Earlier in his career he had been vice-captain to Frank Worrell and, as a member of the Moral Re-Armament organisation, was a man who brought his Christian faith right into the West Indies dressing room. The MRA preached the Four Absolutes: absolute honesty, absolute purity, absolute unselfishness and absolute love.

"I don't remember him lecturing me," recalls Clive. "He wouldn't try to change you. No, not at all. But he was a man who had a very strong faith."

It was a faith that not all of Conrad's team mates appreciated all of the time.

"Wes Hall told me once that, on another India trip, Conrad had been captain in a game against a Commonwealth XI. The boys had travelled through the night and arrived very tired, having had almost no sleep. When Conrad tossed up, Wes could see from the dressing room that he had called right and was mightily relieved, knowing he could get his head down for a few hours.

"But Conrad came back to tell the team that they were in the field straight away. 'What?' shouted Wes. 'Why the hell did you do that?' 'The Lord told me', replied Conrad. So Wes says, 'Well, I hope He also told you He was happy to open the damn bowling.'

The West Indies first innings grew further. As the Indian spinners became worn out, Hunte and Lloyd put on a century stand, and Clive's hitting was sweet. By the time he was caught behind, near the end of the day's play, he had made 82.

'Looking very scholarly behind thick-rimmed spectacles,' wrote the Indian journalist Dickie Rutnagur, 'this left-hander hit the ball off the back foot with startling power; and the manner in which he battled his way out of a period of immense torment in his maiden Test innings marked him as a player of fine temperament.'

There was more to come. In the second innings Clive came to the wicket with the game in the balance and his skipper at the other end. They needed 192 to win, and it was 90 for four.

"There's no rush," said Sobers. "In fact, let's wait for Chandrasekhar to get tired. But I would like to get to the horse track across town some time after three o'clock, because a jockey friend of mine who's riding there has given me a very attractive tip."

Clive took account of this unusual order and made 78 not out to Sobers' 53. The first Test was won, Clive had scored 160 runs for once out and the captain made it comfortably to the races.

"I was very impressed," recalls Sobers. "Clive played extremely well, and I was left with a very strong impression of his ability. He was a very attractive player and a brilliant fielder. And he looked like he understood the game."

"I was still in awe of Garry on that tour," says Clive. "I would often have the hotel room opposite him, and he would call me across the hallway to have a drink and a chat. I wasn't much of a drinker, but he would pour me a small whisky from the little jug he kept. 'Here, this is good for you,' he'd say. It was difficult to believe I was sitting there listening to him talk about the game. This was the man I used to watch out for at the gates at Bourda."

It was a tour for looking and learning, and Clive observed a lot.

"We were very good individually and so there was not much talk about strategy. I think Garry's view was that these players were big enough to know what to do. He was such a great player that he would take the bat or ball and everything he did would come off. So you didn't question too many things. It was a thrill to play with him because we all looked up to him so much. Don't forget that, when we were young, we all wanted to be Garry Sobers, or at least be like him.

"I think at that stage of my career I would have enjoyed a little more guidance, but I was very impressed with how he handled situations on the pitch, how he changed the bowlers around. He was good to watch."

But there was someone else who could advise Clive, and he was staying in the same hotel when the team reached Calcutta. Sir Frank Worrell was on a lecture tour, and his visit coincided with the second Test.

Clive did not know Sir Frank well but, like almost all young West Indian cricketers, he had the utmost respect for who he was and what he had achieved.

There had been no play on the second day of the second Test at Eden Gardens because, first thing in the morning, the crowd had set fire to some of the stands. They were angry that more tickets had been sold than there were seats. Clive and a few of his team-mates hurriedly threw themselves into a car as the fires and the trouble spread, but Charlie Griffith was less fortunate. He ended up running the three miles back to the hotel.

That evening many of the side argued that the riot was a strong enough reason for them to abandon the tour and leave the country. Clive did not know what to do so he knocked on the door of Sir Frank's hotel room.

"I knew him from being twelfth man against the Australians in '65 when he was the manager," says Clive. "That's when he first saw me. I suppose I felt that I was still a very young man on that tour, and Frank was a person that the guys often spoke about with affection."

Worrell gave his advice freely, making the point that the West Indies' own supporters were not the most placid in the world and, should there be a disturbance some time in the future at a Test ground in the Caribbean, whatever course of action the players took now would be remembered then. The players decided to stay in India, and Worrell's words would prove to be prescient.

"If Frank hadn't died so soon afterwards," says Clive, "I believe our cricket would be in a much better state today. He was an icon. Everybody liked him; he was astute, prudent, a brilliant person. He would have been President of the Board and I think we would have had many fewer problems because he was so well respected. There would be a better system."

Worrell also spoke to Clive about why he had not been selected for the 1966 tour of England. He convinced him that it had actually been a good thing. Imagine, he said, if you had not played the moving ball well on those seaming wickets. If the tour had not been a success for you, it may have taken several more years to work your way back into the side. Here, in India, the pitches are more like those back home – and look how well you have started.

"It was sound advice, and it softened the blow of not going to England," says Clive – before adding with a smile, 'Of course we didn't discuss the possibility that I may have done damn well on that tour!"

The interrupted Calcutta Test was won, the final match in Madras was drawn and Clive had played well enough to keep his place. In between the first and second Tests he had scored a hundred, his first in a maroon cap, against the Prime Minister's XI; after the Test series he made another hundred in the game against Ceylon in Colombo, and at Nagpur, before the flight home, he scored 51 and 95 against the Board President's side. He was the leading run scorer on the tour, with 720 runs at an average of 60.

"After that, I felt that they couldn't drop me," he says. "I was thinking that if I played well I would hang on for a couple of series. But I never really imagined that the place was mine because it was generally assumed in the West Indies that I was not at the front of the queue. There were supposed to be other young guys in line before me: Charlie Davis from Trinidad and the Jamaican players, Renford Pinnock and Teddy Griffith."

The India tour changed Clive. He had been away from home for the first time, he had eaten different dishes and had seen a different life. More new experiences were to follow soon. During the tour, Wes Hall had asked Clive if he wanted to play as a professional in England at a place called Haslingden in Lancashire. The fast bowler had decided to take up a job with a brewery rather than play there himself, and the club needed a replacement. Clive had been forced to leave the civil service to begin his Test career and had no job to go back to in Georgetown. Being paid to play cricket in England was an attractive idea.

• • •

Haslingden's last home game of the season is not going to be played. It may be September but the rain and the foul westerly wind from the Irish Sea have a February feel. The players, unchanged, sit in the bar playing cards, waiting for the inevitable decision from the groundsman who is peeling off his waterproof leggings in his shed.

"I'm not going out in that again" he says, watching the rain bounce around the threshold of his open door.

Behind him, to the east, the low slope of the Pennines is the sponge that soaks up the rain. In front, and soon to be lost to the cloud, is Musbury Tor, the flat-topped hill that seems to have had its peak smacked down by a giant shovel. On top of the clubhouse, the sodden flag – 'H.C.C.' in gold on a maroon background – is trying to shake itself dry.

• • •

The weather in April 1967 had been very similar when Clive first saw the ground at Haslingden. He had arrived in London from the Caribbean and had flown up to Manchester. From there he was driven north to his new home, a large two-storey pub built of light brown stone called The Woolpack Inn. It was across the road from the club. From the middle of the square, batting at the southern end, Clive could see his bedroom window over the midwicket boundary.

Even by local standards, 1967 had a wet spring. The westerlies flew over the top of Musbury Tor and brought rain which spattered against the windows of The Woolpack. In the livestock auction at the northern end of the ground, the sodden animals steamed; cattle on Thursdays, sheep on one or two other days of the week. When he could, Clive kept fit by skipping in the back yard, using a rope which belonged to the landlord's grandson.

"I was so bloody cold," Clive remembers. "The landlady, a wonderful woman called Lily Cook, gave me an electric blanket, and I would plug it in and leave it on day and night. When she found out, she ticked me off, 'You can't do that,' she said, 'you could get electrocuted.' 'At least I'd be warm when I died,' I said to her."

Clive was still young, only 22, and the man who was to be his club captain, John Winter, recalls him being "shy and reserved. From his quiet manner it would have been difficult to imagine that this man would one day be a great captain of the West Indies."

John Winter had lived all his life in Haslingden. As a small boy in 1938 he had sat on his doorstep one Sunday night and watched George Headley – the 'Black Bradman' – walk past the front door on his way to the Anglican service at St James's church. Headley was the professional at

Haslingden for five seasons before the Second World War and, as he sat in the pew that summer evening, his Test batting average stood at nearly 67. In the Lancashire League he had scored almost five thousand runs. For what they had received, Haslingden were truly grateful.

Clive knew that great players were nothing new around these parts. For forty years or more, Test cricketers had been coming to the county to be paid to play. All the teams in the main Lancashire Leagues had a professional, and the appointment was taken very seriously. It was proper cricket, and the clubs paid proper money to their best player. In return they expected runs and wickets. From the West Indies alone, apart from George Headley, there had been Learie Constantine and Manny Martindale, Clyde Walcott, Everton Weekes and Basil Butcher. Conrad Hunte, Seymour Nurse and Wes Hall.

In 1967, Clive's opponents included the Australians Neil Hawke and Frank Misson, Charlie Griffith and Chester Watson from the West Indies and the England Test cricketer, Johnny Wardle.

"The league was used to some wonderful players, so he had a lot to live up to," says John Winter.

"I already knew what George Headley had done at Haslingden because we'd always look and see the records of the West Indians in the leagues," says Clive. "I knew about Everton Weekes at Bacup, Frank Worrell, who had played in the Central Lancashire League, Roy Gilchrist, a feared bowler in those days. So I was aware of who I was following and what they had achieved. I admired them too because up in the leagues, that was competitive cricket. If the pitch was wet, they didn't come off. Imagine those soaking outfields, bowling eight-ball overs in waterlogged canvas boots. So when I arrived, I appreciated that not only had there been a great man at Haslingden in the past, there had been great West Indies players all over the place and people expected you to do as well. It was very prestigious. A lot of great players had passed through."

Years later, Clive would sit and chat with George Headley about their experiences in Lancashire League cricket. They had other conversations too:

"George would always tell me about how life was for a West Indian cricketer in the 1930s. He spoke about how hard he found it being black in the West Indies side because most of our leaders were white. He was our first black captain, just once in 1948, and of course he should have led the side before he did. George knew that there had been an injustice done, but he never spoke with any bitterness. George was not a rebel. When I look at the Test runs he scored, he did so well, given that he had so few opportunities. They were right to say that Don Bradman should have been called the 'White Headley'."

Aside from knowing that great things were expected from West Indian professionals in the league, Clive knew little else about life in the north of England.

"I had no idea what to expect. It was a cultural shock to be in a new country, seeing how things were done differently. When I was on the bus, children would shout out, 'Mummy, there's a black man', and of course I had never heard that sort of thing before. One Sunday morning I was being driven to an away game and saw a long queue of people. I said, 'Boy, this is a God-fearing nation.' I thought it was like home. My team-mate, who was driving, said, 'Actually, they're waiting for the pub to open.'

"When I played, I was the only black guy among twenty-something white fellows. But I never felt intimidated or singled out, because I believed in myself. I would think of Garry and the way he walked in to bat. I have always felt comfortable in Lancashire because I was always made to feel welcome. I was treated so well."

On the bus, in the street, at the shops, Clive was recognised almost everywhere he went around Haslingden. The locals were very warm, and, he says, "really wanted to do things well for the professional."

"People in the town knew who I was, they said 'hello' and asked you in for dinner. One time, when I had moved out of the Woolpack, I missed the last bus home after the game and this couple not only invited me to stay the night at their house, they moved into the spare room and let me have their bed."

It was the sort of hospitality that was not easily forgotten and it helped shape the way Clive felt about Lancashire people.

"I think I never went anywhere other than Lancashire because I fitted so nicely in this county. But my decision to stay there for my whole career was also an act of loyalty to the people who made me feel so at home. I couldn't play for anybody else, I just couldn't."

Even when Clive thought he detected local intolerance about his colour, he was proved mistaken.

"I was living in Great Harwood with Keith Barker and his family. Keith was from Barbados, but he'd lived and played in Guyana. Like me, he was a pro in the leagues. One day we were out in the street, bending down, washing my car, and this guy opens his door and shouts, 'Hey, Blackie, Blackie.' We both drew ourselves up to our full height and looked at him in amazement. And he was so embarrassed! 'I'm so sorry,' he said. 'I didn't see you there. I was just calling for my dog.' Sure enough, as he was speaking, this black labrador came trotting along the pavement."

Friendly though they were, Haslingden were not one of the strongest sides in the Lancashire League. The club had not won the title since 1953 when the Indian Test all-rounder Vinoo Mankad was in the team. During his own time, Clive was unable to inspire Haslingden to similar glory and his two seasons there were successful, but not outstanding.

He scored a century in his first game and several more followed that year. Clive finished the season leading the league averages, having scored 861 runs at more than 50 per innings. His looping Georgetown leg spin had been abandoned in favour of seam-up – "my fingers were too cold to get any purchase on the ball and I didn't get much turn in the damp" – which brought him 47 wickets. Yet the side rarely took ten wickets in a match and finished the 1967 season fourth from bottom. Clive's qualities as a powerful and aggressive batsman were probably tempered by the type of cricket he was playing. The matches were timed: a two o'clock start and a seven o'clock finish. Fifteen minutes between innings.

Most sides would decide to stick Haslingden in if they won the toss, knowing that despite their professional's prowess, there would have to be a declaration to allow Haslingden enough time to try to bowl out the opposition. Very big individual innings were rare and a score of 150 to 170 for a side was about par. The wickets were uncovered, often wet, and took spin and seam.

"Timed cricket was new to me," says Clive. "I began by playing like I did in the West Indies, hitting people on the up but after a while I realised the pitches weren't great, the ball was doing a bit and you had to play more defensively."

One reason why Clive came to the league was to improve his batting. As he adjusted to the pitches, some bowlers thought they had worked him out.

"He was very powerful with the bat," says John Winter, "but perhaps in the first year he had a weakness outside the off stump to balls going away from him. He got caught behind a few times and I think some of the teams decided he was vulnerable and started to bowl it there."

Nevertheless, Clive still managed some memorable innings. At home, on a relatively small ground, he soon had the ball chiming off the metal pens in the cattle auction. The groundsman was often tucking his trousers into his socks to search for balls clattered into the nettle patches; sixes were hit over the scoreboard and one ball was discovered rolling in the road 150 yards from the middle.

For the first time, people began paying on the gate not only because they wanted to see a game of cricket, but because they wanted to watch a match in which Clive Lloyd would be playing.

On one occasion at Church, the two captains squelched their way into the middle to toss up and decided very quickly that it was too wet to play and that the game should be called off.

"Should it by buggery!" bellowed the club's chairman when told of the skippers' decision. "Clive Lloyd's playing for Haslingden. Have you seen the bloody ticket money we've taken? Tell the groundsman to get back out there, find a dry part of the square and cut a fresh bloody wicket."

"So they got the mower out and did just that," says John Winter. "Clive played a great innings that day."

Apart from entertaining the spectators, staying in the middle meant that Clive had to spend less time in his own dressing room. It was nothing to do with his team-mates, whose company he enjoyed. Rather, it was because Haslingden had a particularly basic pavilion. No inside toilets, no hot water, no electricity, and gas lights which, for all but the expert, were best left alone.

"It was the first time I'd ever seen a man pee in the sink," recalls Clive. The quarter-of-an-hour break between innings meant that other things were done in a hurry too. Tea was eaten from a basket on the dressing-room table.

"A quick sandwich, a slurp of tea and a bite from a Holland pie and you were back out in the middle."

• • •

Clive did not have to experience his first Lancashire winter that year; after the good start to his Test career he had been selected for the series against England which began in the West Indies in January 1968.

In the first match at Port-of-Spain in Trinidad, *The Times* reported that Clive's batting looked 'fiendishly good'. As he neared a century, Ken Barrington was bowling leg spin to him. Barrington threw one up, and Clive straight-drove him down the ground. The ball crossed the rope for a four but was within a foot of being a six. Either way it meant that he had reached his first hundred in a Test match. He was applauded around the ground and noticed that the England fielders were also giving him a generous hand. Cowdrey. Graveney. Barrington. The names on the kitchen radio were clapping the Crown Street Kid.

"I was so happy," remembers Clive. "What made it even better was that I got the same score that Tom Graveney had made in the first innings, 118. I mean, here I was playing with people I used to admire when I was young. It was a very formidable side. And people were now saying, 'who is this bespectacled lanky guy?'

"Just look at Tom Graveney, I loved to watch him batting. The West Indies *love* Tom Graveney. He said he would have loved to live in the West Indies. I'm sorry he didn't say he would have loved to play for us. This man was so elegant. He was elegance personified. The way he drove, the way he stroked the ball. Colin Cowdrey, he was a master craftsman too.

These are the England guys I grew up listening to. Colin would make runs any time against any bowling. I know how good he was. He and Tom were great players. I remember Colin just caressed this ball; a drive to me at cover one time and this thing hit my hands as if the ball was a rocket. All timing, all wrists."

"Clive helped change the course of the West Indies," believes the Caribbean cricket writer and commentator, Tony Cozier. "In 1968 the Black Power movement was in vogue, and this was very much in the air in Trinidad. Clive came in and was hammering the ball all over the place. One particular straight drive off Jeff Jones seared the grass, hit the sight board and rocked it. Now the crowd at Port-of-Spain is renowned for its wit and, down to our right, near the press box, one guy stood up and shouted, 'You want black power? *That's* black power!' That innings set Clive's place in the West Indies side at that stage of his career."

At the Jamaica Test, Clive got to know Colin Cowdrey more intimately than he expected. The West Indian Basil Butcher was well caught down the leg side by the England wicket-keeper Jim Parks and, on the way back to the pavilion, slapped his pad with his bat. The crowd believed the player to be giving them a sign that he had not touched the ball, and bottles were thrown onto the pitch. Then the arrival of armed police in gas masks cranked up the tension.

"Mmmm. That's right," says Clive. "We had a little bit of a riot."

Tear-gas grenades were set off to disrupt the trouble-makers behind the fences, but the wind was blowing in the direction of the pavilion where the players were now sheltering. In the dressing rooms, Clive found himself underneath a table with the England captain. The wet towel he had wrapped over his mouth and nose had little effect and his eyes were streaming.

"Ah Clive," said Cowdrey cheerfully, speaking with muffled bonhomie from behind his own sodden towel. "You know the first time I encountered this sort of thing was when I did cadet training at school."

In between spluttering and retching, Clive managed to let the England captain know that this was his first time. That evening, as it became clear that England would remain in Jamaica to complete the Test, Clive recalled the words of that "wise old bird" Frank Worrell, who in India, had urged moderation after the Calcutta disturbance.

As with the first two Tests, the third one in Barbados was drawn. There was a lot of rain and in the second innings Clive went in at 79 for three, with his side still 21 behind. He ended the match 113 not out, his second century in three Tests and the game was made safe.

At Port-of-Spain the sequence of draws was broken by one of cricket's more famous declarations, when Sobers was irritated by what he saw to be England's conservative play.

There is even a chapter in his autobiography called *Boring England*. "I always thought cricket should be a game with people challenging each other, not looking to see how you can draw. It seemed to me that England looked for a draw first and a win second," he wrote.

On the final day of the game, Sobers set England 216 to win in 165 minutes. They did so and afterwards, in the dressing room, Clive was distraught.

"I was part of the best team in the world, and we had played by far the best cricket in the series. With hindsight we should have given them a stiffer target, considering some of our main bowlers were injured. That was the first time I had lost a game playing for the West Indies, and in those days I was a bad loser." He pauses. "In fact, I still am. Basil Butcher got five wickets in the first innings but, to be honest, he was never going to do that again. It was a once in a lifetime thing. I thought we should have gone on and just batted for a draw. But we decided to bring the series alive, which we certainly did."

Because the fifth Test was at Bourda, Clive was brought some small measure of consolation. He was playing a Test match on his home ground. Batting in front of his mother and other members of his family, he made 31 and a single. No big innings this time but nevertheless it was, in his words, "a dream that had come true". Sylvia was delighted to watch him at work, and the cricket writers were not too displeased either. In its report of the series, the *Wisden Cricketers' Almanack* paid particular attention to Clive:

> The most exciting player of all was Lloyd, the large, spectacled left-hander, who could hit the ball with tremendous force off either front or back foot. Defensively he was as yet not the complete player, but he was a most dangerous opponent, capable of rapidly changing the course of a match, and in a side noted for fine ground fielding he was brilliantly prominent. He was an exceptionally fast fielder in the covers, swooping and pouncing on the ball to save innumerable runs, and none could take chances with his throwing.

• • •

With two centuries in eight Tests, Clive left the Caribbean to return to England and his second season with Haslingden. It was a life with few embellishments. Lloyd the young international cricketer carried his own kitbag and travelled mostly by bus between his digs and the ground. For a while in 1968 it looked as if Clive would break George Headley's club record of 1360 runs in a season. He finished just short, but again achieved the best average in the league, 61.30, having scored 300 more runs than the next most successful batsman.

He had been selected for the International Cavaliers in televised Sunday matches, and at the end of the summer at Lord's and Scarborough he played for a Rest of the World XI against England. It was clear that topping the averages in the Lancashire League would not be the summit of Clive's achievements in England.

For a while several first-class counties had been hoping to sign him, especially now that in 1968 the rules for engaging an overseas player were made more straightforward. Lancashire, Gloucestershire, Hampshire and Warwickshire were all interested.

But Clive had already made the choice for himself. While he was playing for the West Indies against England, a telegram had arrived from Manchester and he had accepted an offer to play for Lancashire.

"Warwickshire offered me the most money," remembers Clive, "but that wasn't the thing. The Lancashire contract was worth £2,500 and the offer from Warwickshire was a lot more, nearly twice as much. For a time I wondered about going to Hampshire; Danny Livingstone and Roy Marshall were there from the West Indies. But then I just decided it was between Lancashire and Warwickshire."

It was really only going to be Lancashire. Clive had fallen for the place, and he would soon take his seat in a dressing room whose occupants were going to play some of the most exciting cricket the county had seen for years.

"I remember seeing him in a raincoat, shuffling along behind the nets at the start of the 1968 season," says Jack Bond, the Lancashire captain and the man who had wanted the county to sign Clive. "People were saying 'who's that?' and we said, 'It's Clive Lloyd.' Even though he had played Test cricket he wasn't that well known. But seeing the size of him, six feet five inches, in a murky April in his raincoat with that funny stoop, he was quite something."

Clive's contract at Haslingden allowed him to play eight matches, other than league fixtures. So in May he played his first game of first-class cricket for a Lancashire XI, making one against the Australians. Two months later he was asked to play in a 2nd XI game against Derbyshire. His chauffeur was to be Jack Simmons.

"'Would you please pick up another player at Haslingden?' they said. 'His name is Clive Lloyd.' I didn't know who he was. I arrived in my Vauxhall Velux, and Clive climbed in. Plenty of leg room for him and enough of a journey for him to nod off." The two young men heading to Derby were about to play the first of their several hundred games of cricket together.

It was the beginning of a long friendship, but before it could develop Clive was leaving England again to play Test cricket. His time with

Haslingden was over, and the West Indies side was off to Australia and New Zealand for the winter of 1968/69. It was a tour which made it plain that the side could no longer be referred to as world champions.

During the five Test matches in Australia, the West Indies dropped 28 catches. They would probably have still been beaten even if half of those had been held, thinks Clive, but perhaps the humiliation of their 3-1 defeat would not have been so great.

"We were being well and truly thrashed," he remembers. "The experience of all those chances going down never left me. It was because of this series that, when I was in charge, I insisted that our fielding must be as good as it possibly could be."

Aside from the fielding, Clive had become concerned by the lack of runs he was making. In the five first-class games he played before the first Test, an 87 not out against Queensland was his best score. He had arrived in Australia, said one newspaper, with a great reputation as a dashing batsman 'hailed in many quarters as the likely successor to Garry Sobers' but, for the first time in his international career, he was in scratchy form.

Yet, in the opening Test at Brisbane, Clive made 129 as the West Indies won their only Test of the tour. Just as he was regaining his touch, he was forced to miss the next Test. In the state game against South Australia, he had been hit on the arm while fielding and ruptured a vein. He was in some pain and heard about the West Indies' innings defeat on the radio next to his hotel bed. The depressing news from Melbourne did little to dull the ache in his arm, but he was cheered briefly by a pick-me-up from home. He had seen off the boxer Lennox Beckles to be voted as Guyana's sportsman of the year. It was the best piece of news he would hear about his career for a while.

Four times in the series the Australians scored more than 500 and in the final Test at Sydney, with a first innings lead of 340, the Australian captain Bill Lawry denied the West Indies the dignity of following on, padded up himself, and declared only when his side has set the opposition a total of 735. Australia won the match by 382 runs.

The West Indies were suffering. The series loss in Australia would be followed by a 1-1 draw in New Zealand. That single victory in New Zealand would be the West Indies' last Test win for more than four years.

"You could see the reasons for the decline," Clive says. "Wes Hall was not as quick, Charlie Griffith was coming to the end. We needed a new set of players. We had an ageing side, but we hadn't planned for the future."

CHAPTER FIVE

YOU'RE LOOKING SWELL, HUBERT

Late summer, 2006

Harry Pilling is sitting in the front room of his bungalow. His dog is on its best behaviour at his feet, hoping for another of the boiled sweets that Harry keeps in his tracksuit pocket. Harry puts down his pint of tea and has a big draw on his cigarette.

"We got a lift together once after a game and we passed my local, The Three Crowns. I said to Clive, 'Fancy calling in for a quick pint?' Well, my pub was all gumboots and effing and blinding; there were some real rough characters drinking in it. Clive came in, and they loved him. He had a pint and they loved him."

• • •

Harry Pilling lived through a revolution at Lancashire County Cricket Club. He joined the ground staff in 1959 aged 16. Seven pounds and ten shillings a week with no winter pay. Cyril Washbrook was in his last season as first-team captain; he had been in charge for six years and his rule was absolute.

"I was the boss and they knew I was the boss," Washbrook once commented of his relationship with the rest of the dressing room.

"They call it the good old days, but they weren't always," says Harry Pilling. "Sometimes you'd be playing and you wouldn't be told what the team was for the next game. They'd pin it up and there'd be three names missing and they'd fill them in depending how the lad in question got on in the second innings."

Peter Lever played for the club for 17 years and, like Harry, was taken on at Old Trafford in 1959.

"The atmosphere at Lancashire in those first few years was awful. There was a lot of talent yet we won nothing. The club was run through fear. In the 2nd XI dressing room – which was known as 'the dogs' home' – your mates would say, 'Oh? You've been picked in the first team? Bad luck.'"

By the early 1960s, the championship had not been won since it was shared with Surrey in 1950, and not claimed outright since 1934. To make matters worse, the county's great rival, Yorkshire, would finish first six times before the decade ended. To use a local expression, Lancashire were in the cart. It would take the leadership of Jack Bond, a man who had spent a fair portion of that decade in the Lancashire 2nd XI, to bring some success to Old Trafford.

"Jack was a great man," says Harry Pilling. "He wouldn't expect you to do anything he wouldn't do himself. Many's the time he went in up the order if other players were struggling. He always led from the front, did Jack."

Jack Bond became Lancashire captain in 1968 and, like Cyril Washbrook, he made absolute demands of his players – fitness and loyalty, for two – but there was also a resounding difference. He wanted the side to have fun. Lancashire had got into the habit of playing cricket efficiently but with little enjoyment.

"If you enjoy playing," says Jack, "the public will enjoy watching you."

• • •

Len Hopwood played for Lancashire before the Second World War. In the early 1970s he would write in the *Manchester Evening News* about the fuss caused in 1938, when it was thought that the great black West Indian all-rounder, Learie Constantine, might come to the county.

> He was the most exciting and electrifying cricketer of his era. He was pre-eminent in Lancashire League cricket. As a three-day cricketer he was equally spectacular with his flamboyant batting, bowling and fielding. Rumour grew that Lancashire wanted that attraction. In those days the thought of a black chap playing for Lancashire was ludicrous. We were clannish in those less enlightened times. All hell was let loose when it was heard that negotiations were going on. In the dressing room we wanted none of Constantine. We would refuse to play. Constantine never did become a Lancashire player. We had nothing against him personally. He was, in fact, very popular with us. But the thought of a black man taking the place of a white in our side was an anathema. It was as simple as that.

• • •

"You can't imagine, after a decade of purgatory for the likes of me and Harry Pilling, what it was like to have Bondy in charge," says Peter Lever. "Clive arrived, so did Farokh Engineer, and it was a different world."

"Lancashire has always been a club ruled by politics," says the opening batsman David Lloyd. "But these were more than changes, it was a flaming revolution."

"I think we were quite lucky to get Clive to come to the county," says Jack Bond. "Maybe he took to the Lancashire humour straightaway and in Haslingden there was a homely feel. But I think Old Trafford was a big selling point. He was going to play at a Test match ground pretty much every day."

"It was a time when there had been a development in the way people thought," says Clive. "I brought a West Indian flavour to the side; Farokh was flamboyant. I would play my shots, and I think the guys realised that there was no need to be cautious, to be staid. And, of course, they suddenly had to live up to the changes. Now it wasn't just Brian Statham or Ken Higgs who did everything. We all complemented each other. The batting was strong, and the bowling was equally good. Jack Bond was also very strong on the importance of fielding. Before long we were chasing down totals, setting big scores ourselves and bowling sides out. What's more, it was a brand of cricket that people wanted to see. Old Trafford would sell out for the one-day games and the Roses matches. They'd close the gates by 10 o'clock in the morning."

In 1969, that was all to come. Clive's county career began slowly that summer because the West Indians were touring England and Clive was selected for all three Tests. He scored only 183 runs in the series and, when he did play for Lancashire in the second half of the county championship, he was unable to make a big score.

"I think I was lulling my new team into a false sense of insecurity," he laughs.

In 1969 a new limited-overs competition on Sundays had been set up called the John Player's County League. Clive had limited success in his eight games, scoring two fifties, but there was triumph for Lancashire. Jack Bond, in his second season in charge, brought the county a trophy at long last.

"I think Jack's great strength was that he knew about teamwork," reflects Clive. "He knew the value of respect too. The fact was that he was such a good man personally, meant that we didn't want to get out of line. We were playing for him, we wanted to please him, to do well for him. I have the greatest of respect for Jackie. He knew how to get the best out of you. He knew that I wasn't there just to play for myself, that I wanted to help other players get into the limelight. Even his wife, Florence, was lovely. She used to wash all my underwear and there aren't many county captain's wives you can say that about."

Once again, Lancashire folk were making Clive feel welcome. In the dressing room he struck up particular friendships with Harry Pilling and Jack Simmons.

"Jack is a man I have liked for so many years. Ever since he drove me to that 2nd XI game in 1968. He is the chairman of the club nowadays, but has no airs and graces. Forty years ago what struck me was that he was a real team man who didn't mind anybody doing well. It's little wonder we're still very good friends today."

Harry Pilling was the joker in the side.

"He was such a funny guy and I really enjoyed batting with him. He knew how to work things out. He played to his strengths and that worked well when we were at the crease together. He was always messing about, a real prankster. 'Here's one of those down-to-earth Lancastrians' I thought when I first met him – and I couldn't help but like him."

Harry was one half of a Lancashire double act. His mate and sidekick was the all-rounder, John Sullivan, who had been an amateur boxing champion. He once punched a man to the ground because he had heard him insult Clive. Among the other players, Harry and John were known as 'H. Dirt and J. Filth'.

"Sullivan and Pilling," chuckles Clive. "If you couldn't be happy with those guys, you couldn't be happy with anyone. They were a hell of a duo. They would get up to all sorts of things. Sully would piddle in the bath while you were in there."

"Lloydy had these massive hands," remembers Harry. "Whenever he'd see me he'd put his fingers round my neck as if to throttle me and say, 'How's my boy?' He always called me 'my boy'."

"Clive and Harry had a few lovely knocks together," says Jack Simmons. "Watching them talk in the middle was like looking at a bucket and mop side by side. When they were taking quick singles, Clive's across in six or seven strides and Harry's little legs are going nineteen to the dozen to keep up with him."

"A great bloke, Lloydy," Harry told the *Guardian* newspaper around this time. "'E'll run just as 'ard for your runs as 'e will for 'is own. Only trouble is that sometimes ah'm freetened ah'll get trodden on."

When they batted, their contrasting attributes often led to difficulties for those who had to bowl at them.

"Imagine bowling at Clive Lloyd and Harry Pilling," considers Peter Lever. "One's six foot five and the other's five foot three. One's right handed, one's left handed. One's butchering it off the front foot, one's a superb cutter and puller of the ball. So what do you do? You bowl at Clive and he'd play through the ball and smack it straight back over your head off the front foot. For the same ball, Harry would drop onto his haunches and glide you square of the wicket."

The question of what was a good length also seemed to occupy Harry's mind when it was time to have a wash.

"After one of my first games I was the last out of the shower," remembers

Clive. "Most of the boys had gone, except Harry, who was loitering by the table, fully changed. 'What are you hanging around for, man?' I asked him."

"I'm waiting to see if what they say about you lads is true," was Harry's frank response.

. . .

In the 1970 season, Clive made up for the runs his county did not get from him the year before. He made over a thousand in the championship, and showed plenty of the skills that cricket-watchers had long known about in the West Indies.

Opposition bowlers were soon trying to work out ways of stopping Clive scoring, and the England and Kent bowler, Derek Underwood, believed he had the answer. It was rumoured on the circuit that Underwood had developed a special delivery for Clive that he would find unplayable. Sure enough, he clean bowled the Lancashire man in the county game at Dartford. The trouble was, by that time Clive had scored 163.

On seven occasions Underwood was hit out of the ground for six, with one of the shots breaking the window of a nearby house. It was reported that one of the neighbours called the police to try to get the bombardment stopped. Every time the ball was being fetched from the gardens, Kent's Barbadian all-rounder, John Shepherd would call out with increasing amusement:

"Was that the special one, Deadly?"

As in the championship that season, Clive came top of the Lancashire averages in the John Player League, which the county retained. They also won the one-day knockout competition, the Gillette Cup, against Sussex. Clive made only 29 in the final at Lord's, but he made a big impression on his captain that day.

"When Clive got out," recalls Jack Bond, "it looked like we were up against it at 80-odd for three. He came into the dressing room and kept his pads on for a long time and he hung his head. There could have been a tear or two. As it turned out, Harry Pilling won the game for us, and from that point on, I think Clive realised that he didn't have to do it all by himself. What I realised then was that here was a world-class player who'd come to Lancashire to give his all. That was why he was so upset. He could have come and looked after himself and done his own thing. But he took as much pride in his county as anyone in the side. And it was that which impressed a lot of the lads."

. . .

Clive's good form in 1970 assisted his selection for the Rest of the World XI that played five Tests in England. The matches had been arranged hurriedly because the scheduled tour by South Africa had been called off. The republic's long isolation from international sport, caused by its belief in the race laws of apartheid, was beginning.

The Rest were led by Garry Sobers, and the team was picked to bring some pizzazz to what would otherwise have been a very quiet summer.

Clive had the pizzazz. All of cricketing England was hearing of his skills both as a batsman and as a once-in-a-generation cover point at Old Trafford. Against a strong England side and with players such as Barry Richards, Graeme Pollock, Eddie Barlow and Mike Procter around him, Clive made hundreds for the World XI at Trent Bridge and Edgbaston, where his gifts were enjoyed by his team-mates on and off the pitch.

"Clive Lloyd was hilarious," recalls Mushtaq Mohammad, the Pakistan all-rounder. "In the dressing room at Edgbaston there was a map of Britain on the wall, and Clive was pointing out the cities: 'Glasgow, Newcastle, Leeds, Manchester.' When he reached Birmingham he jabbed his finger at the map, saying, 'And here, this is where the boys are beating that ball.'"

"We had some fun," says Clive, "but the whole situation seemed so silly. We weren't allowed to take on South Africa, yet here I was playing alongside half of their team in a Test match."

Apart from the Rest's victory by four matches to one and his own batting, Clive's strongest memories of that series are of the organisation of the games and the way the players were treated. The Tests were sponsored by the brewers, Guinness, and £13,000 went to the winning side. The team was well looked after. Clive was pleasantly surprised to be offered his own room in the hotels where they stayed; in the West Indies side, only a few senior players had that privilege.

"I learned a lot," he remembers. "It was very interesting for me to look at all these players and see how great some of them were. It made me realise how far the West Indies still had to go."

• ◦ •

The bonhomie and the lightness of touch that characterised the Rest of the World matches was not be found later in the year when the West Indies took on India over five Tests in the Caribbean.

"Things I'd begun to notice in my first few series were still there," says Clive, "and had become more obvious. Wes Hall and Charlie Griffith had retired, there was little fresh blood around and this time the Indians caught us out."

India had never won a Test against the West Indies before, let alone a series, but they beat the home side at Port-of-Spain in the second match and drew all the other games. Clive's frustration at his team's performance was compounded by his own poor luck. He batted well but was run out three times, on one occasion because he had collided mid-pitch with Garry Sobers.

"That was just one of many things that went wrong," he recalls. "For some reason, we had a different manager at each of the Test venues – someone from that territory – so it was impossible for Garry to get any help or the team to have any sense of continuity. The other thing was that we used too many players. I almost took to introducing myself to my new room-mates at each hotel. Looking back, I suppose it was no surprise that we lost. It was a depressing time, perhaps as low as that side got, and I remember thinking that two of the remedies were professionalism and planning. No side, however talented, can just get by hoping for the best. That whole experience left me with the very strong feeling that a cricket side should never leave anything to chance."

With the series lost, Clive returned to England for the 1971 season. He cheered himself with the realisation that he was looking forward to going back to Lancashire.

Sullivan and Pilling. Engineer. Simmons, Bond and Lever.

The names brought a smile to his face.

. . .

Chelmsford. 30 June 1971

It was the quarter final of the Gillette Cup, Essex versus Lancashire, and Jack Simmons in the Lancashire dressing room was asking himself a question.

"What the bloody hell's Lloydy doing?"

In the middle, Clive was at the non-striker's end miming to his team-mates. In the air, he traced the unmistakable features of a curvaceous woman. Out went his hands for the bust, in for the waist and out again for the hips. Then he pointed to the front gate. The mime and the pointing were repeated several times.

Simmons watched with increasing perplexity. Then his face brightened.

"Oh. Oh yes, I've got it. Waveney must be outside."

With a thumbs up to the square he set off to fetch Clive's fiancée.

. . .

Waveney Benjamin had not been a cricket fan before she knew the man who was to become her husband. "But what do you do for a living?" she asked him on the night they met, when Clive told her that he played cricket. And this from the young woman whose first cousin was Basil Butcher.

Like Clive, Waveney grew up in Guyana, but unlike him she was from the countryside. She came from Port Maurant in Berbice. At the invitation of her sister, she had travelled to England in 1967 and passed her nursing exams. When she met Clive, she was working at the Bexley Heath psychiatric hospital in Kent.

One evening in 1968 Clive was in London at the home of his cousin, Oscar Gibbs. Oscar was Lance's brother and had a place in Shepherd's Bush. A neighbour popped in and, while chatting to Clive, told him that there was a beautiful Guyanese girl visiting their house. Clive reached for the Old Spice.

Waveney was eating her supper sitting on the floor, listening to music when the doorbell rang. She barely had time to slide her plate on a tray underneath the record player and straighten her skirt before Clive was in the sitting room. He had come, he said, to say 'hello' and out of curiosity, to see if he recognised Waveney from Georgetown. Oh and by the way, would she like to come with him to a party that evening?

Waveney accepted Clive's invitation. That night they danced plenty. He had fallen for her.

Later, back in Shepherd's Bush, Waveney said goodnight to Clive and closed her front door. Except that it would not shut because Clive's foot was in the way.

"Clive," she said with a smile. "This wouldn't happen at home."

"Ah," replied the keen young cricketer, "but we're not at home, are we?"

Waveney smiled again. "Goodnight," she said. Clive spent the night on Oscar's sofa.

· · ·

Within a year, Clive had proposed. And when Waveney turned up at Chelmsford their wedding was just ten weeks away. She had timed her visit well. The game she watched was the sort of contest which the Lancashire fans had grown to love. A tight finish with a brilliant knock by Clive Lloyd.

Lancashire batted first, and they lurched from 16 for three to 40 for four, then 59 for six. Yet Clive remained, even when Essex were convinced they had him caught behind. Stuart Turner got Clive to play, there was a loud click and the wicket-keeper Brian Taylor caught the ball jubilantly. Essex were delighted. Surely, with Lloyd gone, they would win. But Clive stood still.

"There was a very good reason for that," he says with some indignation. "I didn't hit it. The noise the Essex boys heard was my bat clipping my boot as I drove. They were very excited probably because they thought I was the danger man and they'd got me."

"Oh bloody hell," remembers David Lloyd. "There was this almighty noise and Essex to a man convinced themselves that Clive was out and they'd been robbed. For them it will always be a thick outside edge. There are pubs in Chelmsford where they still talk about it today."

Clive transformed the Lancashire innings, as Brian Chapman reported in the *Guardian*:

> Lloyd spread havoc or delight, depending on the point of view, across the field. He was not so much driving as condemning the Essex bowlers to strokes with the lash. Even spectators perched at telescopic distance on a roof outside the ground must have sensed the drama.
>
> Lloyd surmounted his 100 with a ringing six into the square leg crowd off Turner, and followed it by depositing Acfield's off spin on top of a thronged beer tent adjoining the sight screen.

The scores for the Lancashire top seven read: 1, 2, 0, 109, 10, 0, 3. Essex had to score 204 to win and lost by 13 runs.

In the semi-final Lancashire played Gloucestershire at Old Trafford in a game which famously did not finish until after quarter to nine at night. Rain at lunchtime had created delay and Lancashire, wanting 230 for victory, were well behind the rate on 120 for two when Clive attacked the South African quick bowler Mike Procter, hitting the first five balls of one over for four, four, two, four, two. But wickets fell, including that of Clive, and the light grew increasingly murky.

At 8.40 the last train back south had departed from the Warwick Road station, the sky was almost dark and, in front of 23,500 spectators who were going nowhere, David Hughes joined his captain Jack Bond in the middle. There were five overs to go, and 25 runs were wanted. The captain offered sensible advice: "Don't go daft. Take things as they come." By the time the next over from the off-spinner John Mortimore had ended, Hughes had belted 24 of the runs needed for victory.

Brian Johnston was commentating for the BBC as Jack Bond hit the winning single:

> *Lancashire are in the final! Lancashire have won by three wickets, and the crowd is converging on the field. I haven't seen anything like this since the Oval in 1953 when we regained the Ashes. Everybody surrounding the players. Lancashire have won one of the most extraordinary cricket matches I think I have ever seen.*

Eric Todd, covering the match for the *Guardian*, caught the mood of the county's followers in these years of one-day triumph: 'I wonder whether any county other than Lancashire could and would have rounded it off with better timing and in such exhilarating fashion.'

The final was against Kent at Lord's and was described by *Wisden* as 'possibly the best and most exciting of all the Gillette Cup finals … the result hung in the balance until almost the very end.' Clive made 66, Lancashire's top score, but it appeared that Kent would win until Jack Bond took a stupendous catch to end the innings of Asif Iqbal for 89.

Soon after, Clive matched his captain's athleticism to run out Bernard Julien and the cup was safe.

"I can see it now," says David Lloyd. "Clive swoops in and goes round the ball from the wrong side, picks it up and knocks middle stump out of the ground with the keeper, Engineer, standing up. Magnificent."

Such feats were no longer a rarity. There had been many instances of his brilliance in the outfield since he had arrived in England.

"Billy Ibadulla sticks in my mind," says Clive. "It was a Cavaliers game, and I was at cover. I dived and caught the ball on the bounce, fell over and was on my backside when I threw down the stumps. Billy was just standing there with his mouth open."

Then there was Glenn Turner, who in 1970 was on 99 and was run out needing a single to score a record tenth century in a season for Worcestershire. "It was not a ludicrous run," said Turner. "It was just that man Clive Lloyd."

Lancashire had perhaps the best fielder in the world, even if Clive did not look it. He was tall and rangy, not squat, close-to-the-ground and explosive. His feet were huge and his arms were long, so long that just before the first Test against England in 1968/69, he had trodden on his own hand while fielding and spiked it with his cricket boot. The shamble and the shuffle did not suggest rapid reactions, yet his appearance was a camouflage.

The excellence had been developed many years previously on the uneven outfield of Demerara Cricket Club. Being too young to bat or bowl, fielding had been the only way Clive could get noticed and he threw himself at anything. At Haslingden, his captain believed the Lancashire League had not seen such a fielder since the days of Learie Constantine in the 1930s.

"Lloydy just had brilliant reactions," says his Lancashire team-mate David Hughes. "He was pencil-thin but he had a rocket of a throwing arm, long strides and was quick to the ball. But he didn't pull the arm all the way back. It was a sort of quick movement in mid-stride, never a long launch. It all came from the shoulder. And he was deadly accurate too. The last man I remember being as accurate was the Rhodesian, Colin Bland. Nobody would take a run to Clive's right hand."

"He was better than Colin Bland," is the judgment of Peter Lever. "He didn't hit the stumps as often but he got to the ball much more quickly.

Some of the things that he did, we would just laugh at because we knew we couldn't match him."

Jack Bond would usually place Clive at cover point, even though he would not stay there for long. He wandered around square of the wicket on the off side. Even though the skipper felt that, technically, Clive was out of position, he would never bother to correct him.

"It was his quickness as much as anything. And even though he was a tall man, he was so good with his hands. You'd think he'd find it difficult to get down repeatedly, but he had no trouble at all."

"First, it was anticipation," says Clive of the way he went about fielding. "I wanted to predict where guys were trying to hit the ball. So I was on the move. They'd see the gap but I was already on the go, in a position, ready to strike. I also had telescopic arms which helped, so batsman thought the ball was past me, but I'd still get to it. Then, after a couple of years there was the matter of respect. Some singles the batsmen wouldn't take because they knew I was there. So I saved runs too. One thing followed the other. I ran people out and that stopped the next guy going for what was probably an easy single."

The Yorkshire batsman Doug Padgett has cause to remember Clive's fielding ability more than most. Peter Lever recalls a Roses match in 1970.

"It was Old Trafford, a three-day championship game. Saturday, Monday, Tuesday and a John Player League game on the Sunday. Lancashire batted all day on the Saturday so Dougie doesn't get his pads on until we stick Yorkshire in for the one-day match.

"He joins Geoff Boycott, who knew how to collect runs, and Dougie's soon at the non-striker's end when Boycs pushes one and sets off. 'Yeees!' he shouts and then sees Clive darting towards the ball from cover. 'Noooo!' he yells as he's turning round, and Dougie, on a nice fresh green square, slips and is on the track with his legs in the air like a beetle on its back. I race back to the stumps from my follow-through and Clive underarms it to me and I take off a single bail. Poor Dougie gets up off the floor, brushes himself down and walks towards the pavilion with mud all over his backside.

"The next day, Monday, and it's back to the championship. Boycs and Doug at the wicket, me bowling. This time Geoffrey has a look. No Clive Lloyd at cover, so he turns a straight ball off his toes. 'Yeees, come one,' he shouts, but this time Clive is fielding behind square on the on side. Three yards into his single Boycs spots him. 'Nooooooo! Get back!!' So up go Dougie's feet, he's flat on his behind. Clive wangs the ball to me, one bail removed, and he's off again.

"It's now Tuesday afternoon and it comes to their second innings. Boycs is ready. Cap on, chewing gum in. Phil Sharpe's ready. Dougie's due in at three but he's nowhere to be found. Not in the toilets, not in the pavilion, nowhere. 'Oh, Christ,' says Brian Close. 'Get bloody padded up someone – and you,' he says, pointing to the twelfth man, 'find Doug.'

"Eventually the twelfth man goes to the car park, spots Dougie's car where he can see smoke coming out of the top of the driver's window. He bends down and there's Dougie, fag on, reading the newspaper. 'What do you want?' barks Doug without taking his eyes off the sports pages. 'The skipper has insisted that you go and pad up,' said the twelfth man. 'Tell him,' said Doug, folding up the newspaper and dropping his cigarette into a puddle, 'to find some bugger else who wants running out. I will not be batting today, young man. Now piss off.'"

. . .

As well as retaining the Gillette Cup in 1971, Lancashire had finished third in the County Championship – and, on 12 September, the side had the chance to win the John Player Sunday League again.

The day before, Clive had to secure another prize. He married Waveney. The nuptial Mass was celebrated at St Augustine's, the Catholic parish at Grosvenor Square, south of the city centre in Manchester. Clive wore a pin-stripe five-button suit topped off with a big bow tie and a carefully-trimmed goatee. His team-mates dressed up and were there too. The reception was at Old Trafford. It was not an especially late night, but the next day Lancashire surprisingly lost to Glamorgan and so missed out on the chance to win the Sunday League on run rate.

"I do not know what happened," says David Lloyd. "But I can swear that it was nothing to do with the party. After all, we were professional sportsmen, so give us some credit. Normally in those days when Glamorgan came to Old Trafford, they expected – and got – a good hammering."

It was a late-summer disappointment, but Clive had an interesting winter to look forward to. The West Indies were playing New Zealand in the Caribbean in 1971/72; a chance for him to score some big runs in international cricket again. Before that, Australia were due to play a series against the Rest of the World XI and Clive had accepted the invitation promptly.

It was a decision that very nearly cost him his life.

. . .

The Rest of the World XI was again led by Garry Sobers, although his side was not as strong as the one he had captained against England. Ian Chappell started a series captaining Australia for the first time. It was a genuine overseas tour, planned to last three months. First came games against Victoria, New South Wales and Queensland in November. By

December the first international match had ended in a draw at Brisbane and the second had been won easily and early at Perth by Australia.

It was on this tour that Clive faced the Australian fast bowler Dennis Lillee for the first time.

"I think Dennis is the greatest of the international bowlers I have batted against," he says. "There is not a Test batsman who he hasn't troubled at some stage. Apart from anything else, he had such a beautiful action, a real case of poetry in motion. He would be as difficult on a slow wicket as he was say, at Perth, because he was always trying something, always making you work hard against every delivery."

On the second day of the four-day game against South Australia at Adelaide, Saturday 18 December 1971, the Rest were in the field. Clive, as usual, was at cover point ready to swoop on a careless single, dive to turn a four into a dot ball or throw himself at a catch, high or low.

Ashley Mallett drove and Clive leapt to intercept the speeding ball. He caught it in his right hand but landed heavily on the hard ground and the catch was gone. His right shoulder had taken the impact of his crashing fall and as Clive lay on the ground he realised he could feel nothing. He was paralysed.

. ● .

Tony Greig's face was above him, peering down and blocking out the sun.

"Come on Lloydy, get up."

"No," replied Clive, "I can't. I don't feel my legs. They're numb."

Greig bent down, and his face changed in an instant. Clive could hear him shouting. He wanted the doctor to get onto the pitch.

"As long as I live, I'll never forget what happened that day," says Greig. "Clive was a freak fielder with a gift that meant the ball hit him straight in the middle of the hand, no matter how it came. He went for this catch, and he twisted in the air and landed in the same twisted shape. It was a brilliant, brilliant effort. But he collapsed in a heap. Immediately we thought it was extremely serious. I mean, he was in agony."

Two medics in peaked caps brought a stretcher to the square, and Clive was moved onto it. A searing pain was carving into his back. With Greig carrying the handles behind Clive's head and the two medics at the other end, he was lifted from the Oval, his hands holding on to the wooden frame of the stretcher. His big feet looked like the hands of a clock stopped at ten-to-two. Still in his whites, he was taken straight to hospital.

"I think Rohan Kanhai travelled with me," says Clive. "The pain grew harder to take as I lay there in the first hour or so. The doctors took some X-rays, and they told me I had cracked my spinal cord. There was, they said, a possibility of permanent paraplegia."

The extent of his injury was withheld from the newspapers. The manager of the World XI, Bill Jacobs, told reporters the next day that he was pleased with Clive's condition but it would be unlikely that he would play in the Melbourne game starting on New Year's Day. Within 48 hours, the story had changed a great deal: 'He has no chance of playing again on the tour,' reported *The Times*.

Clive lay in his bed, weakened by the great pain which he felt somewhere deep in the middle of his body. At night he was given painkilling injections but would sometimes have to ask the nurses for supplementary tablets, which they were reluctant to give him because of their strength.

He was alone, fearful, his new wife was thousands of miles away. His life as a cricketer seemed over.

The drugs made him dream. The sunlight streamed in shuttered shapes onto his bed. He was a boy again lying in Georgetown Hospital and he could hear Sylvia talking loudly to the nurse. 'Move his bed. He's not staying there. I don't want him under that clock. You think I want my son to die?'

"It was a traumatic time," recalls Clive. "Once I'd survived, I really did wonder if I would walk again. There was no immediate promise from the staff that I would. I was thinking, 'Well, this is the end', you know? It brought home a lot of things to me, and the only conclusion I could come to was that I was down here for a purpose."

For some days Clive was unable to do anything. Then, when the doctors were certain that he was ready and the pain was manageable, he began a course of physiotherapy. First lying on the bed and later, as he responded well to the treatment, standing up.

"What they did was actually lower me into a frame and tell me that they were teaching me to walk again because my legs hadn't been working. I will never forget putting my feet on the ground for the first time in two weeks. Oh that pain! The pins and needles!"

When it became clear that his recovery, if there was to be one, would not be immediate, the word in the cricketing world spread. One of Clive's first and most regular visitors was Sir Donald Bradman.

"He just turned up. He would come for an hour, maybe two. He did so several times. We had some terrific chats. One thing I remember was that he loved talking about the laws of the game; their development, the way they were applied. He also told me that the West Indian batsman he enjoyed watching the most was Everton Weekes. 'My favourite of the Ws,' he called him."

During their conversations, Bradman told Clive that he should consider seriously the idea of bringing Waveney to Australia and living there. He would, he promised, be Clive's sponsor, should he decide that was what he wanted.

Sir Donald was not the only visitor, and almost all the others who came seemed to bring a bottle of spirits with them. Soon Clive's bedside cabinet was full and jangled like a moving milk float every time it was opened. As New Year approached, he decided that the nurses deserved a drink; a little Caribbean punch.

"They'd been so good to me, so I threw everything in. My recollection was that the punch went down very well. So well in fact that one of the nurses fell asleep on an empty bed. I had to shuffle over and wake her up and say, 'Listen, you're supposed to be on duty.'"

Despite the trauma that his spine had suffered, Clive was otherwise as fit as he had ever been in his life and he was making a recovery that was far exceeding his doctors' hopes. From the first physiotherapy, to being supported with a frame, to standing on his own and taking a few steps, Clive was slowly repairing himself.

"I think I was helped by my own mental fortitude," he says. "It was not the first time I'd been in a tricky situation and I had built up deep reserves of determination. This was another innings to be rebuilt."

When he spoke on the phone to Waveney, he let her know of his progress, and confided to her his concerns that his cricket career was over. He had too, another more fundamental concern. The sort that would trouble any recently-married young man.

"Of course he was worried about the cricket, that was his life," Waveney says with a laugh. "But I remember too that he was – how shall I put it – very anxious that we would be able to resume, to the fullest extent, all aspects of our married life."

To cheer him up, Sunil Gavaskar, Graeme Pollock and some others in the World side had learned and rehearsed a song – a parody of the 1960s musical hit, *Hello Dolly*. Seizing on Clive's middle name, by which he was occasionally known, they called it *Hello Hubert*:

> *Hello Hubert!*
> *Well, Hello Hubert!*
> *It's so nice to have you back where you belong*
> *You're looking swell, Hubert,*
> *We can tell, Hubert,*
> *You're still glowin', you're still crowin'*
> *You're still goin' strong.*

When the song was word-perfect, the harmonies honed and the cast assembled, a phone call was made to the ward on which Clive was staying, so *Hello Hubert.* could be sung down the line.

"Oh, I'm terribly sorry," said Clive's doctor, "he's not here. As part of his recuperation, Mr Lloyd has been taken out by a couple of the nurses for a scenic drive around Adelaide."

"That bastard," said a voice on the other end of the phone, "and we thought he was ill."

CHAPTER SIX

THE MOST IMPORTANT PIECE OF NEWS
– AND I HEAR IT SECOND HAND

By February 1972, seventy days after being carried from the field at Adelaide on a stretcher, Clive was playing cricket again – for Guyana in the Shell Shield, but not for the West Indies. In the words of Tony Cozier, he was 'strangely omitted' from the first three Tests against the New Zealand tourists, and in his absence – in a five-match series in which runs were scored easily on slow pitches – other West Indian batsmen made the most of their opportunities,

In the first Test in Kingston the Jamaican Lawrence Rowe became the first batsman to score two Test centuries on debut, one of them a double hundred. In the third Test in Bridgetown the Trinidadian Charlie Davis hit 183. Clive forced his way back into the team for the fourth Test by scoring a hundred in each innings for Guyana against the New Zealanders. But in the Bourda Test, he was run out for 43 when going well, and Alvin Kallicharran on his debut took his place at the wicket and scored a century.

Clive did not make runs in the final Test. Four months earlier he had been playing for the Rest of the World in Australia and was being mentioned as a possible successor to Garry Sobers as captain. But now he was told that he had not been retained in the group of players expected to be picked for the series the following season against Australia. If he was to play for the West Indies again, he would have to force his way in.

It was a surprising decision, as the administrator Peter Short made clear in an article in *Playfair Cricket Monthly*: 'Selectors do strange things from time to time and West Indian selectors are no exception, but this must rank as one of the most glaring omissions of recent times.'

"These were pretty bad days for me," recalls Clive. "I had been injured, I was trying to come back, and now this news was a knock to my confidence. I think some people in West Indies cricket had hoped that this would be the end, that my career was over. When I returned to play after being in hospital in Australia, it was a shock to them because they thought they'd seen the last of me."

. . .

If Clive did not feel completely welcome in the West Indies, he certainly felt wanted in Lancashire, and again in 1972 he did well for them. Despite missing some games because of injuries, Clive made nearly 900 runs for his county and, for the third year in succession, played at Lord's in September in the Gillette Cup final.

Would Lancashire be able to make it a hat-trick of wins under Jackie Bond? Warwickshire had Bond's side at 26 for two when Clive went in. He looked a little different because he had left his glasses in a case in his kit bag and was experimenting with contact lenses. Warwickshire had set Lancashire 235 for victory and, in ten years of the competition, only twice had a team successfully chased so many runs – and never in the final.

Clive began slowly by taking six runs from the first eight overs of his innings. But once he and his contact lenses had settled in, his caution evaporated. David Brown, the Warwickshire fast bowler, was hit for 10 runs from two balls.

'Not for half an hour or so did Lloyd reveal the awesome power of his driving, but once he had done so, that was it,' wrote John Woodcock in *The Times*.

"He ran me out," remembers Harry Pilling. "We were both going well and I played a square cut straight to the fielder. I looked up and Clive was almost in front of me. In that split second I knew what I had to do next. I thought, 'He'll win it for us' so I ran past him and was out easily. 'Win the match,' I said as I disappeared."

The score was 122 for three when Pilling departed, and Frank Hayes stayed with Clive until it reached 209. Then at 219, with the game all but won, Clive was lbw to Bob Willis. He had scored one of the competition's finest hundreds.

'There have now been two great innings in the final,' Woodcock went on. 'The first was by Geoffrey Boycott in 1965, when he made 146 against Surrey; the second, by Clive Lloyd, when his 126 against Warwickshire enabled Lancashire to win the trophy for the third successive year.'

'No one in the world could match the power of his driving,' John Arlott wrote in the *Guardian*. 'His straight drives thumped into the covers at the Nursery end and the pavilion railings. No one, not even his older cousin Gibbs, could quell his urge to win the match.'

"What a knock," says David Lloyd. "He just kept whacking David

Brown into the stands. Bob Willis came out of it with decent enough figures but Clive climbed into everybody else."

The defeated Warwickshire captain, Mike Smith, confessed, "You cannot bowl at a bloke when he plays like that."

"I passed the Warwickshire coach Alan Oakman after the match," recalls Clive, "and I said, 'Hi, Alan, you alright?', and he replied, 'I was until I saw you go out to bat.'

"I suppose it was one of my best innings in limited-overs cricket, as well as being one that I remember very fondly." He smiles. "Of course I got after Lance a bit that day too."

The Warwickshire off spinner ended up wicketless and without a maiden in his ten overs from which 44 runs were scored. He was one of four West Indian Test cricketers playing for the county that day, the others being Deryck Murray, Rohan Kanhai and Alvin Kallicharran.

"We were chatting and Lance was saying, 'Oh I should have done this, I could have done that.' I cut him off and said, 'But Lance, you didn't. Look in the scorebook' and we laughed. He could be a relentless competitor. He was like me – we both hated losing."

Clive had much to thank Lance for. It was because of his older cousin that he had used a proper bat in the garden of Crown Street when he was growing up, rather than one cut from a palm frond.

"I think Gray-Nicholls began to wonder what a lower-order off spinner wanted with so many bats," says Lance. "Most of them went to Clive."

"Lance was such a big influence," says Clive. "I always wanted to be a cricketer like him. When he came back to Georgetown from a tour he would bring me a present, some clothes or something. I was a young man trying to emulate what Lance was doing.

"Lance was never a great batsman, though," he adds mischievously. "Whenever the West Indies used to play in Trinidad and Lance came out to bat, the crowd would start singing 'A-aa-men, A-aa-men', because they knew the end was nigh. Even so I remember a big stand of ours for Guyana against Jamaica in 1966."

The cousins put on 122 for the ninth wicket. Lance made 18.

. . .

Clive was named man of the match for his winning century in the Gillette Cup final of 1972. He was also the first man to be given the Learie Constantine Memorial Award – a prize for the best fielder in the final.

Yet despite the joy of the day, it ended in discord. "All these guys from the West Indies had seen me bat," says Clive. "Deryck, Rohan – who was going to be the Test skipper – they knew what I could do. When it was all over, Cecil Marley came up to me. He was the President of the West

Indies Cricket Board of Control. I don't know what he was doing there, but he had watched the innings. He said, 'I'm going to speak to the rest of the Board and try to get the selectors to reinstate you on the list of those wanted to play against Australia.' I said to him straightaway, 'You don't have to. I can't be bothered.' Just like that. I really meant it. I had had enough with them. I was angry because he knew as well as anyone that on many occasions I had saved the West Indies – and had done so playing a different style of cricket. When I was on the go, I brought people enjoyment, yet I was being told that I still might not get in the team."

Clive was true to his word. Within weeks he was flying to Australia to play grade cricket for the South Melbourne club in Victoria. The contract was to last for the whole of the English winter, and he told reporters that he did not know if he could 'fit in' the 1972/73 Test series against Australia in the West Indies.

"I was playing for Lancashire and batting really well. I no longer cared if I got picked for the West Indies. I was happy playing for the county and most of the fans thought I was a good thing. I thought my Test career was over. I was pretty low and had started to believe the people who were saying that I was not good enough. But I was annoyed, too. Here I was, heading to Australia with Test hundreds, plenty of fifties and a pretty good average, and I couldn't get in the West Indies side. I mean, if you have Test hundreds, you must be able to bat."

The West Indies Board may not have believed in Clive's worth, but there was a man in the Caribbean who did. It was Forbes Burnham, the Prime Minister of Guyana.

It had been almost seven years since Guyana had gained its independence from Britain, and in that time Forbes Burnham's power had increased. The country was now a 'Co-operative Republic'. The big industries – sugar production and bauxite mining – would soon be nationalised, relations with Cuba and countries from the Soviet bloc were becoming stronger and more money was to be spent on the armed forces.

Burnham was a man who wanted his country to be strong, to have heroes. In Clive, he may have seen such a hero. He contacted the Australian Prime Minister, Gough Whitlam, and asked him to ensure that Clive could be released from his commitments to the South Melbourne club so that he could return to Georgetown. Burnham's plan was that Clive should be playing cricket in Guyana under the noses of the selectors. By the middle of January 1973, it was done.

"Forbes Burnham was a man before his time," Clive says. "He had vision, there's no doubt about that. He took the initiative and, looking back now, it proved to be a pretty inspired decision, didn't it? He turned out to be a pretty good judge. I was very grateful to him and always will be. That's not to say it wasn't a tricky situation. Here was a politician getting involved in cricket business. It was a pretty public happening, and I was thinking at the time that I would have to get runs to prove him right. I didn't want to look like an idiot after all this fuss. I didn't want to make Forbes Burnham look stupid either.

"The thing about Burnham was that he was a man who made things happen. I remember a few years later I was in his office one time, and the conversation had got round to the Kaieteur Falls, Guyana's great waterfall. He said, 'Have you seen it?' and I said I never had. He spluttered and reached straight for the phone and shouted into the receiver, 'I'm here with Clive Lloyd and he's never seen the Kaieteur Falls. Arrange for a plane with…' and then he turned to me and said, 'Who else hasn't been there?' and I replied, 'Well, there's Roy and his wife …' So he carries on, 'Yes … a military aircraft with a dozen seats to fly over the falls … yes … this afternoon.' And that was that. The trip was arranged!"

Looking out of the window of the aircraft later that day, the vastness and beauty of his country was made plain to Clive.

"We have a lot to be proud of in Guyana," he says.

Even though Clive was back home, thanks to his prime minister, and was playing Shell Shield cricket again, he was not selected for the first Test against Australia. But he was named in the twelve for the second match in Barbados. It was due to start on 9 March 1973 and, the day before, the all-rounder Bernard Julien chipped a bone in his arm while batting. Clive assumed that he would now play in his place. But he was about to be greatly surprised.

On the morning of the match, Clive was knocking up at the ground when one of the selectors, Jeffrey Stollmeyer, came to talk to him. He informed Clive that he would not be playing and that Keith Boyce, who was not in the twelve but who was on the island, would play instead of Julien.

There was an element of logic in the decision, as Julien was an all-rounder, expected to open the bowling. But, after all that had gone before, the rejection was too much for Clive to take.

"I could not believe what I was hearing," he says. "I was furious."

He stormed back to the dressing room and refused to leave it.

Clive felt humiliated. He suspected that the intervention of Forbes Burnham had embarrassed the Board, and that this was their response.

"I truly felt on that morning that my Test career was over," says Clive. "Sitting in the dressing room I could not see a way back. My anger caused me to be insensitive and selfish – and that's not the real me. All I wanted to do was to get back to England and play for Lancashire."

Clive was consoled by Wes Hall, and also by Clyde Walcott who had done much to reinvigorate cricket in Guyana. He was a man who had observed Clive develop as a cricketer and knew of the talent that he had.

"Clyde talked me round," reflects Clive. "He comforted me, he knew me from home, he'd been my first captain and he said, 'You have a great part to play in West Indies cricket.' I can't really describe how important his words were. What he said really made me change my whole way of thinking. Before then I just wanted to finish with cricket; I didn't want to play for the West Indies again. His words proved to be prophetic."

Walcott's words were all the more effective because no-one of influence had spoken to him in such a way since he had begun playing Test cricket. Not long after Clive's dressing-room outburst in Barbados, the unpredictable nature of West Indies team selection was to be seen once more. No sooner had Clive been dropped, than he was back in the side for the third Test – and he was opening the bowling. The pitch at Port-of-Spain for the third Test was a spinners' track, and in both innings Clive took the shine off the new ball.

"What did I bowl?" he says now. "Right-arm optimistic."

It was not the first time that an opening batsman had seen Clive at the end of his run-up before the morning's first delivery. In the 1972 Gillette Cup final, Clive had hurried though 12 overs to restrict Warwickshire at the start of their innings.

"He loved to bowl and I used him quite a bit," recalls Jack Bond. "He bowled a natural away swinger and with his height it was difficult to pick the length. I would like to have bowled him more often but we wanted him to bat number four and play those long innings."

"That day at Lord's he got through his spell before anyone knew what was happening," laughs David Lloyd. "Twelve overs of complete crap and he got away with it! They were treating Clive as if he was a mixture of Wes Hall and Charlie Griffith. But whenever he bowled he kept things tight. He ran up with this ungainly action but on the right pitch, wicket to wicket, he was very effective. Gentle little outers they were, just swinging a bit. To compare him to one of today's occasional bowlers, I guess he'd be the same pace as the England batsman Ian Bell."

"Ian Bell?" says Clive. "Oh no, quicker than that." He pauses to think. "Paul Collingwood," he decides. "Possibly a little quicker than the fellow Collingwood."

• • •

The third Test match against Australia in Trinidad was a significant one in Clive's cricket career. Not because he opened the bowling but because it marked the end of an uncertain phase in his professional life. For as long as he played for the West Indies, he would never be dropped again.

"Things had changed quickly," says Clive. "My views had changed too. The thought that the Board was trying to destroy my career had gone. I was so pleased to be given another chance but I think, too, that the selectors realised they had made a mistake."

The fourth Test was at Bourda and, in front of the people who knew him best, Clive made 178, his highest score in a Test match. The experiment with contact lenses had been abandoned because the dust from the pitch irritated his eyes and, in a new pair of gold-framed glasses, Clive drove and swept the Australians to all parts.

It was not a match-winning innings though. The game was lost by ten wickets as the West Indies, watched by Forbes Burnham and other Caribbean leaders gathered in Georgetown for a summit, made only 109 in their second innings. The fifth Test, back in Port-of-Spain, was drawn, and another series had gone by without the West Indies winning a game.

. . .

An opportunity for the West Indies to improve would not come till the second half of the English summer of 1973. Before that, in May and June, Clive was back with Lancashire, who, after their Gillette Cup successes and Sunday League titles, were undoubtedly the best one-day side in the country.

"There were four qualities that made us such a strong team for that sort of game," says Clive. "The first two were balance and restriction. The side worked well together and all of the bowlers were tight. They could be relied upon to put the ball in one place. Jack Simmons was known for being miserly with runs but so too were Peter Lever, Ken Shuttleworth, Peter Lee and David Hughes. So sides would usually struggle to get away from us. Then there was the matter of confidence. We started to win, and kept winning, and that made us feel that we would always triumph. No target was too high to chase and, if we failed with the bat, no score was too low to protect – that's how we felt. Finally, I think our fielding was better than that of any other side. I was quick in the covers, but David Hughes was also an exceptional fielder, so with us on each side of the wicket, we could keep the runs down and put a bit of pressure on."

After that third cup win at the end of the 1972 season, Jack Bond had decided to retire as skipper. He had brought the county five trophies in as many years and had utterly changed the way cricket was played and watched at Old Trafford.

'Beer is now drunk openly on the pavilion side,' noted a feature on the county in *Wisden*, 'and many a member feels he is entitled to remove his collar, and sometimes his shirt, to enable him to watch the game in comfort. Old ideas and ideals have been sacrificed in certain respects, but Lancashire cricket is now vibrantly throbbing with enthusiasm and skill … An hour of Clive Lloyd at his best must still remain one of cricket's major joys. That Lloyd is not Lancashire-born may worry the few but not the masses. Cricket today has broken down age-old barriers and Old Trafford has figured prominently in the transformation. Who could ask for more?'

Jack Bond's successor would be charged with maintaining Lancashire's new spirit. Clive felt established at the county and ready for the responsibility.

"They asked all the players who should be skipper," he recalls, "and they said they wanted me. When I didn't get it, several of the guys spoke to the chairman, Cedric Rhoades. 'What happened?' they asked. It was reported back to me that Cedric told them he wasn't sure that the committee could accept that a black man should captain the county."

The job went instead to David Lloyd, who says that he had expected to be appointed. "They had very nearly gone back to an amateur captain," he says. "A guy called David Bailey. It was a very close thing and there was a contingent of the club that certainly wanted it, but Jack Bond wanted me to do it. I had captained on odd occasions when he hadn't played and I knew they were lining me up to do it. I'd been told that. Sometimes Jack and I would stay in the same hotel together away from the rest of the team. It was expected in those days that the captain would be around in the winter to be an ambassador of the club. Because he was away playing Test cricket, Clive was not a runner."

"I think I should have been made captain," says Clive. "I had the respect of the players. Being in the West Indian team didn't make any difference as I was back every summer anyway. I was young and enthusiastic and would have tried to get a lot of new players. I think, had I been given the captaincy in 1973, then the county would have been a lot more successful in the years that followed."

Clive had lost out, but consolation came in the form of more Test runs against England. The West Indies were captained by Rohan Kanhai for the three-match series, which started in late July 1973, and it was the best Clive's career had known.

At The Oval in the first Test he put on more than 200 with Alvin Kallicharran and scored his third century against England. In one over from the England captain Raymond Illingworth, Clive pulled him for two fours; the first got him to 99 and, in premature excitement, a few West Indian supporters ran on to the square. They returned by the dozen the next ball as he repeated the shot to reach his hundred.

"A guy ran up and gave me a swig of something. He said, 'Drink this' and it was rum and orange juice," remembers Clive. "Boy, I felt that."

That game was won and, at Edgbaston in the second Test, Clive made 94. At Lord's in the final game, when Kanhai and Sobers both passed 150 and Bernard Julien scored a century batting at eight, Clive made 63. At last, after more than six years, the West Indies had won a Test series.

"That tour was a turning point for the team and for me," says Clive. "I was confident again, and felt that I was established at last. That was so important. And the side had won after so many mishaps. It felt like the worst was over."

The tour was also the last that Garry Sobers would play away from the West Indies. After the innings victory at Lord's, Clive watched from the dressing room as the man who had been his first Test captain saluted the crowd from the balcony with a drink in his hand.

"He was a great man and he just knew that he was great," reflects Clive. "And that's how he played. Garry would always try different things. He was a guy who didn't like draws, he just wanted to win. Nothing fazed him. I've been there when it was flying around and then seen Garry go out with that walk of his and he just made it look like a different game. If fellows were having a rough time, he'd just do his own thing for them."

In less than a year, after a drawn series in the Caribbean against England, Sobers would be retired, and Rohan Kanhai would be gone too. Their departures were a clear sign that a particular era of West Indian cricket had drawn to a close.

It was time to look for a new leader.

• • •

In the last week in May 1974, Clive was at Headingley sharing a beer with a writer from the *Daily Mirror*.

"It shows how times have changed," he says. "We drank with reporters in those days."

Clive had done well in the Roses match, scoring fifties in both innings.

"Congratulations," said the journalist as they sat down with their pints.

"Thanks," replied Clive. "It was a good pitch, but I was pleased with the way I got onto the front foot."

"No. Not that. I meant 'congratulations' on becoming the captain of the West Indies."

"It was amazing really," says Clive. "The most important piece of news in my life as a cricketer – and I hear it second hand! That's how it was in West Indies cricket, I was the last person to know."

Little more than a year previously, Clive had been unable to get into the team. Now he was charged with shaping its future. He was 29, a good age to lead. Old enough to own some hinterland; young enough to hold his own with his peers.

"My first thought was, 'Well, this is a challenge!' but I don't recall being frightened or overawed. Since I was a kid there had always been challenges, and this was the next one.

"The captaincy was thrust upon me, and I had to make it work. It wasn't as if I had been groomed for the job. So, I wanted to do things my way, while at the same time I wanted to take what I'd learned from Worrell and Sobers. In the early days of the job, I found I had to work out some stuff as I was going along. But I knew from the beginning that there were two things I wanted to change, two things that I thought would help us to succeed.

"One – I was determined to get rid of insularity. I wanted the fellows to understand that we were all one, there was to be no island rivalry. Two – I told them that, if we were successful, we'd be in a strong bargaining position to try to get better pay. I used to do the bargaining with the Board for the players' fees before each tour, and I told the team, 'The only way anything will change is if we can become the best.'"

Clive's first tour as a Test player had been to India. Eight years later, in November 1974, he went back as captain.

The wicket-keeper, Deryck Murray, was his vice-captain. Andy Roberts on his first tour would take 32 wickets in the Tests. There would be debuts for Gordon Greenidge and Vivian Richards. The side of the future was taking shape – and there was some experience on hand, too. Clive was greatly assisted by the tour manager, Gerry Alexander, the last fair-skinned man to captain the West Indies.

"He was very good for me," says Clive. "I found him very charming, very helpful. He had this gift at team meetings to get all the guys talking because he'd make some outrageous statement – you know, playing devil's advocate – and the boys would be fired up to speak their minds. Gerry was very fiercely West Indian. When I think of people who have loved those maroon colours, he's one that comes to mind. The fact that he is fair-skinned makes no difference. He loved the West Indies as much as anybody else."

The tour consisted of five Tests in India and two in Pakistan, as well as a week of cricket in Sri Lanka, and the captain and manager only had one minor disagreement in their four months together. It occurred when Clive discovered that, in his enthusiasm, Alexander had been tinkering with his field.

"My Lancashire pal Farokh Engineer was sitting next to him during one of the matches, and he told me later that Gerry had been calling over the balcony, which was close to the pitch, getting players to move into different positions. When I found out, I had to tell him, 'Look, Mr Manager, please refrain from that activity. If you want to speak to the players, do it at the meeting, or send a message onto the pitch.' He understood it was my territory."

With Alexander to back him up, Clive thrived on the responsibility and set a pattern for his captaincy; the job was making him an even better batsman. In the first Test, in the victory at Bangalore, he hit 163. Then, in the fifth and deciding Test at Bombay, he hit the highest Test match score of his career – 242 not out. His first five Test centuries had taken him seven years to compile. Now five more would come in only 16 months.

On the Indian part of the tour alone, he scored more than a thousand runs. Reporters following the side wrote that his batting possessed a 'spectacular belligerence'. It was 'contemptuous' and 'tempestuous'. The Indian bowlers were 'bludgeoned' and 'overpowered'.

A win against India and a draw with Pakistan was a good start for Clive Lloyd the captain.

"I felt we had a side with players who could do things, win things," is how he describes it.

The next challenge would come in the summer of 1975. England was hosting cricket's first World Cup.

CHAPTER SEVEN

HE BROUGHT THE PRUDENTIAL CUP TO WE

Saturday 21 June 1975

Lord's on a sunny London Saturday. The weather has been hot for a fortnight, and today is just as fine. It is the longest day of the year, and the occasion is the final of the Prudential World Cup between Australia and the West Indies.

In the bottom corner of the Grand Stand – the end nearest the pavilion – some of the West Indies supporters have their shirts unbuttoned, some are bare-chested. Others are wearing waistcoats, rosettes and ties.

Beneath a primrose-coloured balcony sign advertising Sandeman's sherry and port, the younger fans throw themselves around, blowing into curled brass horns and clattering beer cans together. Home-made flags are flown. A couple of policemen with their shirtsleeves rolled up and their helmets planted on the ground sit about the crowd. A huge man with bodybuilder's muscles, wearing scarlet flared trousers and a bright yellow vest, steps over the whitewashed boundary board and vigorously pumps an old-fashioned school bell.

> *Let us put our hands together*
> *And give three cheers for a man so true.*
> *Clive Lloyd the Guyanese captain was impressive*
> *Julien and Roberts too.*
> *When England invited our players*
> *They never t'ought such a thing would be,*
> *A superfine team of West Indian cricket masters*
> *Will go down in history.*

• • •

Cheshire. Summer 2006

Clive is in his sitting room, watching a recording of the final.

"Real cricket fans at Lord's," he observes. "It's not quite the same these days."

His Yorkshire terrier, Millie, is dozing behind his head along the top of the sofa while Clive sips from his cup of coffee. One sugar, a dash of evaporated milk from the tin in the kitchen cupboard.

"Hmm," he says, looking at himself come out to bat. "I was pretty slim there. We should keep these pictures."

• • •

The West Indies had come to England for the first World Cup believing it was a competition in which they could do well.

"The side was not especially young," remembers Clive. "Rohan Kanhai was back and he was 39. Lance was in the squad too and he must have been 40. But what we did have was players who could bat and bowl and I always thought we were the best fielding side around. At least as good as Australia."

Even though the West Indies had played just two one-day internationals in their history, the notion of limited-overs cricket was not new to them. Only Maurice Foster and Collis King in the squad of 16 had not played in the Gillette Cup or the Sunday League. Roy Fredericks had done so for Glamorgan, Deryck Murray had played for Nottinghamshire then Warwickshire where he was joined by Alvin Kallicharran, Rohan Kanhai and Lance Gibbs. Vivian Richards was at Somerset, Bernard Julien at Kent, Keith Boyce at Essex and Vanburn Holder at Worcestershire. Both Andy Roberts and Gordon Greenidge had been signed by Hampshire. Clive, of course, knew a bit about the one-day game from his adventures with Lancashire.

There were eight teams in the competition. The six Test-playing nations plus Sri Lanka and a collection of club cricketers who represented East Africa. The West Indies were in the hardest group, Group B, with Australia, Pakistan and Sri Lanka. Two sides would go through to the semi-finals; that meant one of the better-known teams would go home early. In the middle of the tournament's first week, that side looked likely to be the West Indies.

Clive's team had defeated Sri Lanka so promptly in the first match that the crowd of five thousand at Old Trafford stayed on to be entertained by an exhibition match between the two sides. It was a little different when the West Indies played Pakistan at Edgbaston the following Wednesday.

Pakistan, who had to win to stay in the World Cup because they had already been beaten by Australia, made 266 from their 60 overs. This was a good score.

"There were no fielding restrictions in this competition," says Clive, "so if a captain wished to defend a total by putting most of his men in positions on the boundary, then scoring anything near five an over was a challenge."

When the West Indies batted, they made their runs quickly but players kept getting out. Six for one, 31 for two, 36 for three, 84 for four.

Clive was soon at the wicket.

"It wasn't a hopeless situation by any means. I'd played enough one-day innings to know the value of patience. I knew how to build an innings, then accelerate. I would set myself small targets and take some calculated risks."

Yet from the non-striker's end Clive watched while Kanhai, then Richards and Julien got out. His wicket-keeper and vice-captain, Deryck Murray, came in at 145 for six. Both men believed the game could still be won.

"I was the floating lower-order batsman in that side for the World Cup," recalls Deryck Murray. "Six, seven, eight, whatever suited the game situation. We still needed 120-odd that evening, but I wasn't particularly worried, because Clive was in and going well."

The pair had put on just seven runs when Clive was caught behind from a leg break bowled by Javed Miandad.

"Oh boy, Miandad. He was jumping around like a kid locked in a sweet shop. He was so excited but you see, I didn't hit it. The wicket-keeper Wasim Bari apologised afterwards. 'Bit late now,' I said, 'but thank you anyway.'"

Now it was Murray and the tail. Keith Boyce came and went and, when the number ten, Vanburn Holder, walked to the square, Deryck could see from the Edgbaston scoreboard that 101 runs were needed and just two wickets were left.

There was a hell of a noise in the ground. The crowd was made up of three elements: about seven thousand Pakistan supporters, the same number following the West Indies and a third group who had just come to see a good game of cricket. It was now the Pakistanis that cheered the loudest. Green flags flew as their supporters looked forward to a semi-final that coming Saturday.

The cheers grew when Holder was caught at cover by Pervez Mir. Andy Roberts, the West Indies number eleven, walked out to bat.

"Last man in, but we couldn't afford to lose," says Deryck Murray, "because the loser is almost certain to go home. There were 64 runs left, with 15 overs and a couple of balls to be bowled. Now, in normal circumstances, four runs an over is not unmanageable, but we cannot make a single mistake. So Andy's job was to not get out. We talked and decided we needed two twos an over, and a few singles here and there."

The few singles, here and there, were scored as Murray and Roberts were helped by the Pakistani field placings.

"Their men weren't in the right positions. In their eyes it didn't matter if they got the final wicket or not because they believed they had the match sewn up," says Deryck.

In the dressing room, many of the players could hardly bear to watch.

"I hadn't given up all hope," Clive says, "but it did look like we had thrown it away. Some of the side had changed and packed their bags. I do remember that a friend of mine, Gordon Andrews, had come and sat with us. He had bought one of those crates of pale ale with him. We both had a bottle and he was saying, 'You'll win this, you know' and I replied, 'How can you be so sure?' and he said, 'Well, I've just come from the betting shop and put a big wager on you to do so.'"

Others in the dressing room were less certain of victory. Bernard Julien had phoned the hospital where his friend, the Pakistan captain Asif Iqbal, was recovering from an operation for haemorrhoids. Julien enquired after his health, told him the score and offered congratulations in advance of his team's victory.

Out in the middle, the attitude was more robust.

"I never thought we were going to lose," says Andy Roberts. "But let me tell you that the only two people in the ground who thought we were going to win were myself and Deryck Murray."

The longer the pair stayed in, the less comfortable Pakistan became.

"Gradually their tactics changed," says Deryck. "We were now making them think about things, not the other way around. Andy grew in confidence, and the whole balance of the game altered. We could see them getting worried. Their supporters had gone quiet, and ours were cheering every run we scored."

Without a mishap, the West Indies' last two men had put on more than half of the remaining runs they needed. They kept going. With five overs left, they wanted another 23.

"When I first went in, I had a look from the middle and the balcony was deserted," chuckles Roberts. "Then one by one they came out. Twenty runs away, 15 runs away, and the area outside the dressing room filled up more and more."

With every over that passed, Clive opened another bottle of pale ale. With four overs to go, a maiden was bowled. Eighteen balls left, 251 for nine, 16 needed. In the next over, to huge delight in the dressing room, Roberts hit a four. Then there was a moment of horror. A misjudged two and Murray looked certain to be run out by a throw from long leg, but Pakistan fouled up the return to the stumps.

One over to go.

'In awful tension, Majid called up Wasim Raja to bowl the last over, West Indies needing five to win,' noted *The Times*.

Nothing came from the first ball. The second was a long hop and Roberts hit it hard. A single was scored, and then – accompanied by whoops from the West Indian fans – the anxious and ill-directed throw from the Pakistan wicket-keeper Wasim Bari gave him a second. Roberts hit another two from the next ball. Two deliveries left and the scores were tied.

One to win.

Wasim bowled a fast leg break, Roberts clipped square on the leg side, Murray dashed. The match was won.

"The ceiling nearly came down in the dressing room," smiles Clive. "Guys were jumping on one another, some were weeping. Pieces of cricket equipment flew through the air."

In the chaos, Clive's friend Gordon Andrews smiled to himself and felt for the betting slip in his trouser pocket.

Such a magnificent performance
That make spectators jump, skip and hop,
With heroes of such fame
We can always win that famous Prudential Cup

"Put us under pressure and we will crack. That was what people thought of us before that game," remembers Andy Roberts. "But we showed that we were as good as anybody."

"This game was so important to us," says Clive. "We were still in the World Cup, but it proved something else too. In a crisis we had, almost for the first time, retained our self-belief. That was so significant. A lot of West Indians had left the ground before the finish. Afterwards a friend of mine rang me up and he said, 'How many did you lose by?' I said, 'We won.' He replied, 'Clive, don't be silly. What really happened?' People couldn't believe it. One other thing it showed was that our bowlers could get runs for us; they believed they could bat. We didn't have number elevens!"

"From that day," says Deryck Murray, "we realised that it was not just the stoic English that could fight back from devastation to win; not just the Australians that had the aggression to do so; we could do it too. The game went some way to changing some of the things about West Indian cricket history that needed changing. And it was Clive who made it happen; he began the journey."

The journey continued. The West Indies beat New Zealand in the semi-final. The Australians were waiting for them at Lord's.

• • •

Clive peers closely at the television. Gordon Greenidge and Roy Fredericks are opening the innings wearing tight little sun hats. Greenidge's is sky-blue. The names of the two sides appear on the screen.

Lillee, Thomson, Gilmour, Walker.

"You see," remarks Clive. "Four fast men, but I don't remember anybody complaining about that."

Clive watches Fredericks hook Lillee for six, fall and knock both bails from the stumps with his toe. Twelve for one.

Greenidge and Kallicharran are both caught behind and the score is 50 for three. The television pictures show Clive walking to the wicket, looking down at the turf. His pads, almost the size of ironing boards, flap with each stride. In the middle waits his old skipper, Rohan Kanhai. Silver hair peeks from under his cap.

Clive's first ball will be from Lillee. He takes his guard of middle and leg and waits as the bowler approaches. Just before the Australian lets go of the ball, Clive's back knee flexes and he lifts his foot from the ground. It is an unconscious trigger movement he makes before every delivery.

"That's so strange," he says. "I never knew I did that. It wasn't until someone pointed it out that I realised. It seems I had always done it, but had never been aware."

Lillee bowls again, and the ball is too full.

'Effortlessly timed off his pads by Lloyd,' says the television commentator, Jim Laker. 'That's going to beat Walker to the ropes. Slightly downhill here at Lord's and, with this quick outfield, the ball gathering pace the whole way down to that Tavern boundary.'

"I felt in pretty good nick straight away," says Clive. "It was just one of those days where you had a feeling that everything would go right. The ball came off the middle nicely; I was seeing it well. I was expecting to get runs."

The screen shows Clive hook Lillee mightily for six, and then smash a good length ball, not a half-volley, for four.

On the sofa, Clive smiles a little.

"I used to do that instinctively," he says. "I had the ability to pick up the good length ball early and, with a flick of the wrists, despatch it over mid-wicket for a boundary. The bowler would be confused, thinking, 'What do I bowl next?' It was easier for me to do it because of my height. What was a good ball for the bowler was a drive for me."

Another big shot off Lillee, but this time Clive pulls without control. His left hand comes away from the bat and Ross Edwards, the best fielder in the Australian side, at mid-wicket drops the catch.

"Big moment," says Clive, reaching for his cup.

Had Clive been caught, when his score was just 26, the West Indies would have been 83 for four.

Whistles blow and bells ring. Under the Grand Stand a banner is unfurled. It reads: 'West Indies – world champion, will tie the kangaroo down.' The painted kangaroo is bound with rope, and is being pulled along by a West Indian cricketer in whites and pads.

On go the batsmen. Forty to Clive. Kanhai is still there but, for 11 overs, he does not score a single run.

"It's difficult to imagine out-scoring Rohan," remarks Clive. "I mean, he was always such a big figure in my life: Guyana and the West Indies. I remember he kept coming down the wicket, encouraging me by saying, 'Go on, stay there.' He knew I was hitting it well that day."

On the small screen, Clive continues to hit well. Max Walker's final five overs go for 49 runs. Most of the blows are hit by the West Indian captain who charges through his half-century and then keeps up the attack to take the game away from Australia.

> *When our wickets started to tumble*
> *well if you hear how West Indians bawl,*
> *But when C. L. demonstrated the meat of the bat*
> *the writing was on the wall.*

Lloyd and Kanhai keep going. Clive cuts, slashes and drives through the 60s, 70s, 80s and 90s.

In the BBC's radio commentary box, John Arlott is broadcasting:

> *And they've scored off the last 15 balls. Now difficult not only to bowl a maiden over, but apparently to bowl a maiden ball. One-eight-five for three and Gilmour – my word, how life can change between Wednesday and Saturday – still a useful bowler and still not the easiest problem for Lloyd to solve. Gilmour comes in, bowls, and Lloyd hits him high away over midwicket for four. The stroke of a man knocking a thistle top off with a walking stick. No trouble at all. And it takes Lloyd to 99. Lloyd, 99 and 189 for three and umpire Bird having a wonderful time, signalling everything in the world, including 'stop to traffic coming on from behind'. But he's let Gilmour in now and he comes in, bowls, and Lloyd hits it to cover, there's his hundred, only half-fielded out there on the cover boundary – and the century's up, and the whole crowd seething with leaping West Indian delight. I can only say it was worth this, it's worth the treatment it's getting. I thought I saw a policeman applauding. Ha! What an innings. A hundred off 82 balls in a hundred minutes. Two sixes, 12 fours, and even Kanhai outshone.*

Clive points at the television.

"You know that was my favourite shot of the day. The technique, I mean. Just one run, but it came off the bat so sweet."

He watches himself raise the bat to acknowledge the crowd. A man in the Tavern Stand presses his hands together as if in prayer and bows deeply three times. The MCC members get up from the white benches outside the pavilion to applaud. Clive Lloyd has just scored one of cricket's great hundreds. He does not sprint down the pitch punching the air to bear-hug Rohan Kanhai; he does not point his bat meaningfully at the dressing-room balcony in a show of macho camaraderie. Neither does he kiss the badge on his cap. He raises the bat and holds it up for a few seconds before wiping his forearm across his brow.

"It was an innings that will stay with me," is how Clive describes his hundred. "But the pitch was good and I felt, if I stayed in, I could get some runs. Thomson bowled me some unplayable balls that took off from a good length. And we all know how good Dennis was and that he would try different things. So it was always going to be a battle."

Before the over is finished Clive will be out. Gilmour bowls down the leg side, the batsman follows the ball and behind the stumps Marsh takes a low catch. Gilmour appeals, but without certainty.

Clive chuckles when he sees Marsh's hopeful face on the screen. He holds the ball up in his glove.

"He doesn't seem too sure, does he? I think I hit it. When we were having a beer later, Marshy told me, 'Look. If there's one player I wouldn't steal out, it's you.' So, I took that as a mark of respect."

The camera pans back to reveal the length of Clive's walk to the pavilion. It is not polite Lord's applause that he hears, but a wall of noise accompanying him to the dressing room. All are on their feet.

On Monday morning the newspapers will print the tributes.

John Arlott in the *Guardian*:

> Lloyd is often a hesitant starter. Now, however, he middled his first ball with monumental certainty and, without further ado, launched himself upon an innings of majestic power. He moved with lithe, almost languid, smoothly muscular speed of a tiger; he hit with the unstrained leverage of inborn timing.

John Woodcock in *The Times*:

> His innings will always be talked about while those who watched it are still alive. To dwarf so many of the world's leading batsmen as Lloyd did, was of itself a mark of greatness. Physically, and in terms of cricketing authority, he towered above the rest. He was larger than life. To have such gifts of height and power and timing is one thing; to use them at a time like this is another. Lloyd made the pitch and the stumps and the bowlers and the ground and the trees all seem much smaller than they were.'

Clive gets up slowly from the big sofa. His dog has woken up and wants to get out of the room.

"I appreciated bowling second," he says as he walks back to the sofa, having shut the door. "I would trust my bowlers to defend most totals. I knew they could bowl straight, and from county cricket I knew we could contain. Not only that, we had a few fellows with pretty handsome arms in the outfield."

He looks at the screen and sees the BBC presenter Peter West.

The Australians are batting. To win, they need to make 292 in 60 overs. No team batting second in England in such a game has made a higher score.

'Here's the seventh over of the innings,' announces West. 'It's 25 for none, and the bowler is Keith Boyce bowling to McCosker.'

"Ian Chappell will never forget this day," says Clive. "I think he was so sure he would beat us."

The Australians do their best to chase the total they need to win the first World Cup. At 80 for one off 20 overs Chappell's side are doing more than enough. Clive comes on to bowl.

"Uh-huh. Here comes the rubbish," he says, raising his eyebrows.

But, in his first over, Ian Chappell tries for a single on the leg-side and Vivian Richards whistles in from mid-wicket to break the stumps with a sideways flick. The non-striker Alan Turner is out.

It is the first of three deadly throws from Richards. Chappell's brother, Greg, will see his wicket destroyed when the Australians have made 115, and the captain himself will underestimate Richards' power while dashing for the bowler's end at 162.

"We talked about this before the match," says Clive. "I said to Viv, 'The Australians are not the best runners between the wickets.' We supposed there might be a couple of run outs. But in fact, we underestimated."

When another sharp throw, this time by Vanburn Holder at backward square leg, runs out Max Walker, the match seems all but over. Australia are 233 for nine and only Dennis Lillee is left. He and Jeff Thomson will have to make 59 from seven overs.

The West Indians in the crowd certainly think the cup is theirs. Thousands of supporters are standing on the boundary edge, waiting for the last wicket to fall.

They keep waiting. Between them, Lillee and Thomson bring Australia closer to their target.

"Of course I believed we would still win," says Clive, "but at the back of my mind was what happened in that game against Pakistan, when Deryck and Andy got us out of an even worse position. With the crowd so excited it was a pretty tense situation."

With three and a bit overs to go, and 24 needed, Australia can still win. Then Thomson hits a catch to Roy Fredericks at extra cover. From all around the ground the crowd career towards the players in the middle.

But the umpire, Tom Spencer, has his arm outstretched. It is a no-ball, not a wicket. Fredericks tries for a run out, and the ball disappears into the blur of legs. Lillee and Thomson start running for overthrows in a chaotic sea of bodies. Where is the ball? The two batsmen turn for another. At the stumps, Deryck Murray looks bemused with two dozen people standing around him as the game goes on. It is as if he has decided to start a game of cricket on a very crowded beach. A policeman is leaning over the stumps to put one of the bails back on.

On the sofa, Clive slaps his knee with his palm. "Oh boy. I think Thommo was wanting about seven from that," he guffaws.

Eventually the game restarts.

The Australians get another run as Lillee heaves wide of Clive at deep mid-on and the captain runs round, picks up and throws back to the bowler in one movement. Then a leg bye, next a dashed single into the on side.

Nine balls to go, eighteen needed, as Vanburn Holder comes in for the fourth delivery of his last over. Thomson misses but comes down the pitch anyway. Is there a run? The ball is in Murray's gloves and the wicket-keeper throws it underarm to break the stumps. Out! Run out! This time it is out!! Here come the crowd and the players risk being consumed by the galloping mass. Murray grabs all three of the demolished stumps and stuffs them under his arm. He sprints for the pavilion like a boy with a purloined chicken being pursued by the constabulary.

"Run to get in, lads!" shouts Clive at the screen. "Run!!"

Cricket's first World Cup has ended chaotically, deliriously – and for the West Indies, successfully. They are champions of the world and Clive Lloyd is their captain. He is man of the match, hero of St John's Wood, hero of the Caribbean. He brought the Prudential Cup to We.

Now he is the greatest one of all time
His batting and bowling was superfine
Captain of all captaincies
He brought joy to the West Indies
For all the world to see
He brought the Prudential Cup to We.

• • •

Clive looks content on the sofa as he watches the television. He sees what must seem like a thousand people patting his back.

"Oh yes, that was tough," he says. "When you were soaking wet with sweat and the fans would be slapping you on the damp shirt – some of them didn't know how hard they were belting you. But those invasions, they were all part of the game then."

• • •

Down in front of the pavilion, Prince Philip has arrived to present the cup to the West Indies. He is wearing his MCC tie.

Clive accepts the big-eared silver cup from him and holds it up to the crowd.

"So many people," says Clive as he looks at the images. "And a lot of ecstasy. Before the tournament, we knew it would be special, but I don't think we anticipated the intensity of it. The drama of the matches and the fondness for the cricket felt by those who watched it. I remember we stayed in the dressing room until late, drinking and laughing, with the cup. And when we went out to dinner, I was so tired. Jeez, I was tired. A century and twelve overs bowled! I ate standing up because I knew, if I sat down, I wouldn't get up again."

"Rod Marsh and I were in our creams for 14 hours that day," recalls Ian Chappell. "We drank in the West Indies' room for a while before the Lord's staff kicked us out saying, 'We're not serving any more beer.' So we went down to the public bar in the Tavern. Clive in his suit and tie, me and Rod in our creams and we stayed there until midnight, surrounded by people who'd watched the game. It was wonderful because the West Indies' supporters down there made it a great atmosphere. Not gloating at all."

The three players were joined by Mike Procter, the white South African Test player.

"After a while this enormous West Indian guy came over," says Chappell. "He said, 'Hello' and then pointed at Proccy and went, 'Who's this?' I thought, 'Aw shit, it's been such a lovely day, and now it's all going to go wrong.' 'Erm … this is Mike Procter,' I said. 'Mike Procter!!!' boomed the bloke. 'One of the world's great all-rounders. Lovely to meet you!!'"

• • •

"From that night on," says Deryck Murray, "there was an appetite for success. We got recognition, we were young and we thought, 'We like this feeling.' With Clive at the front, we thought we could build on it."

Scouting days with sister Jean. Clive, aged 12, in Georgetown.

Clive's mother Sylvia

Clive's father Arthur

Clive's sisters *(left to right)* Jean, Elizabeth, June and Jacklyn with brother Teddy

Clive is introduced to the Queen, Lord's 1969. Steve Camacho waits.

Supercat meets the Louisville Lip, Dorchester Hotel, London. Waveney is beside Muhammad Ali.

Clive and John Winter, his captain at Haslingden

Clive, Peter Lever, Keith Goodwin, David Lloyd

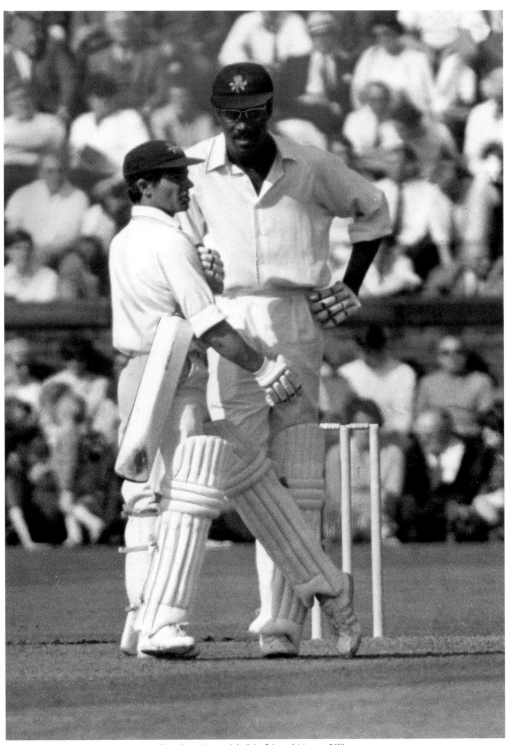

Clive batting with his friend Harry Pilling

The 1975 World Cup winners
Deryck Murray, Gordon Greenidge, Roy Fredericks, Clive and Alvin Kallicharran
"This was the next day," says Clive. "We hadn't had much sleep."

Hitting Dennis Lillee for six. World Cup final, Lord's 1975.

Showing the Cup to the Guyanese Prime Minister, Forbes Burnham.

Lancashire 1971

Standing (left to right): Barry Wood, Roger Tattersall, Ken Shuttleworth, Bob Ratcliffe, John Sullivan, Ken Snellgrove, Frank Hayes, Clive Lloyd, Derek Parker, Jack Simmons, Keith Goodwin, Buddy Oldfield (coach)

Seated: David Lloyd, Farokh Engineer, Peter Lever, Jack Bond, Harry Pilling, John Savage, David Hughes

West Indies 1984

Back row (left to right): Gus Logie, Thelston Payne, Larry Gomes, Jeff Dujon, Eldine Baptiste

Middle row: Jackie Hendricks (manager), Malcolm Marshall, Desmond Haynes, Roger Harper, Courtney Walsh, Milton Small, Richie Richardson Walter St John (assistant manager), Dennis Waight (trainer)

Seated: Joel Garner, Viv Richards, Clive Lloyd, Gordon Greenidge, Michael Holding

Batting for the West Indies, Lord's 1980. Alan Knott behind the stumps.

"What did I bowl? Right-arm optimistic."

Clive with the Australian captain Kim Hughes.

Clive with Vivian Richards, "the West Indian everyone should want to be like."

Clive the manager with Viv Richards, Gordon Greenidge,
Desmond Haynes and trainer Dennis Waight.

Clive and a friend on their 50th birthday.

Something to smile about. Clive and Brian Lara, at the 2006 Champions' Trophy in India.

Clive's children
Samantha, Jason and Melissa

Clive's grandchildren
Maeva, Seren and Naima

"Here's a sportsman I know."
Nelson Mandela welcomes Clive to South Africa.

Clive as match referee.

Barry Richards, Clive Lloyd and Richard Hadlee,
portrait by Andrew Festing,
hanging in the Long Room at Lord's.

AUSTRALIA v WEST INDIES

Lord's. 21 June 1975

WEST INDIES WON BY 17 RUNS

WEST INDIES

R.C. Fredericks	hit wkt b Lillee	7
C.G. Greenidge	c Marsh b Thomson	13
A.I. Kallicharran	c Marsh b Gilmour	12
R.B. Kanhai	b Gilmour	55
C.H. Lloyd *	c Marsh b Gilmour	102
I.V.A. Richards	b Gilmour	5
K.D. Boyce	c Chappell (GS) b Thomson	34
B.D. Julien	not out	26
D.L. Murray +	c & b Gilmour	14
V.A. Holder	not out	6
A.M.E. Roberts		
Extras	lb 6, nb 11	17
	(for 8 wkts, 60 overs)	291

1-12, 2-27, 3-50, 4-199, 5-206, 6-209, 7-261, 8-285

Lillee	12	1	55	1
Gilmour	12	2	48	5
Thomson	12	1	44	2
Walker	12	1	71	0
Chappell (GS)	7	0	33	0
Walters	5	0	23	0

AUSTRALIA

A. Turner	run out	40
R.B. McCosker	c Kallicharran b Boyce	7
I.M. Chappell *	run out	62
G.S. Chappell	run out	15
K.D. Walters	b Lloyd	35
R.W. Marsh +	b Boyce	11
R. Edwards	c Fredericks b Boyce	28
G.J. Gilmour	c Kanhai b Boyce	14
M.H.N. Walker	run out	7
J.R. Thomson	run out	21
D.K. Lillee	not out	16
Extras	b 2, lb 9, nb 7	18
	(all out, 58.4 overs)	274

1-25, 2-81, 3-115, 4-162, 5-170, 6-195, 7-221, 8-231, 9-233, 10-274

Julien	12	0	58	0
Roberts	11	1	45	0
Boyce	12	0	50	4
Holder	11.4	1	65	0
Lloyd	12	1	38	1

Man of the Match: C.H. Lloyd

Umpires: H.D. Bird and T.W. Spencer

CHAPTER EIGHT

IF PEOPLE MISTOOK THIS FOR BLACK POWER, THAT WAS THEIR PROBLEM

Even without the World Cup, the English summer of 1975 saw some of Clive's best batting. In the county championship he scored six hundreds and Lancashire had a chance of winning the title right up until the end of the season. In August, Clive captained the county because David Lloyd had been injured by Andy Roberts when batting against Hampshire, and he kept them in with a chance of the title until rain in the last game at Sussex thwarted them. Lancashire finished fourth. While in charge, Clive also helped the county to the final of another Gillette Cup, their fifth in six years. They had won in 1970, 1971 and 1972, lost in 1974 and now, with David Lloyd recovered, they beat Middlesex to win for the fourth time. Clive scored 73 not out and once again won the man of the match award. 'It would have been a lack-lustre occasion without Lloyd,' reckoned *Wisden*.

Early in the season Clive scored the first of his championship centuries against Surrey at the Oval. He believes it was the best innings he played in his professional career. "It was a wet wicket," remembers Clive. "It certainly wasn't easy."

Lancashire batted first, and at lunch they were 113 for one. Then it rained and no play was possible until the next morning. Then, on a pitch that turned and lifted, Clive was the only man who could cope. Around him six batsmen made a total of 24 runs while Clive, batting with great skill, made 109 not out. In the words of John Woodcock in *The Times*, 'Clive Lloyd played one game and everyone else another.'

"Clive often used to get off the mark by glancing the ball down to fine leg," says one of his team-mates that day, David Hughes. "That was the time in his innings he used to play across the line a little bit and it was then that you had to get him. If you didn't and he started playing straight, the umpire was in mortal danger. He was just immensely powerful. He hit the ball harder than anybody I've seen in first-class cricket. He had this one shot that was almost like a pull off the front foot, and it went different places depending on the height of the ball. If it was a length ball that bounced knee-height, he'd hit it over mid-wicket, but if it got up a little bit he'd pull it off the front foot over deep square. Amazing."

"Explosive is the word I'd use," reflects Jack Bond. "In the dressing room, people didn't wander off and do other things when he was batting because you were expecting something extraordinary. Apart from that, he played very well technically. But he could get onto the front foot and hit it straight or over mid-wicket when other people would look to get back. That must have upset a few bowlers."

Twice in his innings at The Oval, Clive hit a four followed by a six off the next ball.

"I was playing the way I knew how," he says. "And I'm proud of that. I knew the guys were struggling. It was turning sharply but I took the game to Surrey and once I did that I was controlling the situation. But here's the thing: that only happens if you have the ability and the thinking to do so. Batting is all about working things out. That to me is how you assess a great player. When they're confronted by things, how do they counter them? How do I get the better of this guy who's giving me trouble? Do I go in the nets and work it out, do I just try to stay here in the middle for as long as possible? Today, I like the batsman who thinks about how to conquer a situation. That's why I like Lara, Sarwan and Chanderpaul so much. They're always thinking. Where are the runs? Where is the pressure? What won't this bowler like? Work things out and overcome them – that should be the psyche of the sports person. It doesn't matter what game you play; the best of sport is played from the neck up. Because your hands, your eyes and your feet won't always get you runs. I batted pretty well against Surrey that day. The best players know when it's their time – and they make the best use of it."

Not only was this innings of 109 Clive's personal favourite, it contained probably the biggest hit of his career. The six off Robin Jackman, say witnesses, was the longest strike they have seen in their lives.

One of the people watching that day was Brian Bearshaw, the journalist and Lancashire cricket historian. He described the blow in his book *The Big Hitters*:

> The pitch had been laid towards the gasometers and Lloyd was at the Vauxhall end facing Robin Jackman who dropped one short. Jackman later claimed he had slipped – Lloyd said it was an attempted bouncer. Whatever it was, Lloyd hooked it over the traffic in Harleyford Road and into the grounds alongside Archbishop Tenison School. David Lloyd, then Lancashire's

captain, declared: "it was all of 140 yards – I measured it." A few minutes after the shot I went to the point where the ball had departed the ground and where one spectator was still in raptures. "I thought at first it was going to land in the seats," he said. "Then I thought it might hit me, but it just kept on going, over my head." He maintained the ball had cleared Harleyford Road and landed on the lawn between the school and Stoddart House. Some years later I asked the Oval groundsman, Harry Brind, about it. He had no doubts that it was the biggest hit at the ground during his years there and estimated it at 150 yards. "Easy," he said. From the wicket to the edge of the grass, he continued, was 95 yards. "Work it out for yourself," he said. I did, and reckoned it was another 40 yards to the railings on the other side of Harleyford Road, and as it landed well beyond there, it seemed that 150 yards was about right, which must make it one of the longest hits ever.

"It was one of those that hit the sweet spot," is Clive's memory of the shot. "I think Robin was a little surprised by what I'd done to him. Tom Spencer was umpiring and he'd seen a few cricket matches by that stage in his life. He kept telling everyone it was the biggest hit he'd seen."

. . .

At the end of the 1975 season Clive took on his sternest test as captain of the West Indies when the side travelled to Australia for six Test matches. After that, India and England were waiting. The team would play 15 matches, in three series, in less than a year. What Clive learned and experienced during that time would shape the way the West Indies played cricket for another 20.

It was four months since the longest day of the 1975 summer and the great win over Australia at Lord's that had made the West Indians the world champions of limited-overs cricket, winners of the Prudential Cup. Clive's hope was that the West Indians would become the kings of Test cricket too. He predicted that the result would 'hang on a slender thread'.

It turned out to be a forlorn wish.

"We were thrashed," admits Clive.

The Australians won the series by five Tests to one. Lillee and Thomson often bowled at their fastest for Australia, and the West Indies did not play with enough discipline to cope with them. For Clive and his team mates it was a great disappointment.

One of the reporters covering the tour, Henry Blofeld, wrote, 'The West Indies' chances were always going to be severely handicapped if their batsmen were not going to be able to check their desire to play their strokes regardless.'

On the first morning of the first Test at Brisbane, Clive's side went to lunch having scored 125 runs at a great rate, but six wickets had already been taken. The game was one session old and had been all but presented to the opposition. It was because of their play on this tour that the West Indies were nicknamed 'the Hapless Hookers'.

"It took us a while to learn that the grounds were bigger," says Clive with regret. "West Indians have always hooked. That's how we were brought up. We take on the fast bowlers and we still do. But in Australia there was always a man sitting under the ball. By the end I was pretty exasperated. Some of the guys in the side insisted that they could not resist the hook. We were still learning.

"That series hurt a lot. The spirit in the side was yet to develop properly. I took a lot of personal criticism too. People questioned my captaincy – the way I placed the field, the way I led the side. There were times during that tour where I said to myself, 'How am I supposed to handle this situation?' On the pitch I was still working things through."

"I don't think they realised how good they were," is the verdict of Ian Chappell, whose younger brother Greg had taken over the Australian captaincy. "We should never have beaten them 5-1. They weren't a bunch that took long to learn though. In that series, Clive got annoyed at some of the umpiring decisions and he let that get to him, I reckon. As a captain, you have to keep your emotions pretty even because the team picks up on them very quickly. When Clive got cranky, it ran through the side and didn't do them any good. He hadn't been in charge for long, and all the good captains get better as they go along."

"After the tour," says Clive, "people made some hurtful comments that we weren't grooming our leaders properly – but how wrong they were. Yet this was an occasion where the Board must be given some credit because they stuck with me. It is difficult to explain, but the reaction to our defeat says a lot about some aspects of West Indian cricket. I really believe there were jealous people at home that got some sort of strange satisfaction from seeing us fail. They felt in some distorted way that we were undoing a lot of things that previous figures in the game had done. That somehow we were disturbing the past. Now, given my affection for Frank Worrell and my desire to continue the work he did, I found this inexplicable. I wouldn't go so far as to say that these critics actually liked us losing, but they certainly made excuses when we started winning. It's a frame of mind that makes me very sad."

Even though the West Indies had taken a beating, Clive believed morale could be reclaimed. He did not think he was in charge of a bad side. On a very fast wicket, his team had won the second Test in Perth by an innings. Roy Fredericks made a brutally impressive century, one of the most exciting

Test innings Clive says he has seen. The captain himself made 149 and Andy Roberts bowled extremely quickly. The Jamaican bowler, Michael Holding, was playing in his first Test series too.

"Michael was very important. Before the series began, his name was the first I had put on the team sheet. I was aware of what he could do for us. The win in Perth gave me great hope because I knew we had something there," says Clive. "And that was the Test that we had our best side available. In the other games that wasn't the case."

"It's true that we had lost badly to Australia," recalls Deryck Murray, "but what a lot of people didn't recognise at the time was that for three and a half days of the first four Tests, they were all very even contests. As the tour went on though, we didn't perform. In the last two Test matches we fell away."

By the time of the sixth Test at Melbourne, it was 4-1 and soon to be 5-1 to Australia. Team spirit was wilting. David Hughes from Lancashire was visiting the city and sat in the dressing room while Clive battled towards 91 not out in the second innings.

"It was a dismal sight," he remembers. "Clive was guts-ing it out in the middle even though his side were being hammered yet the guys in the dressing room just didn't seem to be that bothered. They were playing table tennis, not watching the game – utterly defeated. They just wanted to get home."

Painful though it was, the defeat proved to be an important part of the West Indians' development as a cricket side. When it was all over, the team vowed that they would never lose like that again. For as long as Clive was captain, they never did.

More immediately, Clive had another issue to consider. Lance Gibbs ended the tour having taken more Test wickets than any other man, 309, yet he was now 41 years old and would not play Test cricket again. The spin bowlers who were needed to carry on his work were not there. Clive had observed Lillee and Thomson and seen the speed of Roberts and Holding. It became clear that other match-winning bowlers were needed to augment his two fast men.

"There was no great plan that 'I must have four fast bowlers'. It didn't work like that," says Clive. "Michael was still learning, we knew that. Andy had great promise. Vanburn Holder was not as fast, but he did a magnificent job. Same with Bernard Julien. What I wanted were fellows who would take me 20 wickets. I didn't simply crave a *pace* attack; what I wanted was a *formidable* attack. I knew I would not be judged on *who* won the games, I would be judged on how many games were won.

"We had players who could do well in the future," he goes on. "Vivian Richards was showing how wonderful he could be, we had two fine bowlers in Roberts and Holding, and it took a drubbing in Australia for us to come back stronger. Sure, the defeat cost us some impetus and it was a low period, but even in the middle of it I still thought that the side was firm, we had things to work with, the players were warming to me and that I was starting to blossom."

. . .

February 1976. After Australia came India in the Caribbean and a victory was needed to help dilute the dissatisfaction of being whipped in Australia. The West Indies won the first Test by an innings with centuries from Richards and from Clive. It was Clive's tenth hundred as a Test batsman and, of the 19 he made in his West Indies' career, 14 of them came after he had been made captain.

After a draw at Port-of-Spain, the third Test was supposed to be played at Bourda, but large parts of Georgetown were flooded, including the cricket ground. So the sides returned to Trinidad, and Clive declared the West Indies' second innings on 271 for six, setting India 403 to win. Only one Test side, Bradman's Invincibles of 1948, had scored that many in the last innings and won.

Andy Roberts missed this game. After bowling very fast for 18 months, he was exhausted and needed a rest. Along with Michael Holding, the West Indies had selected three spinners: Imtiaz Ali, a leg-break bowler from Trinidad and Albert Padmore, the hoped-for off-break heir to Lance Gibbs. The third was the orthodox slow left-armer, Raphick Jumadeen. It was expected that the wearing Trinidad pitch would suit them.

"We had this stupid notion that spinners would get people out in Trinidad," says Clive. "And they've never done so. People who won matches for us at Trinidad were pace bowlers. That's not to say there wasn't turn at Queen's Park – there was – but it turned slowly. There wasn't a lot of bounce, and in my experience it always did something on the first morning. Yet the mythical connection between spinners and Trinidad remained."

As the Indian batsmen walked out after lunch on the last day, their side needed 206 in about four hours, and neither the spinners with the old ball, or Holding and Julien with the new one, could stop them. Only three wickets fell on the final day and two of those were to run outs. India had reached their huge target with six wickets in hand and with seven overs to spare.

It is very unusual for a Test captain to declare his second innings and then lose. It had happened only five times before in Test cricket, and Clive had been playing in two of those games under Garry Sobers, as a winner and as a loser.

"It was a low moment," admits Clive, "but it's important to say, too, that I wasn't put off spinners for life by the experience. It's just that the ones we had weren't winning games for us. We gave India 403 – and lost. Now if that doesn't make a point, what does? I wasn't against spinners. I played them. I picked them. If I'd have had a Shane Warne, he'd have been playing every day. I thought Jumadeen was pretty good. We thought for a while that Padmore would replace Lance. They were given a chance, but the point is that they did not win matches for us. Our fast bowlers were the ones who were winning matches."

Only Jumadeen survived to bowl spin in Kingston for the final, decisive Test. Ali and Padmore were dropped for Vanburn Holder and a pace man from Barbados making his debut, Wayne Daniel.

On a pitch where the bounce of the ball could not be relied upon, three Indian batsmen were hit during their first innings. Holding, bowling from around the wicket in front of his local supporters, was especially fierce.

Gundappa Viswanath had his finger fractured and dislocated. Brijesh Patel edged a ball straight into his mouth, and Aunshuman Gaekwad was hit over the ear. None could play again in the match.

When India had scored 306 for six, the captain Bishan Bedi let it be known that the innings was closed: not because his team were in a strong position but because, as *Wisden* recorded, he 'wished to protect himself and Chandrasekhar, both key bowlers, from the risk of injury.' The declaration, Bedi would say afterwards, was a protest against intimidatory bowling. When his side batted for a second time, he closed the innings on 97 for five, just 12 runs ahead of the West Indies. The reason was that he believed there were no other players fit to go out and bat. Roy Fredericks and Lawrence Rowe took 11 balls to win the game and the series for the West Indies, but it had been their fast bowlers who made the decisive contributions.

"The Indian tactics were not exactly a show of guts," reflects Clive. "The way the game ended annoyed me. I think what Gaekwad showed in the first innings when he got 80-odd was that, if you're brave enough, you'll make runs. This is Test cricket, you know! It's not supposed to be an easy game. As for the bowling, my memory is that there was a ridge at one end – I think they'd had trouble with an underground pipe that raised up the earth or something – so the ball took off when it hit the ridge. I think that pitch and the one we played on at Old Trafford later in the year were the two worst I saw in my Test career. But you play the game. Any talk of intimidatory bowling is false – a false accusation."

• • •

Hove, Sussex. Summer 1976
The England captain, Tony Greig, is sitting on the roof of the pavilion at Hove. His county, Sussex, are playing the touring West Indians in a three-day game. He is recording an interview for the BBC programme *Sportsnight* which will be shown the evening before the first Test at Trent Bridge.

"I like to think that people are building these West Indians up," he says, "because I'm not really quite sure they're as good as everyone thinks they are. I think people tend to forget that it wasn't long ago that they were beaten 5-1 by the Australians … Sure, they've got a couple of fast bowlers, but really I don't think we're going to run into anything any more sensational than Thomson and Lillee, and so really I'm not all that worried about them."

The England selectors have recalled Brian Close, who is now 45, for the first Test, and the interviewer suggests to him that this is 'a panic measure'.

"I think you've got to sum up your opposition," Tony Greig replies. "You've got to try and work out how you're going to tackle them. And one of the things which obviously must be done is that we've got to handle these fast bowlers. It's been the one thing that we've fallen down on in the past, and we're trying to protect against that. Brian Close is a very strong man, a very brave man, and we think he's the best man for the job right now. It really doesn't interest me how old he is … We've got a lot of young batsmen, but I think that quite a few of them aren't quite there yet … So I would rather go for a man like Close now and, perhaps later on in the day, bring in one of the youngsters."

The interviewer presses him further. "So you're saying, in fact, that the recall of Close for the first Test is, at this point, a short-term measure?"

"I should think so, yes," Tony Greig says. "I'd like to think so. I think Closey wouldn't mind me saying that, either. I hope he proves me wrong."

The England captain pauses. Then he says the words that he will never be allowed to forget.

"I think you must remember that the West Indians, these guys, if they get on top, they are magnificent cricketers. But, if they're down, they grovel. And I intend, with the help of Closey and a few others, to make them grovel."

• • •

Clive thinks for a moment. He takes his glasses off, holds them up to the light and replaces them.

"Grovel is not the best word to have used. It was degrading, and the guys didn't take lightly to it. What he meant, I think, was that, when pressure was brought to bear on us, we could capitulate. But because Tony was a white South African, it brought out a bit extra in the players. Tony of course had a little bit of natural arrogance, and all those ingredients meant his statement didn't go down too well."

"Grovel?" asks Andy Roberts. "What I remember is a wonderfully motivating and inspirational speech. It was all we needed for that tour. Every time Greig came in to bat I was thinking 'I have to get him, I have to get him.' We were all fired up whenever he walked out."

In an hour, Roberts and Daniel took wickets and Holding dismissed five Englishmen for nine runs in less than eight overs. England were bowled out for 71 and by Saturday evening, after the West Indies had made 411, Brian Close and John Edrich, the England openers, were back at the crease. Edrich had recently turned 39, Close was almost 45 and a half.

"We always knew we were going to get into trouble," says Tony Greig. "That's why I picked these two blokes, because they could be discarded. There was no real future in putting a youngster in there because I knew what we were in for. It was very dangerous. The truth is that we had to pick a team for a Test match where we knew we were going to be jumping around all over the place. But it was a joint decision of all the selectors. I considered myself to be in quite good company with Sir Alec Bedser, Kenny Barrington, John Murray and Charlie Elliott. These were serious cricketers."

The pair faced 93 balls from Holding, Roberts and Daniel that evening, and several times Close was hit on the body. Holding bowled seven blistering overs without having a run scored off him. Before the close, he had received a warning from the umpire, Bill Alley, for bowling too many short balls. Padmore's off breaks had been used for three overs.

Two newspapers described the West Indies' bowling tactics as 'distasteful' and 'ugly'. Saturday evening, one of them went on, had been '80 minutes of hell'. 'Frequently too wild and too hostile to be acceptable,' was the verdict of *Wisden* which also pronounced that there had been 'condemnation to a man in both the printed and spoken word'.

"First," says Clive, "Brian Close was a brave man. But at that age, should you be really be sticking your chest out when the ball is coming at you at 90 miles per hour? These men were past it, trying to relive 1963, when they had taken on Wes Hall and Charlie Griffith. What was the purpose of picking guys who would not be around in a couple of years? Secondly, there was never an instruction from me to the bowlers to bowl a short, intimidatory line. That was never my way of thinking and it never will be.

"Did Australia diminish the game when they had Lillee and Thomson, Gilmour and Walker? Did England diminish the game when they won the Ashes with four fast bowlers in 2005? We never diminished the game. I have never heard an Australian say we diminished cricket. Not one. They realised that they had enjoyed great fast bowlers too. That Old Trafford pitch was not a good pitch on which to be facing quick bowlers. When the ball hit the cracks, it either went straight up or along the ground. If you were getting the ball to move disconcertingly, you would want to maintain that line. We were branded as cruel and callous that evening, yet it was the pitch that was not up to it."

The West Indies won the game by 425 runs. When it ended, Clive told reporters, 'Our fellows got carried away. They knew they had only 80 minutes that night to make an impression and they went flat out, sacrificing accuracy for speed. They knew afterwards they had bowled badly.'

"This wasn't an apology," he says today. "I don't think we got carried away in the sense that we lost our heads. We weren't bad sports but tactically, the length wasn't right. We should have bowled fuller and they'd probably have lost four wickets that evening."

Michael Holding recalls what happened in the dressing room when the day's play had ended:

"Clive sat us down and said, 'Hey, these guys have been beaten all over their bodies, they have been made to look like fools – but they are still at the wicket. We have to change the length tomorrow, bowl fuller to get them out, not embarrass them.' But what people forget is that it was a bad pitch. There were cracks all over it. And when a ball was not of full length, it bounced awkwardly and got above chest height. You didn't have to bang it in for that to happen."

"My bowlers never tried to maim anybody," states Clive. "If you hit a crack at 90 miles per hour, the ball is going to do something. You get hit playing cricket; it has always happened. But we have laws to cover it. If it's dangerous bowling you can warn the bowler and take him off. The umpires have the right to do so. There are those who never understood that we weren't people who battered and bruised others. On that 1976 tour I remember Clyde Walcott saying to me, 'Clive, when I played, these guys in England – and those fellows in Australia – used to bowl four bumpers an over at us. And why did nobody say anything? Because we used to hook and we took it on and it was part of the game.'"

"It's nonsense to say his bowlers were trying to hurt us," insists Tony Greig. "You can't blame these blokes for trying. I have no problems with what the West Indians did in that Test match. I'll get behind Clive on that. The problem I had was with the umpires; they were absolutely useless. They should have stepped in sooner and given a warning about intimidatory bowling. That's what the laws are for. The other villain at Old Trafford was the groundsman. The pitch just wasn't good enough.

"Boy, if I had been Clive Lloyd that day and I'd been dishing it out, you better believe I would have let those bowlers go until such time as we were pulled into line. It was not up to Clive Lloyd to say to his bowlers, 'Be nice to two of the toughest opening batsmen in the history of the game.'"

"I didn't play at Old Trafford," recalls the former England captain Mike Brearley, "but I played in the first two Tests, and nobody could complain about the bowling in those matches. They bowled their bouncers, of course, and very good bouncers they were, too. It was a new class of bowling, that was what it was. Lots of bowlers waste bouncers. There's either no pace in them, or they're wildly inaccurate, a waste of energy. These guys didn't waste a ball. I think that it took a certain ruthlessness to continue with the policy of four fast bowlers, but it was a realistic policy when you have all that ability and you don't have much in the way of spinners. I agree with Tony Greig. If I'd had those bowlers, I would have used them, too. I think I would have been regretful about it because the art of spin is an important part of cricket, but I would have done it. It's worth saying too that, if Clive had had a Chandrasekhar or a Bedi, I believe they'd have played three fast bowlers and a spinner."

"For years," Clive says, "there have been people who have said we did something unholy by having four fast bowlers. Today even, I read that my players tried to hurt the batsmen, that we were 'wild' or some such phrase. That our play was dangerous, that the age of sportsmanship died with the modern West Indies side. Let me tell you that these things make me very angry."

For a moment, Clive seems as if he may lose his temper.

"I won't have people talking about my players in this way. It's pure, unadulterated rubbish. People better watch what they say. Dickie Bird, who umpired many of the Tests in which we played, has told me that we were the side that gave him the least trouble. Does that not say something? Yes, this sort of loose talk makes me very angry."

• • •

After the big win at Old Trafford, the West Indies won a much closer game at Headingley, the fourth Test, to retain the *Wisden* Trophy. At the moment of victory, players on the West Indies' balcony leapt into each other's arms in delight. The haunting they had suffered for half a year because of their crushing in Australia had been exorcised.

Between the fourth and fifth Tests they visited Swansea, where on the second afternoon Clive's 120-minute 201 equalled Gilbert Jessop's 1903 record for the fastest 200 in cricket history. It was a hot day in a long, hot summer, and the weary fielders had a drinks break during his onslaught – but for which he would have broken the record by several minutes. He hit 28 fours and seven sixes, one of which narrowly missed a parked car 120 yards away in Finsbury Hill.

Then, at The Oval, the West Indies completed a 3-0 series victory. On a dead pitch exhausted by weeks of sun, Michael Holding took 14 wickets bowling as fast as anyone had seen him. Vivian Richards made 291 to extend his record-breaking total of Test runs made in a single year. England had been beaten absolutely by beautiful fast bowling and beautiful batting. In both of his innings in the last Test, Tony Greig had been clean bowled by Holding. His pre-series promise had been made to look a little ludicrous, but the England captain still retained his sense of theatre. Tony Cozier was commentating on the radio when the West Indies declared for the second time in the match:

> *The West Indies have declared, and Tony Greig has gone on his hands and knees – and to the delight of the West Indies spectators, for three or four paces, has in his own words 'grovelled' in front of the West Indies' spectators. Well, that was a good little touch by Tony Greig and I think the West Indies' spectators appreciated it.*

"I don't regret the fact that making those comments spurred the West Indies on," says Tony Greig today. "The reason I regret them is simply because, with hindsight, they were very inappropriate. I cringe when I see them. I have no axe to grind with how the West Indies players reacted to what I said. I would have done the same thing. There are times in your life when you get things wrong and you make mistakes, and that was one of mine. I think the way Clive and the other guys have handled me over the years is unbelievable. Now many of them are my good friends. None of them have borne a grudge as far as I know."

"I don't think Tony meant what he was saying," Clive says. "What he was hoping to express was that he was going to make us suffer. Now I'm not making excuses for him, because it was a bad choice of words. The thing to do is to forgive and forget."

"Those were still the days," says Deryck Murray, "when, as black people, you had to be twice as good to be considered equal. So this was just something else that drove us forward. I think the fact that we all did time in county dressing rooms also helped because, in there, you always had to perform above anybody else to be treated with respect."

"Important things were happening," reflects Clive. "England were a top-class side, and to beat them was very rewarding. We were beginning to move up the ladder. The formation of a pretty strong team had started. From that series onwards, we were proving to other people that there was a purpose in life and a purpose to life. People in the Caribbean knew it, West Indians in Britain knew it. We were now making a mark in sport where the other people before us had done so in education and politics. Many already knew that politicians such as Eric Williams in Trinidad and Forbes Burnham were strong men. Don't forget that Burnham refused to let Garry Sobers into Guyana because he went to Rhodesia in 1970. They were serious about their colour and what it meant to them. They had taken low-paid jobs in London to finish their studies when they were younger. They showed how determined they were to realise their vision. They knew what it was like to struggle.

"So, in the dressing room, the men I captained knew exactly what it meant to win. They understood the past. We talked about where we had come from, what our ancestors must have seen. We knew they must have heard the word 'grovel' for real. These fellows were very strong in all aspects of their lives, not just cricket."

CHAPTER NINE

DON'T CALL ME A LEGEND, AN ICON, A SUPERSTAR, THEN PAY ME NOTHING

The Sydney Opera House. February 2006

Clive is attending the state memorial service for Kerry Packer, Australia's richest man. Packer died on Boxing Day 2005, owning a fortune of about five billion US dollars. He was 68. Clive is listening to an address by the former Australian captain, Richie Benaud, who was a friend and associate of the businessman.

"It does no harm," says Benaud, in his slow, deliberate manner, "for modern first-class and international cricketers to sit back and assess why, in 2006, their financial situations are so markedly different from thirty years ago. Kerry is the reason."

• • •

"Kerry Packer allowed my kids to have a better standard of living," says Clive. "It was because of him that that they got a better education. Now, years later, they have the opportunity to make decisions, to be in control of their lives. I wanted them to grow up in a better environment than I did; and because of Packer, they toured with me; they saw a bit of the world. So I look back now and see that my experience of Packer cricket was about them too. When the kids are home nowadays, we can sit around and discuss sport or politics or life. I think that the partners of my children realise that they've married people of substance. I wanted them to have certain skills, and I am proud of what all of them have done. They don't have to go cap in hand to anyone."

In 1974, three years before Clive and Kerry Packer met for the first time, Packer took over his father's media business in Australia. Consolidated Press Holdings owned newspapers, magazines and two television stations. In televising cricket, Packer saw some potential. The game fitted with his idea of good TV: cheap to make, lots of commercial breaks. Yet to his great irritation, the Australian Cricket Board, which decided who should buy the rights to its product, had a long-standing and seemingly immovable agreement with the state broadcaster, ABC.

Packer came up with an extraordinary solution. If he was not allowed to buy the coverage, why not buy the cricketers and pay them to play in matches that he could broadcast?

Packer's scheme became known as World Series Cricket and, by the end of its two-year lifespan in 1979, sixty of the best cricketers in the world were playing each other, wearing his colours. This Australian businessman had caused an eruption on the landscape of international cricket. The once-predictable view now sported a towering volcano called WSC. The two-year festival changed international cricket, West Indian cricket, and Clive's life.

• • •

In February 1977, Clive was about to start a home Test series against Pakistan. His prediction to his players when he became captain, that winning would bring them more money, had been only partially realised. The fees from the Board were small, and the players augmented their salaries with some private enterprise.

"We were getting a pittance," says Clive. "When we played in Australia in '75/76, the prize money we won and the money we got from running around doing adverts for aftershaves came to more than the official tour fee. Many years later I asked the financial manager of the West Indies Cricket Board why it was that, in the past, the Board seemed to have plenty of money, and he replied, 'Because we never paid you anything.' What a thing to say!"

Deryck Murray has a similar recollection. "We were a winning team and, when we looked at our pay and what other people were getting, we were at the bottom of the heap. There were a lot of old-fashioned judgments still being made. One thing I'll always remember. When we toured England in 1973 it was a short tour, three Tests, and at the end of the first one the English authorities announced that they had covered all their expenses – including the entire West Indies' fee! And we were saying, 'Hang on! Why has our own Board sold us so short??' Even our own Board members didn't respect us!!"

"We weren't gaining anything, the Board wasn't even gaining anything," sighs Clive. "Consider what we would go on to accomplish. If it was today and we'd achieved those things, my God, we'd all be living high on the hog in the West Indies. Don't call me a legend, an icon, a superstar, then pay me nothing."

• • •

Clive and his side were very well suited to an experiment such as World Series Cricket. They were used to earning a living away from the West Indies because most of the side played county cricket in England. Historically, professional cricketers from the region had always left home to earn money. Secondly, Clive's desire to see himself and his men better rewarded created a mood of expectation – and a willingness to explore professional possibilities away from cricket's traditional paths. Clive himself saw one of his responsibilities as captain to be a financial negotiator for the players before each tour. He had successfully got a rise from the Board before the trip to Australia in 1975/76.

Kerry Packer's first plan was to find a team of world stars to take on an Australian XI, and he wanted Clive in the side. One man who had already signed a secret contract to play was Mushtaq Mohammad, the Pakistan captain. Before the fourth Test in Trinidad, he told Clive that he would soon be approached by an Australian with a proposition.

Sure enough, Austin Robertson, a Packer emissary, met Clive at the Hilton Hotel in Port-of-Spain in April 1977. His proposal left Clive staggered.

"He was offering me around 90,000 Australian dollars plus expenses for a three-season contract," recalls Clive. "This was without doubt a very large sum of money; it worked out about three times as much per year as my fee for playing against England in 1976. This was the sort of money that could give a man financial security for his lifetime. I was married and had two daughters, aged three and one. As far as my professional future was concerned, I was in my early thirties and figured I had about three seasons left in the game. That turned out to be a little bit of an under-estimate, but it's what I thought at the time."

"When I saw what Packer was offering, it was a no-brainer," says Joel Garner. "The difference was so vast it was unbelievable. When I started playing you earned a few hundred dollars of the local currency. Now we were talking 20,000 American dollars for three months' work."

The financial benefits of signing for Packer were obvious, but the prize came at a price. Clive believed that he would have to resign from the captaincy of the West Indies.

"For two days I thought about what I should do. I was thinking that, if I took up the offer, I would be finishing my international cricket career altogether. I didn't think that there was any way back if I went to play for Packer. I thought that once I signed, that was that."

After much thought, many conversations with his wife and a few with Tony Greig, who was in the Caribbean and had declared himself as a recruiting sergeant for WSC, Clive signed for Packer.

"When I think about those days now," he says, "it's clear that we were crossing from one world to the next. In the first part of my career for the West Indies, we played some damn good cricket far from home and, to be honest, stayed in some pretty crappy places. But it was all about playing for the country, being a household name, being somebody. In the 1950s and 1960s in the Caribbean, cricket brought you social status. The guys who walked through the gates at Bourda in their maroon blazers on the morning of a Test match were elite people – that was the perception. You were no longer some little kid from Guyana, but a man who people of different colours and classes held in awe.

"But there was another side to it all. By the 1970s we were professional sportsmen travelling in economy class from the West Indies to Australia. Some of us couldn't even get our legs into the space behind the aircraft seats. It was the old way, and Packer was right when he said that we didn't know our worth.

"We all knew that the world cricket hierarchy wouldn't accept change, but most of the West Indies Cricket Board accepted it because they were broke and they knew we weren't paid properly. You see, the grounds were small in the West Indies so the gate money was always limited. It cost a bit for a side to tour the West Indies because of the distances the teams travelled and, of course, the deals made with the TV stations were struck by amateurs. If the Board had been able to pay us well, we wouldn't have gone anywhere. It's obvious. We weren't looked after properly, and we wanted to make a statement. It was not about being rude or disrespectful, we were just fighting for the same as anybody else: a better life. We gave our best years to a sport and yet, when we looked at what the tennis players or the golfers were getting, we were being given pocket money in comparison.

"They tell this story about Arthur Ashe, the tennis champion who was a guest at the Centenary Test in Melbourne in 1977. It was the time that the whole Packer thing was gaining momentum. Arthur looked around the full stadium of 80,000 people and said to one of the players, 'Wow. Look at all this gate money. You'll be doing well from this.' And the bloke replied, 'Not really, we get a couple of hundred quid, that's all.'

"So something had to happen. The risk was that we would destroy our careers but we felt that we had to make a stand. You can't have athletes from other sports being paid properly and cricketers playing for the love of it. We had to spend more time away from home because the tours were important to us financially. In my first two and a half seasons in charge we played 27 Tests and we were playing attractive cricket. People would come and see us and not only were all the seats sold out, but they'd run out of pies too. So someone was making a few quid out of it. It all makes me think even more highly of the Martindales and the Constantines, those West Indian men who played cricket for almost nothing to such a high standard. They had little to look forward to after they retired. We were looking for better things, we wanted to be able to hold our own in life after we stopped playing. And if we were banned or lost our Test status, so be it."

The West Indies won the Test series against Pakistan by two matches to one. Clive's team had now taken their third series victory in a row, something that a West Indies side had not achieved for ten years. Two more bowlers, fast and young, had played in their first Test matches. Thirty-three of the Pakistani wickets which fell were taken by Colin Croft from Guyana, who was helped by the very tall Barbadian, Joel Garner.

Within three weeks of the series ending, the first plans for WSC had been made public. On a wet Saturday evening at the beginning of May, Clive was on his way from Manchester after a championship game against Gloucestershire, to a Sunday League game at Canterbury against Kent. The England captain Tony Greig was hosting a party for the touring Australian side at his home in Brighton, where he dictated a statement to the press: 'There is a massive cricket project involving most of the world's top players due to commence in Australia this winter. I am part of it along with a number of English players. Full details and implications of the scheme will be officially announced in Australia later this week.'

When the announcement came, the extent of Packer's ambition left the cricket authorities aghast. Now, it was not just a World XI against Australia, there would be a West Indies XI too. Some of the best cricketers in the world had signed contracts that had made them whistle. Players from England, Pakistan and South Africa, and many Test stars and good young players from the West Indies and Australia, were going to be involved. There would be full-length matches and one-dayers as well. Games would be played at night; the ball would be white and not red. Winners would get thousands of dollars; losers would get nothing.

It was exciting yet risky. Clive, who was about to have an operation on his knees which would bring his darting days at cover-point to a close, was eager to speak to the man responsible for this great upheaval.

Packer was staying in London at the Dorchester Hotel. Clive was flown down from Manchester and chauffeured from the airport.

"His wealth was obvious," says Clive. "But did this fellow know anything about cricket? That's what I wanted to find out."

In fact, Kerry Packer was not a bad club player. When he had doubts that the Australia off-spinner Ashley Mallett should be given a World Series contract, Packer proposed that he himself should bat against him and if Mallett got him out, he would offer him a deal.

After their meeting, Clive felt reassured.

"We got on straight away," he says. "He was measured but at the same time had an aggressive personality, and I think he saw both those qualities in the way we played our cricket. It was the start of what was to become a close relationship. Perhaps he liked my attitude as well – you know, ruthless but reserved – and the manner in which I conducted myself and the team. I wasn't really someone who would be seen bawling or fighting. I came to admire him because when he said things, he meant them. He went the full distance."

As the WSC roster grew, Clive had been asked to suggest likely West Indians to play in the side that he would captain. Only Alvin Kallicharran declined a contract. Almost all of the West Indies' players seemed happy to accompany their skipper on this journey.

"Lloydy telling me it was OK made such a difference," recalls Desmond Haynes, who was to sign in 1978. "If *he* thought it was good, how could I disagree?"

"I didn't know if the guys would follow," reflects Clive. "All I said when they came to me for advice was this: 'I have a contract, I am going and, if you want to join, it's up to you.' I believed all along that the fellows should make up their own minds. But I think what it showed was these men thought something of me. They didn't have to go to Packer; they were young – much younger than I was – but they came. It meant so much to me that they did. And that is why nowadays I can't get upset with them about stuff that may have happened over the years, disagreements we had, because I still feel so strongly the camaraderie of those days. These fellows made a brave decision. I mean, the money was good but at the start we genuinely didn't know if it would work or not, so their careers could have been over. But I suppose part of the reason why they went ahead was because they thought well enough of me and, for that, I will always be grateful."

"If Clive had said, 'No, this is not for me,'" recalls Tony Greig, "the other West Indies players would not have come. There is no doubt about that. Clive was more than a captain; he was a father figure. He was very highly regarded by his players. Clive had something very special going for him as a leader of men. He was quiet, very reasonable when we needed to sort things out. I was never in his team meetings, but it's enough for me to hear what Michael Holding and Andy Roberts say about him today. I have a great regard for both those men, who were not just great fast bowlers but are very special human beings. When these guys talk about Clive, they put him on a pedestal because he brought them all together. People say being England captain is cricket's hardest job, but I reckon the West Indies job is harder."

The uncertainty the players had about their professional futures was real. Many traditionalists viewed WSC with deep suspicion, if not open hostility. The International Cricket Conference ruled that any player who chose to play for Packer would be banned from Test and first-class cricket. For a while it appeared to be a career-ending edict, but it was soon revealed to be a foolish decision. At the High Court in London in the autumn of 1977, Packer successfully prosecuted the ICC for restraint of trade.

At Lancashire Clive felt some of the traditionalists' ill-will. The 1977 season was his benefit year.

"I was told that, when the buckets were going round for my collection, some supporters were saying, 'He's got enough money now. What does he need any more for?' The women who were collecting tried to explain, 'Look, this is for what Clive has done for us since 1968, it's not just for now.' There were also comments in the dressing room from a couple of the guys, but I expect that may have been jealousy because they were not asked to get involved in World Series Cricket."

• • •

On 2 December 1977, Clive stood in the middle of the VFL Park outside Melbourne. It was a huge Australian Rules football stadium with concrete terraces to accommodate 80,000 spectators. Garry Sobers tossed a special coin, Clive won and Ian Chappell lost. The first World Series 'Supertest' between the Australians and the West Indies was soon to start.

Despite the size of the stadium, fewer than 500 people were there when the first ball was bowled. The cricket authorities in Australia had made sure Packer's men would not play in the traditional Ovals, and the wickets had to be especially grown in greenhouses, driven to the grounds where cranes lowered the huge concrete trays into the turf. By the end of the day's play the spectators numbered less than three thousand. Sixteen hundred miles to the north-east in Brisbane a 'loyal' Australia side were starting a traditional Test match against India in front of a much bigger crowd. WSC had not immediately caught the public's imagination.

"Of course I was concerned that no-one watched the first few games," says Clive, "but underneath we were fairly certain that people would be happy to be getting something fresh from this cricket. Not long after it all started, Waveney was operated on by a surgeon in Melbourne who was a die-hard cricket traditionalist. I gave him a ticket to a one-day match and, when I saw him again, he was a convert. On another occasion I was sitting with Jim Laker at Sydney, when we were playing with the white ball, and he said, 'Oh yes, I like this. For the first time, I can see the ball off the bat all the way.' He realised that this was a different concept but one that wasn't destroying cricket. Look at Twenty20 today. Sell-outs at Lord's and everyone loving it. The game has evolved and moved on. Packer helped that happen. Is cricket dead? Of course not."

Even though the crowds which saw the Supertests and the one-day games in the first season of WSC were small, they were witnessing a high standard

119

of cricket, not least as practised by the West Indies. The Australians and the World XI captained by Tony Greig knew that they were being tested to the limits of their skill.

"Bob Willis?" said one of the Australian players when asked to compare the pace of the England bowler with the speed of Michael Holding, "Bob was a bloody off-spinner compared to Michael."

Another Australian, Bruce Laird, was struck by the intelligence, never mind the speed, of the bowling sent down by Holding, Garner, Croft and Roberts.

"They were so disciplined. You got no width at all. I can't remember cutting them more than half a dozen times in two and a half years."

"The cricket was a lot harder than Test cricket," says Desmond Haynes. "Getting a forty was like getting a hundred. The wickets were as fresh as golf greens and helped the bowlers, so even guys such as John Snow, who was supposed to be too old, were very useful. They made batting difficult."

"You had the cream of the crop playing," says Clive. "The best cricketers in the world were around at the same time, and that doesn't happen every day. The cricket was tough, there was no doubt about it, because most of these guys had played so much, so they played with knowledge. Thinking cricketers are always more difficult to bat against and more difficult to get out. And in the field some of the catching was tremendous. A few of the pitches were pretty lively, and you had to bat very well to get runs. It was just a pity that these innings weren't officially recorded."

• • •

The status of the West Indian players who signed for Packer was different from the position of their English and Australian opponents, who had, in effect, been banned from playing Test cricket. First, the all-but penniless West Indies Board knew its claim over the players was weak. Secondly, most cricket supporters in the West Indies were behind Clive's side. There was no real feeling, as there was in other countries, that the players had been disloyal. 'Indeed,' wrote Michael Manley in his history of cricket in the West Indies, 'empathy between player and public was automatic, fashioned in the crucible of the common historical forces.'

When the ICC had first tried to stop Packer cricketers playing elsewhere, the Board had substantial misgivings about such a course of action, but agreed for the sake of unanimity. The president, Jeffrey Stollmeyer, stated that it would have been 'foolhardy' to vote against the ICC's will and display a 'chink in the armour' of the cricket authorities. He was less happy after the failed High Court action when the legal bill arrived, which all of the ICC members met between them. 'The West Indies were made to pay their full share,' he wrote. 'I have always thought this was morally indefensible.'

But it would be wrong to say that the Board was on the players' side. It was embarrassed by its impotency – and a confrontation between the team and the Caribbean administrators was deferred only because there had yet to be a clash between WSC fixtures and traditional Tests in which the West Indies were due to play. Tension came quickly to the surface when the official Australia Test side came to the Caribbean in March 1978 for a five-match series. The much-weakened team was captained by Bobby Simpson, who was 42 and had been brought out of retirement to lead the young 'loyalists'. The West Indies, on the other hand, were made up of nearly all the same men who had just finished their first season playing WSC, so few people were surprised when the first two Tests were won by the home side within three days.

These were to be the last West Indies Test matches that Clive would play for some time.

"Strange things were happening," he says. "Deryck Murray had been captain for a one-day game before the Test series and had no say in who played – he was just handed a team list including the twelfth man. Then when the Tests began the selectors told me at the last minute that Viv would be vice-captain instead of Deryck. You see, Deryck was our senior pro and our shop steward. I think the Board were trying to flex muscles that they hadn't shown earlier."

The relationship between the Board and the players was deteriorating, and there were two developments that worsened it further. The Board insisted that the WSC West Indians should let it be known whether or not they would be available for selection to tour India later that year – a series that would clash with the Packer season. Secondly, the Board had made advances to three young players – Colin Croft, Desmond Haynes and Richard Austin – who had informally been offered contracts. Soon afterwards, the three players accepted much better deals from Packer. Once again, the Board had lost face.

"The third Test was at Bourda," recalls Clive. "We were two-up, had a winning side and so I expected the selection meeting to last ten minutes. I had heard rumours that the Board was planning something. What I didn't expect was a six-hour stand-off at the Pegasus Hotel, followed by me walking out having decided to resign."

At the selection meeting, Clive was presented with a team sheet for the third Test. Murray's name was not on it. Those of Haynes and Austin had also been removed.

"I was furious," says Clive. "I told the selectors that they were being vindictive and that I would have no part of it. They wanted to get rid of guys – Deryck and Des – who had just helped us win a Test match. It made me mad that the selectors were bowing to pressure from the Board. They were saying stupid things in that room like, 'Are you telling us we can never drop anyone now?' but these weren't cricketing decisions. It was simple malice. After the meeting I left the hotel and it was the early hours, two, three o'clock. I spoke on the phone to Joey Carew, who was one of the selectors, and I told him I was going to resign because I couldn't put my name to such a side. He said, 'Oh, you'll feel different in the morning,' and I said something like, 'Look at your watch, Joey – it is the morning.' And that was that."

After 29 Tests as captain, thirteen wins and nearly two and a half thousand runs at an average of over fifty, Clive's leadership of the West Indies Test side had come to an end.

Later that day, in his resignation statement, Clive wrote that 'the time had come for the West Indies Cricket Board of Control to make very clear the principles underlying the selection of the present team.' He added that it was 'incomprehensible' that a player such as Deryck Murray had been dropped. He finished by writing, 'My agreeing to play in World Series Cricket organised by Kerry Packer has not interfered in my resolve to use my skills in the interest of my people in Guyana and in the West Indies whose help and encouragement have made me what I am.'

Clive's decision brought an immediate response from his players. Gordon Greenidge, Joel Garner, Vivian Richards, Andy Roberts and Colin Croft all said they would not play in the third Test, or the rest of the series.

The Board had anticipated such a show of loyalty. Fresh players, not contracted to WSC, were quickly discovered in Guyana with their kit, even though there was a regional airline strike. The Board wanted to make it clear that the decision of Haynes, Croft and Austin to change their minds was the last time it would be duped. It believed that the men had told them one thing, then turned round and done another.

"What a coincidence," chuckles Clive. "I think that some of the new players were, you know, 'on holiday' in Guyana. It had suddenly become a very popular tourist attraction. These guys had their beachballs under one arm and their cricket boots under the other. When I rang Waveney in the UK and told her I had resigned, she said that the new team had already been announced on the radio and that Alvin Kallicharran was the captain. At the hotel in Georgetown, when the boys who had been dropped went back to their rooms, a different player's bags had already been left on the bed."

As the furore in Georgetown continued, there were news conferences, statements, claims and clarifications. In the midst of it all, one more man flew in – on a private jet. Kerry Packer arrived to fight the corner of the WSC players. He attacked the Board for their inflexibility before taking his contracted players to Barbados to relax at the Sandy Lane Hotel. While there Packer told Clive that, after all the fuss, he deserved a holiday. Clive agreed. Suddenly, he had some time on his hands; no more Test cricket and the second season of WSC was still months away.

"He took me to Las Vegas," says Clive. "Kerry liked the roulette wheel, he was quite a player. I stayed with him for a while – but not too long. I was quite happy with my little winnings so I took them with me and went to bed."

• • •

World Series Cricket had big plans in place for its second season, beginning in November 1978. More players had been signed, and more money had been thrown at promoting the games. There would be more night matches, which had proved a success in the first season, and the players would be given coloured kit. Yellow for Australia, sky blue for the World XI and a delicate shade of pink for the West Indians. WSC also benefited from a dilution of the animosity felt between Packer and the cricket authorities in Australia. Fifty thousand people turned up to see the Australians play the West Indies at a floodlit Sydney Cricket Ground. The game was a great spectacle and a roaring success. WSC at the SCG. That night Kerry Packer sat happily at the heart of the country's cricket establishment.

As he was giving the crowds more, Packer expected more from his players. The schedule was hectic. Teams were travelling day and night, by coach and in the air, to games big and small across Australia. Professional cricket was taken to places where it had rarely been seen. If a side were bowled out cheaply and lost quickly at one of the big venues, they would be told to get out there and play a second match to give the crowd value for money.

"The organisation left something to be desired," remembers Clive. "On one occasion, we got back to the hotel from a night game at 2 a.m. and I told the boys that they'd be back in the lobby in six hours because it was an 11 o'clock start for the next match. But I have fond memories of playing cricket up-country. It would be difficult to forget seeing blokes in string vests, wearing cork hats, drinking beers at six in the morning – and they were getting international cricket! At one of these venues, Roy Fredericks was playing and missing, playing and missing on a juicy pitch, and one of these local guys shouted out, 'C'mon Fredericks, get on with it, yer mug! I've seen more runs in my wife's tights!!'"

Getting chirped by a dinky-di Aussie was one thing the West Indies' players were able to smile about. Being administered a serious ticking-off by a furious Australian billionaire in their own dressing room was an experience few of the side wanted to repeat.

Some of the West Indies players – though not all – had been saying that they were unhappy with the way WSC was going. Their complaints included the scheduling of matches, venues that were too far away and team buses that left too early in the morning. "All the sorts of things that players notice," says Deryck Murray, "when they're not in form." Another cause of dissatisfaction was the pink kit. Officially it was referred to as coral, but to the players it was undoubtedly pink.

"It was a maroon that was not as dark as it should have been," laughs Clive. "Some of the guys did feel they had dressed up as fairies rather than cricketers. I've seen a few odd things in dressing rooms over the years, but Joel Garner's enormous boots painted pink will always come pretty high up on the list. Still, the opposition didn't have much to say when he and Andy Roberts were running in to bowl at them wearing pink."

On 27 December 1978, there was a particularly poor performance by the West Indies in a day-night game against the Australians at Sydney in front of 15,000 people. They were bowled out for 66 and were quickly beaten by six wickets.

As the side were getting changed, Kerry Packer decided to make a visit and give them the benefit of his wisdom. In easy-to-understand language, he told the players that what they were doing was not bloody good enough. He was paying them to perform, he said, not swan around at his bloody expense. If they didn't like the way he did things, there were Qantas flights leaving every day and he'd make sure they were on the next bloody plane. And another thing. He had heard they didn't like their pink uniforms. Well, tough bloody luck. If there was any more whingeing, he'd make sure they'd be given matching bloody handbags to go with them – to suit the way they'd been playing.

"He dressed us down properly," says Michael Holding. "He abused us with every curse you could think of and told us exactly what he thought."

In the hushed dressing room, most of the players stared at the floor while Joel Garner bit his cheeks to try to stop his giggling.

"It was my game off," he remembers. "When you got offered a game off in WSC, you took it. Mr Packer had such a mouthful to say that it lasted three or four minutes. I have to admit I was laughing – not at what he was saying, but at the way he was putting it over. I was thinking, 'This man's crazy.'"

Clive was one of the players keeping quiet, but only because he had known what was coming. The ticking-off was his idea.

"We had one or two guys who were acting up," he recalls. "I said to Kerry, 'You're paying all this money, you'd better have a word.' I think the guys realised that he was serious and wasn't just putting up the cash for them to do what they liked. His language was a bit sparky and there were a few 'Fs', 'Bs' and 'Cs' flying around, but I think he made his point successfully."

It was not all obscenities though. Packer also came with a strategy. After the expletives, he offered the players a vision. He told them that he thought they could be the best of the WSC sides and the greatest of all teams. If they were prepared to make it work, he would be prepared to assist them.

"We took that as a challenge," says Deryck Murray. "Not just to our manhood, but to the way we played cricket."

"Kerry Packer gave us an inspirational speech which helped changed the fortunes of West Indies cricket," believes Andy Roberts. "We did not take a backward step after that."

• • •

The West Indies started to play some very good cricket in the second season of Kerry Packer's tournament. They got different uniforms too. Clive's side won the one-day series and revealed new levels of athleticism in their play. They had employed an Australian trainer, Dennis Waight, who made them much fitter. His appointment, says Clive, was significant.

"Dennis changed so much for us. We got along famously and his contribution – getting us stronger, full of energy – was unheard of in cricket in those days. Trainers didn't exist. It was all part of what I wanted, and that was to make us more disciplined, because discipline brings success. We did stretching exercises, so the guys became more supple so they could bowl faster. They had stamina so they could bat for longer and field more aggressively. Their improved condition helped their concentration so half-chances at slip and gulley at the end of a day's play were held instead of dropped. Dennis played a part in all that. We would get off a plane after a long flight and, within an hour, he'd have us running through the streets. Sure, some of the players used to say, 'I hate you for this,' but they didn't mean it because they could see the good Dennis was doing."

"We'd never had a single person dedicated to us before," says Michael Holding. "We'd never heard of track suits. You played in whites. But Dennis told us that we weren't fit enough. He got us running and stretching and training, and learned what each of us needed."

"I had a very memorable introduction to the side," laughs Dennis Waight. "I'd been at a hotel in Perth, drinking most of the day with Jeff Thomson and Len Pascoe, and we were giving it quite a serve. At about midnight Thommo said, 'Oi, your boys have arrived.' So I wobbled out, and Clive, Vivian, Andy and Michael were all sitting on one sofa in the hotel foyer, just having got in from the airport. I said, 'Mr Lloyd? I'm your trainer', and Clive took one look at me and said softly, 'Oh blimey.' 'When are we ripping into it?' I said. 'Six a.m. prompt,' said Clive. As I left, I heard them mutter, 'We won't be seeing that fellow in the morning.' I went straight to the receptionist's desk and said, 'Ring me at 0430, keep ringing, and, if that doesn't work, knock the door down.' Anyway I got up and felt terrible and had a 20-minute cold shower, but in those days I was pretty fit so I went for a good long run and arrived back in the foyer to hear Clive say, 'I told you he wouldn't turn up.' I tapped him on the shoulder and said, 'Where have you been? I've been waiting outside!' I stayed for the next 22 years."

Waight had been a rugby league trainer in Sydney before he joined Packer, and he had certain ideas about what his new team needed.

"Cricket is played on the ground and so you have to run. Nowadays the boys are always in the gym. I don't mind the weights, but we seem to have more injuries so I think that should be cut down. My training was simple. I told them, 'We're going to stretch for half an hour every day, we're going to do 500 sit-ups in a session, we're going to do a lot of press-ups and we're going to run hard every day.' At first, when I told Clive of my plans, he said, 'You're going to have a rebellion on your hands.' But he also told me he would back me to the hilt. And all the time we were together he kept his word. The players came round to me – sure, winning a lot helped that – but they definitely got fitter. After a while the physio side of my job was virtually nil because we never had any injuries."

By 1979, in the peak of their physical condition, the West Indians played a series in the Caribbean against the Australians. There was a strong desire among cricket-lovers there to see the best cricket on offer – and that meant Packer cricket, not the weakened official Test side that had just lost a series in India for the first time. The local Board was in no financial position to refuse the tour.

"I would accept Mr Packer's money for our Board's survival," wrote Jeffrey Stollmeyer, "but I could not bring myself to attend any of his matches."

"Jeffrey and I never really clicked," says Clive. "We had something in common of course because we both captained the West Indies. But there was little else. We were from different eras. I remember, later in my career, I had led the side for a long time and we were in Trinidad and a friend of mine said to me, 'Are you coming to Jeff's for dinner tonight?' And I said, 'A dinner at Jeffrey's? I hadn't heard there was one. I've been skipper for seven years now and he hasn't ever invited me in for a bite. I don't expect he's going to start now.' My friend said, 'Well, in that case, I don't think I'll go either.' It was as if it was still the days of the elite; now I'm not saying there was a colour issue going on between us, but let's say we never quite gelled."

Had Jeffrey Stollmeyer seen any of the five Supertests, he would have recognised that he was watching a fine contest.

"It was as hard-fought a five-match series as I've played in," remembers Ian Chappell. "We played above ourselves throughout and the West Indies were a bloody good side."

Roberts, Croft, Holding, Garner and Daniel all bowled some brutally fast spells throughout the series, and their efforts were backed up by some brilliant ground work.

"They knew they were 15 to 20 runs better than any other team in their fielding alone," Greg Chappell says in *The Cricket War* by Gideon Haigh. "So they had the confidence and arrogance of knowing that, whatever we made, they could make more. It took a lot to get up knowing they could always raise themselves a cog no matter how we played."

In the first Supertest in Jamaica, Clive made 197 in the second innings as the West Indies won by 369 runs. After a draw at Bridgetown, the Australians won the third match in Trinidad by 24 runs. At Georgetown in the fourth match there was a second draw – but not before the teams had been barricaded in their dressing rooms because of a riot.

It started when spectators became angry after a delayed start, even though the outfield seemed dry. At one stage, the Australians were piling kit bags against the door as it was being pounded under the weight of would-be intruders.

"Just goes to show," says Clive laconically, "that the customer mustn't be taken for granted."

"It was pretty bloody serious, actually. Oh shit, yeah," remembers Ian Chappell. "We were holed up in the dressing room for 45 minutes. Some of the guys had put on helmets and were carrying up-turned chairs to protect themselves. I kept near the security guy because he had a pistol. After a while there was a shot outside and I said to him, 'Oh great, the police are here,' and he said, 'No, that's the other side firing.' Afterwards we found out that some of them had been trying to set fire to the wooden pavilion from underneath."

When the fifth and last game was over in Antigua, with the series shared 1-1, both sides drank together in one dressing room.

"Rodney Marsh turned to me and said, 'This is terrific'," says Ian Chappell. "I said, 'You know why, don't you? It's because there's so much respect between the two sides.' We had belted each other's brains out and neither team had given an inch – that's respect for you."

"I was delighted by some of the cricket that we'd played," says Clive. "That time was so important for several reasons but, in terms of the cricket, it's difficult to overstate the importance of the whole Packer thing for us. Our game, our attitude was very different from the past when we had always showed sides too much respect. By the end of World Series Cricket all that changed because we saw for the first time that the Australians had a soft underbelly and they weren't as tough as they seemed. They had some great cricketers, but we found out that they suffered under pressure. That was a huge discovery. From then on, they didn't beat us for a decade and a half."

The series played in the West Indies brought WSC to an end. By the spring of 1979, Kerry Packer had reached a compromise with the cricket authorities which suited him. The exclusive television rights to Test matches which he had coveted in the first place were now his and, under the terms of the peace settlement, his organisation would control the future marketing of Australian cricket.

"When it had ended and we had come back as the official West Indies side, two things happened," says Clive. "First, it was confirmed in people's minds that it was us they wanted to watch. They still felt we were the West Indies. Secondly, I think they realised that we had been right to go. I was always telling the players, 'We must win everything we can in WSC.' I didn't want people saying, 'They're just playing for the money, so let's support the boys who stayed at home.' And for the same reason when it was all over, I knew we had to do well again, to assure the people that we could still be the number one – that these guys they were watching were the best eleven cricketers in the Caribbean."

"WSC was a very good thing and came at the right time," believes Deryck Murray. "When Clive took over, we wanted to become the best team in the world and we were building on it. What WSC did was throw us – all the top cricketers in the world – into conflict with the establishment. That gave us a unifying force. It felt like it was the players against the world but, uniquely for the West Indies, the public fully supported us and that gave us added impetus. The prize money structure was significant, too. It was 'winner take all' in every game, so we certainly learned how to win! Don't listen to the propagandists who say it was all a circus. This was the highest level of cricket that men had played."

The West Indies benefited hugely from WSC. The one-day game in particular was ideally suited to the way Clive's side could play: fast, straight bowling, aggressive, intelligent batting, brilliant fielding. When World Series Cricket ended, no team was better placed to take advantage of the experience.

Clive's captaincy also benefited. His personal authority increased because he was the sole man in charge of his team. There were no Board members bearing down from on high, no managers deciding itineraries and strategies. Clive led on the pitch and off it.

"We had plans," he says. "Things weren't just happening by accident. We all played together and spent time with each other. We talked about tactics and worked things out. The team spirit flourished. Time and again we sat down and talked cricket. We gelled because we knew one another pretty well and we respected one another. Of course there were clashes from time to time, but we never got into a situation where two guys hated each other. We were professionals – that had never been more obvious

– and that glue kept us together. We embraced a discipline that the West Indies did not have years before.

"After Packer it was like a door had shut on the past. We had some power, we had better conditions, we had some money, we had some negotiating muscle. The players, not the administrators, could call the shots a bit more. We weren't there yet, but we were getting there. Above all, the cricket played by these fellows from the West Indies had got pretty good, too."

WORLD SERIES CRICKET SUPERTESTS
LEADING BATSMEN

Qualification: 500 runs	Matches	Innings	NOs	Runs	Average	100s
B.A. Richards	5	8	1	554	79.14	1
G.S. Chappell	14	26	1	1416	56.64	4
I.V.A. Richards	14	25	2	1281	55.70	4
L.G. Rowe	9	15	2	570	43.85	2
D.W. Hookes	12	22	2	770	38.50	2
C.H. Lloyd	13	21	3	683	37.94	1
C.G. Greenidge	13	23	2	754	35.90	1
I.M. Chappell	10	27	2	893	35.72	2
R.C. Fredericks	10	18	–	621	34.50	–

LEADING BOWLERS

Qualification: 30 wickets	Overs	Maidens	Runs	Wickets	Average
M.A. Holding	272.5	48	799	35	22.83
A.M.E. Roberts	468.1	102	1209	50	24.18
J. Garner	331	43	867	35	24.77
D.K. Lillee	573.3	101	1800	67	26.87
C.E.H. Croft	293.2	56	872	30	29.07
R.J. Bright	464	97	1249	42	29.74
L.S. Pascoe	270.3	38	960	30	32.00

CHAPTER TEN

WE FAILED, AND THEN WE SUCCEEDED

Soon after World Series Cricket came to an end, there was an opportunity for the West Indies to show how good they were at playing in a 'traditional' tournament. The second World Cup was to be contested in the English summer of 1979, and Clive's side were defending the title they had won in 1975. There were no English Packer players involved, and the re-entry of the Australians who had signed up for WSC was delayed by their Board. Clive's side were not troubled by such delicacies. Of the 14 men chosen for the competition, seven had played in the first World Cup and ten had been involved with Packer. Only three young players – Larry Gomes, Malcolm Marshall and Faoud Bacchus – had no experience of either.

"I think, in our own minds, we believed that we were the best side in the world and it was now a matter of showing people that it was so," says Clive. "The side had changed a little; I think that, if you compare the two World Cup squads, you might say that we had fewer all-rounders this time, but our bowling was stronger. Vanburn Holder and Bernard Julien had gone, but we'd picked up Colin Croft, Michael Holding and Joel Garner. We felt confident that we could keep the trophy. After all, if we'd learned one thing from Packer, it was how to win one-day tournaments."

The team's feeling that they were the best was borne out by the result. In the final against England at Lord's, Clive's side won by 92 runs. Vivian Richards repeated his captain's achievement four years earlier, by making a brilliant hundred, and he was helped by Collis King who smote a brutish 86 from 66 balls. As he was walking through the Long Room to go out to bat, King had discovered that a miniature bottle of brandy had rolled into his glove from his kit bag.

"I could have given it to somebody to hold," he recalled, "but I decided to uncork it and down it. There was a burning sensation in my chest as I took the field, but that encouraged me to do great things on that day. When I met Viv in the middle, he said to me, 'Kingdom, I smell something.'

I asked him what he thought it was. He simply went 'Hmmm,' and I knew it was our day."

King and Richards put on 139 at nearly seven an over, and the final score of 286 was too much for England. Clive collected the trophy, and Vivian Richards picked up his Man of the Match award, wearing a shirt bearing the WSC logo.

"I think Mike Brearley's problem," says Clive of the England captain, "was that he had to get in too many overs from part-time bowlers: Boycott, Gooch and that fellow Larkins. I think Viv and Collis put him away for about ten an over at one point. When they chased they had a good opening stand, but Brearley and Boycott batted too slowly. I was pretty certain that we wouldn't be beaten that day."

Clive had now captained his side to two successive World Cups, yet – for all the celebrations on the day – his achievement was barely recognised by the men who ran the game in the Caribbean.

"Can you imagine what would happen to English men who won two World Cups?" asks Clive. "They'd be given the freedom of London and never have to buy a drink for themselves again. I keep repeating this, but some people don't want to hear. Five million West Indians scattered across the Caribbean Sea and look what we achieved. It was a mammoth task, but I'll tell you what happened. Clyde Walcott, who was the manager, came to me before the tournament began and was a little sheepish. He said he'd been told by the Board to offer me £50 as the captain's fee! This was amazing news. It was as if Packer had never even happened. Fifty quid! Well, I said, 'No thanks' and they later came back with an irresistible offer. They doubled it! Oh yes, the Board was very good to me. I got a hundred per cent rise!! It just showed you what these cricket officials thought about us."

· · ·

As in 1975, the West Indies followed a World Cup win with a tour to Australia. Much had changed since the last time, and Clive was determined that there should not be a repeat of the thrashing his team had suffered in 1975/76.

"This was such an important series for us. We had never won in Australia; no West Indies side had triumphed there. The Packer players were all back. The row with WSC was over so both sides could choose their eleven best cricketers. These games would be contested by two very strong sides and, of course, we had to make right the defeat of '74/75, which was a heavy one, but one that I still don't think truly reflected the way we had played."

England were in Australia, too. One of the consequences of WSC was that the Australian Board had lost a lot of money during the Packer seasons. Having two visiting Test sides in the country at the same time was considered the best way of filling up the kitty. The West Indies played both the hosts and England in the one-day series, which they won, but they only played Test cricket against Australia.

As well as wanting to avenge the defeat of the last tour, Clive had another reason for wanting to win in Australia. He was almost certain that this would be his last Test series.

"I had had both knees done in 1977 because I had been in a lot of pain. I remember one time in a Gillette Cup game that season I was in such a state that, when I came off the pitch from batting, I had to take the stairs one at a time. After the operations, I was better but not completely cured, and the right knee still swelled a lot. By the time we went to Australia I was 35 and I thought that would probably be it. I told the boys as much and the first thing they did was to rifle through my kit bag, hunting for souvenirs. It was Kerry Packer who took me to a knee specialist, Mervyn Cross, when we arrived in Australia and he said, 'If this guy says you're finished, you're finished.' I went to him and he opened me up and hoovered out all of the junk from my knee before the first Test."

Clive was not finished. The operation was carried out successfully and the captain was fit for the second Test at Melbourne after a draw at Brisbane when Deryck Murray had led the side.

The West Indies had played seven Tests at the MCG and they had lost every one of them, but this time, with Clive returned and reconsidering his decision to retire, they won by ten wickets. Just a draw at Adelaide in the third and final Test would bring a historic series win.

They did better than draw; they won by 408 runs. 'West Indies so outplayed their dispirited opponents that their victory was one of the most overwhelming in Tests between the two countries,' commented *Wisden*. 'As usual, their formula for success was consistent batting, irresistible fast bowling and athletically alert fielding.'

Going in at 126 for four in the first innings, Clive scored his twelfth Test century. It was one of his fondest.

"I'd been pretty worried about my form. The runs weren't coming easily, and those I had scored were not hit with much fluency. At the back of my mind was the thought of retirement, so I suppose I wasn't in the best shape mentally. When Lawrence Rowe and I were turning that first innings around at Adelaide, it was not a pretty sight for some of the time. So, when the hundred came, I felt a huge sense of relief."

With a first-innings lead of 125 the West Indies had plenty of time when they batted again to make a very big score. 'Let 'em chase 1000, Cappie,' Andy Roberts was saying in the dressing room.

"I'd never forgotten Bill Lawry at Sydney in 1969," smiles Clive. "He set us more than 700 to win. The man had no pity for our suffering! On and on they went. This wasn't revenge, but I wasn't going to declare early."

The strategy to bat on worked. At the end of the fourth day Australia, chasing 574, were seven down for less than 150. The next morning, after nine overs, it was all over. Two-nil to the West Indies. Winners of the Frank Worrell Trophy. Conquerors of Australia. World Champions.

"You know I think what pleased me most," reflects Clive, "is that nine of us had been in Australia for the 5-1 thrashing and were still playing. One of the criticisms our team always had to endure throughout the years of success was, 'Oh, these guys just turned up, bowled fast and won Test matches.' This is nonsense. This side had grown and developed. We did it together. We failed, and then we succeeded. The same fellows the critics said had no future in '75/76 were still here as world champions four years later. So they must have learned something."

. . .

The West Indies did not have much time to savour their success. Three days after the victory at Adelaide, they were playing cricket again, this time in New Zealand. A three-Test tour had been arranged. A one-day game and a first-class match would be followed by a one-day international; then, two days after that, the first Test would begin. It was a trip which was as disappointing as the Australia series had been satisfying. Rancour quickly replaced contentment. The discipline, respect and success that Clive's side had developed all but evaporated.

"We messed up," he admits. "We were tired. It was the first time we had beaten Australia, and then we went straight there. We treated New Zealand badly by arriving off the back of another tour. I went back recently as a referee, and one of the first things I did was to apologise again for what had happened in 1980. We should have played to the whistle, and we didn't."

At the time, New Zealand were one of the poorer sides. In fifty years of international cricket, they had won just ten Test matches and now they were taking on the world champions. Geoff Howarth was about to captain his country for the first time:

"The West Indies were unbeatable, that's what we thought. But we were determined to play to our potential. They had been through a hard trip in Australia, and I think they were a little blasé and a bit homesick. But they were professionals. Maybe they expected to knock us over in three days. We intended to catch them on the hop."

A New Zealand victory in the one-day international at Christchurch should have acted as a warning for the West Indies. Two days later, at

Dunedin, the first Test match began. The ball kept low and there was what *Wisden* called 'sharp' movement off the pitch. The West Indies did not bat well and, in their two innings, there were seven lbw decisions given in favour of the New Zealand fast bowler, Richard Hadlee.

"We were a professional side, we'd had a lot of tough decisions in Australia and we came through that," reflects Clive. "I don't deny that we got it wrong in New Zealand, but some of the decisions made in that series were blatantly incorrect. The umpiring was so poor. One of the umpires was this fellow, Fred Goodall. I don't mind umpires making mistakes because no-one is infallible, but I think Fred Goodall went a little further. Cricket is a game of fair play, the umpires and captains must protect that at all times, and I don't think the way he umpired in that series had the interests of cricket at heart."

By the last afternoon of that first Test in Dunedin, with the home side needing 104 to win, Clive's side had become exasperated by the number of umpiring decisions that had gone against them. When John Parker was given not out, caught behind off Michael Holding, the bowler kicked down the batsman's stumps.

"We all know that Michael Holding is an honest guy," says Clive. "If a man like him was so incensed as to do something as drastic as that, it just shows you how bad these umpires were."

Colin Croft was playing in the match, and he well remembers the incident involving his fellow bowler:

"The ball didn't brush the glove," he says. "It tore the glove off! Deryck Murray took it in front of first slip. Parker was on his way to the pavilion when he was given not out."

At 73 for eight it seemed as if New Zealand would be bowled out short of their small target, but they won the Test by a wicket.

"From then on it was an awful bloody atmosphere," recalls the New Zealand cricket journalist, Don Cameron. "By the time of Christchurch and the second Test it was getting worse and worse. A local radio station composed a satirical calypso ridiculing the West Indies."

Fred Goodall umpired at Christchurch. There were more debatable decisions and, after tea on the third afternoon, the West Indies would not come out of the dressing room to continue the match. They wanted Goodall removed.

"We refused to play," acknowledges Clive. "It was a protest against seeing and hearing some extraordinary things on the tour. Lots of stuff happened, on the field and off. During the match the officials were telling me that the umpires were not accustomed to such fast bowling. 'What you really mean,' I replied, 'is that they're unable to umpire at this level.' Guys were gloving the ball all over the place, fellows were plumb in front and not being given lbw. 'Our livelihood is on the line here,' I remember saying. 'Why don't we just call this a goodwill tour and forget that these are Test matches?'"

After a delay of 12 minutes, the West Indies were persuaded to resume, but the break had done nothing to improve the relationship between the bowlers and Fred Goodall. After being no-balled, Colin Croft petulantly flicked the bails from the stumps. Soon afterwards he shoulder-charged the umpire as he was in full flight running in to bowl. Croft insists it was accidental.

"If Fred Goodall was in Hollywood, he'd have picked up an Oscar. He was staggering around as if he'd been run down by a truck. I'm six foot six and 230 pounds. If I'd meant to hit him, he wouldn't have got up. It's crap that I barged him deliberately."

Fred Goodall's recollection is a little different: "Colin Croft carried on straight through and cannoned into me. I was knocked sideways to avoid tumbling over."

"I had a word with Crofty," says Clive, "but he had done this once before to Bill Alley who was umpiring a Lancashire game, and that was an accident. You see, Colin runs in very straight, then breaks away."

'It was the height of discourtesy when Goodall, wishing on two occasions to speak to Lloyd about Croft's behaviour, had to walk all the way to the West Indian captain, standing deep in the slips. Lloyd took not a step to meet him,' noted *Wisden*.

"Of course I felt personal responsibility for our lack of discipline," says Clive. "As captain, I have to take the blame for that. I wish those things hadn't happened, and no man wants black marks on his record. As the Australians say, it was 'a bit of a blue'. But it's a lucky man who gets through life without having the odd confrontation. Every boy has had a little fight in the playground at sometime! Or else you wouldn't know what the other side is like. I was captaining men of character, we'd been through a lot together and we were no longer going to take whatever came our way. I think I'm as fair as the next person and I think that I played my cricket hard and, if I got beaten, then no problem, but I don't like incompetence. At the highest level of sport you cannot have incompetence. Are there bad tennis umpires at Wimbledon? I don't think so. If there were, people wouldn't come back the next day."

The second Test was drawn, as was the third in Auckland. Weeks after celebrating being indisputably the best cricket side in the world, Clive's men had lost a Test series, their first defeat in four years. New Zealand had never won a rubber at home before.

"We just wanted to get away," says Clive. "We wanted to forget it and start again. One good thing did come out of it all though. New Zealand beat us and as a result they had teams come straight to them who had not played Australia first. When you have finished in Australia, you want to go home. It was treating the New Zealanders like second-class citizens. When I think of that time now, I think first of the terrible umpiring, but we should not have behaved in that manner. If I had my time over again I'd have handled it differently. Even today I regret that things went so far."

In 2007, when he retired as a referee, Clive was heartened to receive an email from the New Zealand umpire, Brian Aldridge.

> I feel that I must express my appreciation of all the help and advice you gave me whilst in our country, and I will never forget your wonderful sense of humour and the very professional way in which you carried out your tasks. I believe it was your total understanding of the game and what the spirit of cricket was all about that endeared you to not only the umpires but all the players – even on occasions you had to remind them how the game should be played.

"I think we've put things right now," says Clive.

• • •

In the two series that followed the fractious and unsuccessful tour of New Zealand, the West Indies did much to mend what had been broken. During a very wet summer in 1980, England were defeated one-nil and in the third Test, in front of his home county supporters, Clive – in what turned out to be the mistaken words of *Wisden* – hit 'the hundred he fervently wanted on his last Test appearance at Old Trafford'. At the end of the summer his side became the first since Bradman's 'Invincibles' in 1948 to tour England undefeated in all first-class games.

Clive's team was beginning to be compared with the game's best. There was time, too, for the skipper to be given a personal accolade.

On a rare sunny evening during the tour Clive was accosted by the television personality Eamonn Andrews in central London. Outside the Commonwealth Institute building on Kensington High Street, the Irishman, holding the big red book, delivered his famous proclamation. "Clive Lloyd. This. Is. Your. Life." All Clive's team-mates were there waiting, surrounded by a steel band who were playing a specially composed tune. Sir Clyde Walcott was in on the surprise and had ordered a taxi to take Clive and himself to the Institute. "Oi," said the driver as they were about to pull up. "Ain't that bloke there off the telly?" He had spotted a celebrity guest on the pavement arriving for the show. "Never seen him in my life!" bellowed Sir Clyde, terrified that the game was up before it had begun. "Now drive on and keep your eyes on the road!!" The bewildered driver was forced to go round the block once more.

Later that night, three of Clive's sisters, Jacklyn, Jean and Julie who had been flown in from New York, came through the doors as his final guests. Jacklyn said, "Well Eamonn, of all Clive's achievements none has been greater than when he was a skinny lad and he took over the bread-winning role. He's a hero to the West Indies now, but he's been our hero since dad died."

· ● ·

The Test matches continued. In Pakistan in the winter of 1980/81, despite the dead pitches which had been prepared to muffle the West Indies' pace attack, Clive led his team to a 1-0 victory. When the cricket was over, he also led them up the Khyber Pass.

"Clive was very pleased with himself," recalls Dennis Waight. "He said, 'I've arranged the guides and the bus and some food – it'll be a great day out.' 'Happy days, Skip,' we all said as we set off. But the bloke who drove the bus was speeding through these mountainous passes and bends at what seemed like a hundred miles an hour. All we could see out of the windows were the 1000-foot drops down either side. Most of the blokes were terrified when we reached the top. 'Strewth,' we all said as the bus skidded to a halt and we got out. 'Well, at least we'll get a nice lunch,' said Clive. As the words left his mouth, there were these three huge explosions. 'What's that??' we all shouted at the guide. 'Oh, that's the Soviets across the border in Afghanistan firing heavy artillery,' he said. 'Stuff the lunch!' we yelled and jumped back in the bus for another white-knuckle ride down the mountain. The boys ribbed Clive for months afterwards. 'Got any more trips organised, Skipper?' they used to ask."

In February 1981, a couple of months after the Pakistan adventure, Ian Botham took England to the Caribbean, the team's first visit since 1974. Clive made scores of 64, 100, 66, 58 and 95 in the Test matches, and his team won the series 2-0. In a little over a year, 15 Tests had been played and none lost by the West Indies since their one-wicket defeat at Dunedin.

· ● ·

In November 1981, it was time for another trip to Australia. Pakistan were the other visitors and, as well as a three-nation one-day tournament which West Indies won, the two visiting teams each played a three-Test series against Australia. "I didn't like this innovation very much," says Clive. "Three matches often don't give a team a chance to prove a lot."

The West Indies returned to old habits and lost the Melbourne Test. The next match at Sydney was drawn, and that meant that the West Indies had to win at Adelaide to retain the Frank Worrell Trophy.

"It would not have been wise to undo all the good things we had built up," reflects Clive. "Viv Richards had been brilliant for what seemed like years, and I suppose it was inevitable that sooner or later he would have a quiet series. We were certainly up against it at the end. But there was some great bowling on both sides. Lillee was a shade slower but still very clever and Michael Holding bowled really as well as he ever had. They were exciting games to play in."

Holding and Roberts bowled out Australia for 238 at Adelaide, and a century by Larry Gomes gave West Indies a first innings lead of 151. But Australia, with a hundred from Allan Border, were 190 in front with six wickets in hand when the fourth day's play ended. It seemed as if the draw Australia needed to win the series was just a couple of hours of batting away.

"I spent the night wondering how we were going to win this Test," says Clive. "I knew that wickets had to fall quickly and that our fast bowlers needed to be especially motivated."

"'Get the four fast bowlers angry,' Clive told me first thing the next morning," recalls Dennis Waight. "'I want them fuming when they go out to play.' Now, there's a hill in Adelaide at the back of the ground with a statue on top, so I ran them up and down the hill three times: Joel, Mikey, Colin and Andy. They came into the dressing room furious and perspiring like buggery, saying, 'Skipper, what's this idiot doing? We won't last the day.' Clive said to them, 'I only want you to bowl for an hour and half. If you haven't taken all the wickets by then, we're not going to win this game.'"

Clive's bowlers obliged. Six Australian wickets fell for 24 runs, and the West Indies needed 236 to win in about four hours.

The team manager for this tour was Clive's childhood friend and fellow Test batsman, Steve Camacho.

"The night before, Clive and I were in the lift at the hotel and I suddenly realised that we didn't actually have the Frank Worrell Trophy with us. It would have been a damned embarrassing situation if I couldn't hand it over. I confessed this to Lloydy and he said, 'Don't worry, we'll win. Then you won't look silly.' I said, 'You're joking, Clive,' but he was insistent. He was as good as his word and guided us to victory in very aggressive style."

Clive came to the crease with the score on 114 for three, and he hit the winning runs with 17 balls of the match left. He had scored 77 not out, and the West Indies had won by five wickets. As he made his way off the pitch, three of the men he had made so cross that morning raced towards him as if Dennis Waight had ordered them on another training run. Grabbing arms and legs, Holder, Garner and Croft hoisted Clive onto their shoulders and carried him from the Oval.

"That was a very special moment," says Clive. "I suppose it summed up what we thought of each other and how we felt about our cricket. They had always shown me tremendous respect, as I had to them, so there was a bit of mutual admiration being expressed. Something like that had never happened to me before."

Clive's Lancashire team-mate, Jack Simmons, was in Australia that winter and had called in on the dressing room during the Test match at Melbourne.

"Clive was having a snooze with his pads on when I arrived," he remembers. "I didn't want to disturb him and so I was chatting to the rest of the boys who were having a game of pool. Holding and Crofty were there. We talked cricket and I said, 'What's it like to have the best player in the world on your side?' I had Viv in mind because he'd scored all those runs over the years. They turned to me and said, 'Who do you mean?' and I explained myself. They shook their heads and pointed at the bench where Clive was asleep. 'Not Viv,' they said. 'It's the Skipper. He's the one we rely on.'"

. . .

The dressing room was loyal and happy. But not all cricketers in the West Indies were content in 1982. Some may have felt they had been overlooked and had been treated unfairly; others were perhaps angry that they had been dropped for younger players. Others still may have thought that with the talent already in front of them, they would never play Test cricket.

Some of these men decided that they would tour South Africa.

To many people in the Caribbean, the notion of a team of cricketers from the West Indies going to play in a country where prejudice against black people was part of the law was incomprehensible.

Many of the Caribbean governments forbade any contact between their countrymen and women and South Africa. When England had toured the West Indies in 1980/81 the Test match in Guyana was abandoned because Forbes Burnham's government objected to the presence of the replacement England bowler, Robin Jackman, who had played professional cricket in South Africa.

"The cricket authorities and governments were united in their abhorrence of apartheid and their determination to use every possible weapon to fight it," wrote Michael Manley.

Despite this widespread feeling, the rebel side included men who had only recently represented the West Indies: Lawrence Rowe led the team and was assisted, by among others, Alvin Kallicharran, Sylvester Clarke, Colin Croft, Collis King, Richard Austin and David Murray.

"We were always being offered money to go to South Africa," says Clive. "I mean huge amounts, massive amounts, hundreds of thousands of dollars. The sort of money that would have made me comfortable for the rest of my life. But money is not all.

"I was so disappointed when they went. Some of the guys who played on that tour told me things afterwards: one of them got thrown out of a shop, another was told to get out of a train carriage. I couldn't have handled that, and I would never have put myself in that position. When people arrived in the West Indies, did they have to sign a piece of paper making them an honorary black man? No, of course not. It's ludicrous. But that's what these boys had to do in South Africa; they were made 'honorary whites' for the duration. It was demeaning. Think of all the black sportsmen going back to the days of Jesse Owens – those guys fought for a lot. Think about the things we experienced in England in the '50s, '60s and '70s: 'No dogs, no blacks, no Irish' on the guesthouse doors. We experienced bad things in America, prejudices that we had to overcome. The worst thing is for someone to tell you that you are a lesser person because of your colour. I can't accept that."

Soon after the rebels had gone to South Africa, Clive was in a club in London, when he was approached by the manager.

"This guy, the owner, brought out some champagne. He said, 'Clive, I respect you tremendously for what you did by not going to South Africa.' I said, 'Thank you' and took a sip. Then he went on, 'Because, if you had gone there, I would have put arsenic in that bubbly.' And I knew he wasn't joking. But it showed how deeply people felt about what had happened. The guys who went, I doubt very much if they made an impact on people in South Africa to make them change their minds about apartheid. They went for a particular reason. It was obvious to my way of thinking that they weren't going to bring apartheid to a halt, and so they must have been going simply for the money. Yet it was by *not* going, that people began to question the regime. Sportsmen, whether they like it or not, do have a lot of influence, and we should recognise that. If people respect you, when you speak, they will listen.

"I didn't intervene with the guys who went to South Africa. What could I do? It was down to the individual's conscience. If I'd gone, I could have been a rich guy, but I wouldn't have been able to live with myself. It was obvious that they would be given a life-long ban. Many of them never came back to the Caribbean, and some of those that did had a tough time, because people felt so strongly about this issue. They could not have accepted that these cricketers could ever play for the West Indies again. We would have been in deep trouble if it had happened."

The crisis of the rebel tour was widely discussed in the Caribbean during the 1982/83 season. Those who had gone to South Africa would never play for their territories again; some of them would even be prohibited from playing club cricket. Nevertheless, the regional first-class tournament, the Shell Shield, was still a strong competition.

The Barbados team included Gordon Greenidge, Desmond Haynes, Wayne Daniel and Malcolm Marshall. The Leeward Islands were captained by Viv Richards, whose side contained Richie Richardson, Andy Roberts and Eldine Baptiste.

Clive was the captain of Guyana. His side had not won the shield since 1975, the last time he had led them, and in between they had been one of the weakest teams.

"I raise a smile whenever I hear I could only captain pace bowlers," says Clive. "There were a lot of fine cricketers in this competition – established Test players and fellows who were just about to make it. We won that competition with a spin attack."

Leslaine Lambert was the Guyana fast man, but the two off spinners, Roger Harper and Clive Butts, and the leg spinner, Derek Kallicharran, who was Alvin's brother, did most of the bowling. Roy Fredericks was the player-manager. He had set aside his post as a government minister to come back to cricket and, aged 40, scored a century and a double century for his country.

'The Guyanese owed their success to many factors,' recorded *Wisden*, 'the most influential, without doubt, being the leadership of the West Indies captain, Clive Lloyd. His presence and stature helped remove the self-doubt which had afflicted their cricket.'

"It was very satisfying to put Guyana at the top of the tree," reflects Clive. "We won the one-day competition too, and the double of both trophies in one season had never been done before. It was an achievement that made me very proud."

As the regional competitions in the West Indies were being played for, the rebel side were playing matches in South Africa in the first months of 1983. Clive stayed in the Caribbean to lead the West Indies against India over five Tests. There were three draws and two wins for his side. In another few weeks both teams would face each other at Lord's in the final of the World Cup.

· · ·

The West Indies had been undefeated in the first two World Cup tournaments while India had won only one game, against East Africa in 1975. India caused a surprise by winning the first of their two matches against West Indies in the group stage of the 1983 tournament, but there was nobody who expected that they would repeat the feat in the final. The Indian captain Kapil Dev told his players that they had done very well to get that far. Enjoy the day, he said.

On another sunny Lord's Saturday India were bowled out for 183 before their 60 overs had been used up. A run rate of three an over was not hard to achieve on the first morning of a Test match, let alone in a one-day final. The West Indies looked to have won the cup by mid-afternoon, but a calamity awaited.

'Even with the distance of time,' wrote the Indian journalist Dicky Rutnagur, 'it is hard to find an explanation for the most powerful and star-studded batting line-up of that era failing to achieve a modest target on a balmy afternoon at Lord's.'

Against an attack of mostly medium pace, the West Indies players got themselves out. Greenidge was bowled not playing a shot, but at 50 for one Haynes and Richards looked in control. Then Richards skied a hook to mid-wicket, Haynes was caught driving on the up, and Gomes edged the ball to slip. Clive pulled a muscle making his first single and needed a runner. He was soon out for 8 and, when Bacchus fiddled at a wide, the innings was in ruins at 76 for six. India went on to win the match by 43 runs.

"I think we all expected each other to do the work," says Clive. "I said at the time that we batted like amateurs, and that's just what we did."

Malcolm Marshall was so confident of victory that he had already ordered a new BMW car which he expected would be taken care of by his winning prize money.

'What utter folly! I cannot now comprehend my arrogance and stupidity,' he wrote later.

"The way I look at it today," says Clive, "is that we lost only two games in three tournaments over eight years. Both were to India. It was just one of those things, one of those days. But we did not apply ourselves properly. I think if we'd been set another 100 or so we would have won. We should have walked it. A couple of months afterwards we went to India and beat them five-nil in the one day series and won the Test series three-nil. They knew then that they'd played the best side in the world. But it's true we were complacent in that final. And what a big thing we missed out on. A hat-trick of World Cups, now there would have been something to savour. Yes, I think we missed out there."

CHAPTER ELEVEN

HE HAS TAKEN US TO THE MOUNTAIN TOP, WE SALUTE HIM

Manchester. One evening in August 1984

Clive had been tricked. He thought he was going to the Lancashire ground at Old Trafford for a television interview. Instead he walked into the middle of his own surprise fortieth birthday party. A steel band was playing, and there were relatives from the Caribbean and the United States. Clive's three-year-old son Jason, wearing a scarlet jacket, had taken to the floor and was dancing like Michael Jackson. Happy birthday, Clive.

Later in the evening, he chatted to his friends and sipped his gin and tonic in the Tyldesley Suite behind Lancashire's pavilion. His younger daughter, Sam, sat on his knee, and he had his arm around her older sister, Melissa. There was a disco, and people were still dancing. *Let's Groove* by Earth, Wind and Fire filled the room:

Move yourself and glide like a 747
And lose yourself in the sky among the clouds in the heavens.
Oh – let this groove, light up your fuse, it's alright, alright, alright.
Let this groove, set in your shoes and stand up, alright, alright.

It was a fine way to celebrate being forty. It had been a good year.

• • •

After the comprehensive Test and one-day victories in India in the winter of 1983, the West Indies took part in a triangular one-day tournament with Pakistan in Australia and played even better, winning the World Series Cup and ten of their 13 matches.

These victories were an antidote to the talk of decline. Around the time of the World Cup defeat there had been murmurings that Clive's side had gone past its best; the loss that had only just been avoided in Australia in '81/82 was significant, some writers noted. The fast bowlers were not as effective as they had been, observed others. The captain has too many injuries to keep playing, said some.

In fact, the West Indies were getting better. After the one-day series in Australia, the Australians were outclassed in the Caribbean in March and April of 1984. The defeated captain, Kim Hughes, said he'd just played against 'the strongest, most professional and disciplined' side he had known. The five-Test series had been won easily, with the West Indies not losing a single second-innings wicket from beginning to end. Only the poor weather stopped the 2-0 scoreline from becoming more embarrassing for Hughes's Australians.

In the summer of 1984, the West Indians came to England.

• • •

"We had a team meeting before the series started," recalls Graeme Fowler, the opening batsman for England and Lancashire. "The topic was *How to Bat Against the West Indies*. Bob Willis began by saying, 'Malcolm Marshall and Joel Garner are a good opening pair.' 'Bit of an understatement,' I said to myself, 'but go on.' 'Because of their accuracy and their pace,' said Bob, 'just try to pick up your singles off them. Next, Eldine Baptiste,' he continued, addressing me and Andy Lloyd, the other opener. 'You're both left-handed so he's going to angle it across you. He'll cause you problems, so be careful.' 'Fine,' I thought. Then I heard Bob say, 'The off spinner Roger Harper is an exceptional and under-rated bowler. He will keep it very tight.' 'No runs there then,' I muttered to Andy. 'So when Michael Holding comes on,' concluded Bob, 'he's the weak link. He's the one we've got to get after.' *Michael Holding!!?!?? Michael bleedin' Holding??!* Well, by this point I remember thinking, 'C'mon then Bob – you may as well put your pads on and have a bloody go.' Dear me. Michael Holding was the one we had to get after."

Bob Willis was no longer captain of England. The job had recently been taken from him and given to David Gower. It was an appointment, believed *The Times*, that could 'embrace a new frontier' and may last for a decade. Gower himself was not gazing quite so far ahead:

"Look at that West Indies team," he says, "and then our own team sheet. Who would get in the first XI? Not many of ours. Ian Botham as all-rounder? Perhaps I would be selected in the middle order instead of Larry Gomes. All the leading cricketers were on their side. We knew it would be the sternest test of our courage as batsmen. Mentally and physically, when facing the West Indies' bowlers, one knew where one was supposed to be, but the trouble was that if you weren't at the top of your game, you wouldn't bet on hanging around for too long. There was no respite. If you saw off Holding and Garner, well whoopee, you had Marshall to come."

Yet it was the batting of the visitors, not their bowling, that captured the first headlines of the summer. In the first one-day match, at Old Trafford, West Indies collapsed to 102 for seven before being lifted by the astonishing ability of Vivian Richards.

Batting with the tail, he hit 189 not out and took the total to 272. One straight six off Derek Pringle was hit out of the ground at the City End. 'Just as Bradman used to do,' wrote John Woodcock, 'Richards spoilt the game. He turned what might otherwise have been a close match into a runaway victory.'

"It became obvious then," recalls Graeme Fowler, "that it was not going to be a normal summer."

"Viv had been batting so well for such a long time by then. So this sort of innings was no surprise," says Clive. "When he started his career he took a bit of time to get going, but I think the big moment for Viv was in Australia the first time around, when he opened the innings a couple of times. That was when he really thought about his technique, and he got some big scores which gave him impetus and confidence. Then he went to number three, and you have to have those two attributes to bat there. That man has to be one of the best in the side. You can't have a poor number three, because he puts too much pressure on the middle order.

"Watching Vivian bat was, of course, one of life's pleasures, and I enjoyed batting with him too. I think his confidence was so formidable. He had nerves, sure he did, just like the rest of us but his great skill was that he never showed them. And, like all the very best, you knew that once he got through a certain period of bowling, he was looking, and likely, to make a big score. When I think about some of the things Viv did in the middle, I just wonder about his hand-eye co-ordination. I mean it must have been exceptional. His reflexes were extraordinary and people would say, 'Look – he's playing across the line' but, because of Viv's skills, that didn't matter. He did it so easily. In the dressing room he was at once jovial and very serious. Not introspective, but he had pretty strong views. Even so, he always behaved professionally. I think one thing that people don't appreciate is that we really had a team without heroes. Everyone was a superstar and no-one was a superstar. Don't forget we grew up with each other, we knew everything about each other. At the team meetings these men didn't hold back if they had something to say."

"1984 was actually a difficult year for us," says Joel Garner. "We were all very taken up with trying to be successful and several sad things happened. We had players who'd had family members die and it was never spoken about in public. The team kept very close and we supported each other. Things that would normally come out stayed quiet because we respected each other and trusted each other. The privacy we had kept us going.

"Besides that, there were a couple of defining moments. We knew we were going to win well when we saw Greenidge at Lord's; Marshall at Leeds; Holding at Old Trafford, not a wicket in sight, then he comes up with four or five. The enjoyment of that tour is that we pulled each other along at every turn. The self hardly came into it at all. We had a group of fellows who were very good friends – and we still are.

"This is the atmosphere that Clive created, and it is one of his greatest successes. Trust in one another. It was a feeling difficult to describe if you had not been part of the dressing room. Viv Richards, for example. On the outside, everybody looked at him and saw him as invincible, but we knew the different frames of mind he could have, we knew the strengths and the weaknesses of him and of each other. We knew when to get into someone, when to say nothing and avoid them. The greatest thing that happened was that we learned what made another man what he was."

• • •

The first Test was at Edgbaston, and Andy Lloyd, Test cricket's first Shropshire lad, was making his England debut at his home ground. He had already seen Graeme Fowler dismissed, when, after half an hour, he was bowled a short ball from Malcolm Marshall. It would be the last delivery he would face as an England player.

"I was in the dressing room," says Fowler, "and there was a locked door between us and the players' area and another closed door between us and the pitch. The telly was on with the sound turned down. The ball didn't get up as Andy thought and it walloped him on the temple guard of his helmet. I heard the crack through those two doors and I was 80 yards away. 'That's hospital,' we said to each other straight away."

Fowler was right. Andy Lloyd was taken from the ground and spent nine days in the Queen Elizabeth Hospital in Birmingham. He did not play any more cricket that year; his Test career had lasted 17 balls.

From his bed, Lloyd would learn that England made 191 in their first innings, and that the West Indies replied with 606. England had lost the first Test by an innings and 180 runs.

Some observers supposed that Andy Lloyd's injury was a predictable consequence of the unsavoury nature of the modern game. In the weeks before the tour started, *Wisden* had blamed umpires for 'allowing fast bowlers to resort ever more frequently to the thuggery of the bouncer'.

'This has got so badly out of hand that for all but a few highly talented batsmen it is now madness not to have a helmet handy. The viciousness of much of today's fast bowling is changing the very nature of the game.

'A day's play in West Indies, when the West Indians are in the field, may be expected to consist of the minimum requirement of overs, if there is one, and as many as three bouncers an over (perhaps 250 a day), so long as the pitch has anything in it. To add to their menace, many of them are bowled from round the wicket. I am not saying the West Indians are the only offenders, but they are the worst. ... Already each season ends with more broken fingers and cracked ribs than the one before. One day, a white line may have to be drawn across the pitch, as a warning mark to bowlers.'

Clive shakes his head slowly and sighs:

"Look. We played cricket within the spirit of the game. Do you think I'd have been asked by MCC to give the Cowdrey Lecture at Lord's if they thought I'd spent a decade in charge of a bunch of bandits? We were not cruel, neither did we set people up to knock the hell out of them. Our boys were quick and, if you have quick bowlers around, people are gonna get hit. Other bowlers hit people. We always thought that it was part of the game. I never thought Jeff Thomson wanted to kill anybody. Certainly none of my bowlers ever said they liked seeing a batsman's blood on the pitch. Jeff hit me in the jaw, Dennis Lillee got me too. But at the highest level, you are going to take one on the body sooner or later. Then look at Viv. The man wore nothing more than a cap on his head his whole life. Are you telling me he never got bounced? He just took them on, like we all did, and, because of that, there was no cause to call it intimidation. When guys in helmets such as Andy Lloyd start ducking into the ball, of course it looks different. As for a white line on the pitch, why the hell should I be bowling half-volleys to all and sundry?

"There's a lot of nonsense talked about 'four fast bowlers' being a bad thing. Today, the West Indies have four fast bowlers, they came to England in 2007 without a spinner and they got beaten badly. Is that a 'bad thing'? England beat Australia with four fast bowlers to win the Ashes. I didn't hear many people saying that was a bad thing. Now, I think what people didn't like, and I'm prepared to say that I believe they were envious, is that our boys stayed together for so long. They won matches, and then came back four years later and won some more. And then there were the reserves. We had Wayne Daniel in the wings. We had Sylvester Clarke. Eldine Baptiste, Ezra Mosely, Patrick Patterson. All these guys just waiting there. It was a machine.

"Yes, I'm certain that envy played a part in the criticism. These fellows who had been writing about cricket for years didn't like it that the old order had changed. They found that threatening. Sport is not always played to the same system; things change. I think that what some cricket writers didn't like was that they looked at us and they knew that a certain kind of West Indies cricketer had died for good. We weren't subservient and grateful for what we got. We were getting mammoth scores, we were bowling well, we fielded well. We paid attention to detail and were very fit. People were not accustomed to that. They were used to a guy having a career of five years and then he was gone. We were there for 11 years. Nineteen years until we lost seriously. If you were born after 1975, you wouldn't have seen the West Indies lose until you were in your twenties. Some people took that hard and couldn't understand that here was a set of guys that had put something special together. Just like Frank Worrell did. He brought people together. And I think the fact of our four fast bowlers gave some critics an easy target, when perhaps their frustrations were about some of the other things I've spoken about."

"I think the game was fortunate that Shane Warne and Muralitharan came along," says Mike Brearley. "It would have been a great limitation on cricket if it had become all fast bowlers. But I do acknowledge that the West Indian fast bowlers were all very different from each other, and it was always interesting watching them play. And I think too that the bowling wasn't as limited as it would have been in other people's hands."

"Within the game," says David Gower, "there is a greater acceptance of short-pitched bowling than without. It doesn't always make for an edifying spectacle and, as soon as you become a spectator and not a player, you probably wish there was a bit less of it. But what these bowlers did was to find the balance, and so I think you got more short stuff if you got on top as a batsman. Secondly, if they were getting wickets pitching it up, then they would continue that strategy. If you hung around they would try a few short ones to see if it made any difference."

"Of course what everyone ought to know is that we wished we had the same bowlers," insists Graeme Fowler. "A lot of people who didn't like it were just jealous. That's a fact. And besides, it was Australia that started it. Lillee and Thomson. That said, I do remember thinking, 'This is not like any cricket I've ever played.' It was a physical assault. They were assaulting me with the ball. It got to the stage where it was physical defence and you had to work out how to combat that and score runs. It was designed to disrupt you, get you out – and it did."

"Was I frightened?" asks David Gower. "I think it would be naive not to admit to a certain anxiety now and again. Seeing Andy Lloyd getting hit, for instance – that didn't help. They were always going to get you at some stage, and at some stage it was going to hurt. You just hoped it wouldn't hurt too much. The worst time was the waiting; that's what did me in. When you walked out, and you'd picked up your gloves, picked up your bat, put your hat on, that's when it counted. It was actually sitting around watching people struggle, that was the worst part. The anticipation was the most difficult thing to deal with."

The report of the 1984 tour in the *Wisden Cricketers' Almanack* would be accompanied by a picture of the England night-watchman, Pat Pocock, 'ducking for his life' while being greatly inconvenienced by a bouncer from Malcolm Marshall. The picture was titled 'the unacceptable face of Test cricket'.

"The unacceptable face of Test cricket?" exclaims Fowler. "Was it hell! We *never* thought that. We just knew we were involved in a monstrous battle. We never thought this was against the spirit of the game. Our only thought was that, if you can't handle it, then don't do it. Just get stuck in. The West Indies were found guilty of nothing more than being superb."

"They were the best side I have ever seen," insists the England batsman, Allan Lamb. "Better than the Australians today. And the game's ruling body had to change the laws because the West Indies were so good. The ICC brought in this limit of two bouncers an over. That was rubbish. We didn't mind getting bounced. They had the armoury and, if you didn't have the equipment to cope, well, go and suck eggs."

"It's a sad day when a bowler can only bowl one or two bouncers an over. It's wrong," says Desmond Haynes. "The umpires have the power. Let them decide. It's so beautiful to see a hook shot played well. I wanted people to bowl short at me! It was like a half-volley, a four-ball. I always expected to get a short ball from a good bowler."

"The criticism has to be rooted in jealousy. Why else would people complain?" says Joel Garner. "And the answer is very simple. You play to your strengths. It wasn't intimidation. If you take short-pitched bowling away, how many fewer runs would Clive Lloyd, Alvin Kallicharran, Viv Richards and Gordon Greenidge have scored? They conquered the bouncer. Take away the short-pitched ball and you take away one of the joys of cricket. It's such nonsense because, when we were on the end of it, we never complained. The way I see it, we didn't bowl excessive bouncers, we attacked people who had a weakness. Australia do it, and no-one worries. Should we play cricket to appease people?"

The West Indies must have bowled full at least some of the time in 1984. Of the 96 England wickets which fell in the series, 41 of them, or 43 per cent of the total, were either bowled or lbw. Alongside the criticism of the West Indian short-pitched bowling were complaints about the pace with which they got through their overs. In 1984, it was 13.5 overs an hour, slightly better than the England rate of 13.4 overs an hour.

"First, I want to say that we never used a slow over-rate as a tactic," insists Clive. "No, no, no. We never did any of that sort of stuff. We were always trying to get the opposition out. Test matches are different to one-dayers; you have more time to think about things and work players out. That's how players get experience – thinking about the game a little bit more. The point is that we beat England in three and a half days and four days that summer. Would the grounds selling tickets want it over in two and a half? We could have arranged it! So you can't have it both ways. I think the spectators saw some fine cricket when we played, and that was despite the best efforts of the opposition doing all sorts of stuff, preparing slow pitches, turning pitches – to blunt our bowlers – and we still got them out. We had men for all seasons. There were times when we would win Test matches within five days – which is the agreed limit for such a game – and we'd get fined for bowling too slowly. Now I find that so terrible. I think they should give us back our money."

• • •

The West Indian side under Clive Lloyd was known for its fast bowlers. Some would go so far as to say that the captain would not use spin bowlers. During his time in charge, Clive selected 11 specialist spinners and two spinning all-rounders to play in Test matches. He failed to call upon a slow bowler in just two of the 74 Test matches in which he led the West Indies. The combination of Roberts, Holding, Marshall and Garner – the best-known of Clive's fast bowlers – appeared together in seven Test matches, and the most games they played together in succession was four.

Roberts, Croft, Holding and Garner played in 11 Test matches together, while Garner, Marshall, Holding and Eldine Baptiste appeared six times. Sylvester Clarke, Croft, Marshall and Garner bowled in the same game on three occasions and just twice did Holding, Croft, Marshall and Garner play as a foursome. In Clive's final series in Australia, Garner, Marshall, Holding and Courtney Walsh were picked together twice and only once did a Test scorecard list the West Indian bowlers as Holding, Clarke, Garner and Croft.

"These men were special bowlers," says Clive. "This was a time when bowlers weren't just carthorses, they were thoroughbreds, beautiful runners, strong athletes." He smiles. "Here, I'll tell you how things have changed. You know, there used to be these games that touring sides would play in England against the TN Pearce XI? That was Tom Pearce who used to captain Essex either side of the war. Anyway, Tom was captaining Essex in 1948 when Australia made 700 in a day against them. So I asked Tom at Scarborough one time, 'What did you do when your guys were getting hit to all parts? Did you set men back on the boundary?' 'Oh no, Clive', he replied. 'We were enjoying it!' 'You were enjoying it???' I wailed. 'What about the bowlers? Were they enjoying it too?' I couldn't believe my ears!"

Clive is guffawing and wiping his eyes. "Oh boy, can you imagine?? Bradman caning you to the boundary all day long. What about a deep point or a guy on the fence at midwicket? And the captain admiring every shot from slip. Oh, those poor bowlers!!

"When I think of the guys that bowled for me, I think of their contrasting styles," says Clive. "When you batted against them, you had to adjust the way you played. We had Joel with his height and that yorker. Mikey bowled very fast; Malcolm Marshall was skiddy and could do everything; Andy Roberts was a great thinker. He wasn't easy to negotiate. Then there was Colin Croft. He was awkward because he came wide of the crease. The whole thing was awesome. People would say, 'Oh, this is terrible cricket.' But tell me who didn't admire watching Michael Holding running up to bowl?"

"I didn't have a stock ball," says Holding. "Different conditions meant I bowled differently. Of course I had the advantage of being able to bowl at 90 miles per hour which helped, but only rarely did I swing the ball a lot. In England it would go if I bowled very full, but in most countries I depended on hitting the seam regularly and getting movement that way. Whichever batsman I had to bowl to, left or right, I wanted to move the ball away from him. Doing that meant there was no second line of defence. He had just his bat and not his pad."

"I learned my yorker from years of practice in local and regional cricket," says Joel Garner. "It wasn't a natural gift. When I first came into the side in Pakistan in 1977, I suppose I was a second-string bowler behind Andy Roberts and Vanburn Holder. Only later did I get given the new ball. I was expected to keep things tight rather than be a strike bowler, but I quickly learned that wickets were the thing. We had six or eight guys bowling for four places. The ball I bowled most often was the in-swinger to the right hander. If I got one to go away, it was because it went off the seam."

"Joel and myself were the off spinners," laughs Colin Croft. "We bowled the long spells and then Holding and Marshall came back on to administer the shock treatment. You know I started as a wicket-keeper? That's what I did at school but, when I got big and strong, I started bowling fast and by, say, 1969, had a pretty fearsome reputation in youth cricket in Guyana.

"It was not until I played for the West Indies that I fully realised that I bowled from so wide of the crease. So the ball always gave the batsman the impression that it was coming in at him. They reasoned that, if the ball started so wide, it had to dart in. That's why I worked really hard at doing the opposite; bowling a leg cutter that would leave the right-hander.

"The other thing I didn't really appreciate until afterwards was that batsmen thought I was bowling at a drivable length. Nowadays they tell me it was shorter than that and I gave people nothing to drive. Maybe that's why I got so many catches in the gully. The ball they believed could be hit through the covers was shorter than they thought, but was too quick for them to make an adjustment."

Deryck Murray kept wicket to all these men, and to Malcolm Marshall as well.

151

"I think that Michael bowled the fastest," he recalls, "but, if I was forced to choose one of them, I would say that Andy Roberts was the best. I've never played with a more intelligent bowler".

"Apart from bowling with his brain, Andy was just so strong," says Clive. "He's the only man I've seen lift Dennis Lillee off his feet by his lapels. That was in the Old Melbourne Inn one night. He could just bowl and bowl. I think he played for the whole year in 1975. And in so many of our victories he played a big part; by that, I mean he could bat too. Lots of crucial innings were played by Andy to save us.

"The man also had a memory like an elephant. He bounced me viciously one time in the Shell Shield. Usually he didn't say much but he came down the pitch and went, 'That's for hooking me for six in Dominica.' The shot he was referring to had been played five years previously. He'd waited that long to give me his quicker bouncer. As they used to say about Andy's short ball, 'One for you to hit, then one to hit you,' although it was unusual to have a five-year delay between the two."

"Sometimes I wish people would remember me for my out-swinger," says Andy Roberts. "But I suppose being known for having two different bouncers is OK. There are many people in the world who cannot bowl one proper bouncer, never mind two."

Roberts's best-known tactic would be to give the batsman a deliberately slower short ball which would be hooked or pulled for four. The batsman then thought he had the measure of the bowler.

"That was the sole intention," he says. "Then the second one would come on to you quicker. A lot quicker."

Roberts also had a lesser-known skill that brought him a reputation as a man who could make the ball play tricks. Many batsmen would look at the ball in the bowler's hand as he ran in to see which half had been shined. They could then anticipate which way the ball would swing. Men who thought they had successfully predicted that Roberts was about to bowl them an out-swinger often walked back to the pavilion having been hit in front by one that went the other way. What they didn't know was that Roberts had a unique ability to rotate the ball 180 degrees with his fingers while his arm was turning over in the delivery stride.

"It was planned and well thought out, like everything in my bowling. It was something I worked on. I wasn't a big party man, I didn't drink so most nights I would stay in my room and think about cricket. We didn't have lap-tops or DVDs of our matches, so my own memory was my computer.

"My bowling went through different phases. I began as an out-and-out fast man, bowling straight and now and again with a ball that came back into the batsman. Later on, in 1975/76, I changed my action, got my arms higher at the point of the gather and learned to swing the ball away from the right-hander. That became my stock delivery.

"But whatever I did, in my mind, I became a batsman. I used to think what I would be able to do if a particular delivery was bowled at me. That's why the batsman was often presented with the unexpected."

· · ·

The second Test between England and the West Indies in 1984 was played at Lord's. When Clive batted, he scored his 7,000th run in Test cricket. Only one West Indian, Garry Sobers, had done the same. Before Clive reached that landmark, Graeme Fowler had made a hundred in England's first innings of 286.

"I took the applause, Botham was at the other end and shook my hand. One or two of the West Indian side did the same. Incidentally, they were best mates with you off the pitch. Clive let everything settle, then, just as the bowler was about to get underway, he stopped the game and walked the mile and a quarter from slip to my crease and he said, 'Fow' – that's what they called me at Lancashire – 'well played, young master' and walked back.

"There was no-one more thrilled than Clive that I'd got a ton, and that was him all over. He never wished ill on a rival because his philosophy was: *I want them to do as well as they can, I want myself to do as well as I can, and then we'll judge who's the better player.* Now the consequence of that thought process is this: all you can do is look after your own game and do your best. I would suggest that, if you see life like that, then you're living out your days in a pretty happy place."

Having reached a second-innings lead of 341 on the last morning, England declared. The West Indies would have to score their runs in just under three sessions to win.

"It was not a gung-ho declaration," says David Gower. "We thought that, if they had a good day, they might get close."

The West Indies did a bit better than that. Gordon Greenidge bullied the English bowlers and scored a double century as his side won by nine wickets. 'It was Greenidge's day, the innings of his life, and his ruthless batting probably made the bowling look worse that it was,' said *Wisden*.

"It was unbelievable," recalls Graeme Fowler. "Allan Lamb was at cover, I was at backward point and Greenidge was giving himself room and smacking it past us for four. The closer we got, the harder he would hit it one side or the other – he was playing games with us. We didn't blame the bowlers, though, it just got to a stage where it became inevitable. We couldn't stop him."

An England captain had not declared a second innings and lost since Norman Yardley did so against Bradman's Australians at Headingley in 1948.

"It was a mighty humbling day to be a skipper in the field against that," says David Gower. "They won with nearly 12 overs of the last 20 left. To use a colloquial expression, all the wheels came off. The chairman of selectors, Peter May, was keen that we declared early. By the mathematics of the 1960s, that made sense; by the mathematics practised by the West Indies, it was a bit ambitious. None of us expected to lose like that."

"It wasn't the done thing to go on batting," says Fowler. "And that was the trouble. We were stuck in the 1960s and the West Indies were playing 21st century cricket in 1984."

• • •

"What an innings that was," says Clive. "Gordon at his best. A great side must have great openers. And the thing about Greenidge and Haynes was that, aside from their ability, they were so well organised and they had the interests of West Indian cricket at heart. Gordon was the punisher, the more aggressive of the two. Desmond, as a batsman, was more conservative, the solid one."

"My role was a supporting one," says Desmond Haynes. "I would never try to outdo Gordon; I wanted to make sure that our batting partnership was a long one. I don't mean the number of runs we put on in an innings; I mean the number of Tests we played. If he made 89 and I got 11, then it was a hundred partnership and I would be picked in the next game. I was happy to play second fiddle. I always thought that Gordon was better than I was. He was a more complete player. Early on, I was not so good against the spinners, but Gordon was fine to watch. Always working the ball around, sweeping."

"A great number three helps," Clive adds, "and you can't get any better than Viv. And don't forget the middle order. As the side grew, we had Larry Gomes, a wonderful anchorman on whom we could all depend. People could play around him. But so often Gordon and Des gave us a good start, and that was of the utmost importance. We knew that, if we made anything over 300, the opposition was likely to be on the run because we had bowlers who could cause trouble. They loved bowling at a side while looking at a big first innings on the board, and many times we had Gordon and Des to thank for putting us in that position."

• • •

At Lord's, England had been mocked by a batsman. At Leeds for the third Test it was a bowler's turn.

In the first half hour of the game Malcolm Marshall was hit on the hand at gully and fractured his thumb in two places. The doctor, who set his left arm in plaster soon afterwards, told him not to play cricket for ten days. Had he been watching the game two days later, he may have been surprised to see his patient walking out at number eleven, holding his bat in his good hand. Larry Gomes was not out 96 and Marshall had decided to help him reach a hundred.

"It started out as nothing more than a dressing-room joke," remembers Clive. "I made a light-hearted remark in passing to Malcolm and he said, 'Do you really want me to play?' It got me thinking and I said, 'Well, yeah, OK then.' I think it showed the sort of team spirit we had in those days. Nowadays they would just say, 'He's out of the game.' But this fellow wanted to be in the thick of it. I suppose it also illustrated what we felt about playing cricket for the West Indies."

Marshall lasted eight balls. Long enough for Gomes to end the innings 104 not out and for the England bowler Paul Allott to be hit for four by a man holding a bat in one hand.

England may have been able to raise a brief smile about Marshall the one-armed batsman, but there were no laughs to be had batting against Marshall the one-armed bowler. Single-handedly he took them apart with seven for 53 in England's second innings, his best bowling figures in a Test match. One of the wickets was a caught and bowled.

"I have *so* much respect for that guy," says Clive. "I never had any problems with him. He listened. From slip I would just put my arm up to signal for him to come around the wicket, and he would never challenge it. And so, if he ever wanted anything, I would always let him have it because I knew that he was such an intelligent bowler, up there with the best we've had. Even if I didn't think what he had suggested would work, I always let him try because I had a great respect for his knowledge of the game.

"He played against us at Lancashire once when he was at Hampshire. He bowled five of the most beautiful balls against Gehan Mendis and the sixth just slipped down the leg side. Malcolm was effing and blinding because he didn't get it on the spot. You know, this man had just bowled five unplayable balls and the last one strayed, so he was furious. That shows just how competitive he was. These are the things I remember about Malcolm. He was a very intelligent cricketer. He and Andy Roberts were deep thinkers; they didn't just run up and bowl."

England lost the third Test by eight wickets. Clive's side were now 3-0 up with two to play. The series had been won. It had been more than sixty years since England had lost the first three home games of a rubber.

"It was now a question of the margin," says David Gower. "By this stage I was trying to deal with my own emotions as a player and as a captain. I had a certain feeling of helplessness. We'd been beaten badly and whatever I said when I made an attempt to build or maintain an aura of confidence in the dressing room felt a bit hollow."

"We always thought," says Desmond Haynes, "that the England players were put under too much pressure every time we toured the country. From the newspapers and from their selectors. So what happened was that they kept bringing in young players – 21 guys played against us in 1984 – and some of them were making their debuts against one of the strongest sides they'd ever play in their lives. C'mon! That was just such juicy prey for our fast bowlers."

• • •

"We had a team photo taken before the fourth Test at Old Trafford," remembers Graeme Fowler. "Botham was on the front row, looked around and said, 'Bloody hell, in fifty years time they'll look back and think this was a good side, won't they?'" Five days later England had been defeated by an innings and 64 runs.

"I think Beefy's frustration," continues Fowler, "was the knowledge that we were fighting cannons with pea-shooters. He knew we couldn't compete, yet in every Test match we'd got on top of them at some stage. Ian knew we were in a massive scrap and for the first time he couldn't save us by himself. He was upset that there was no repeat of the Ashes in 1981. It got to a stage where it became nothing to do with tactics, but simply ability and courage."

"It's true, we were a very difficult side to throw down by this stage," says Clive. "We had a lot of knowledge. I mean, for nine years some of us had played the toughest cricket together. That's a lot of shared experiences. We had the best openers in the world, our spinner Roger Harper was playing well. Larry Gomes, who was often ignored by people who praised our batting, was having an exceptional series. The middle order was very solid. We had the best of young and old, the best of pace and superb fielding."

There was one England player who had some success that summer. Allan Lamb made three hundreds, at Lord's, Headingley and Old Trafford. He had worked out a way to play the West Indian fast bowling.

"First of all there was a bit of desire there," he explains. "I wanted to prove people wrong because I'd been hurt by criticism of my ability. I'd been told that I was not good enough to play for England.

"So that was the mental drive. At the crease my technique went something like this. First, I stood still. I was always looking to get my balance going forward. If I went a little bit forward, I could always get back; but, if I started off by going back, there was no time to shift forward before the ball was on me.

"Secondly, I looked at the bowling hand. It's fine watching the ball, but I preferred to watch the wrist. A lot of the guys didn't do that. 'Watch the wrist!' I'd say because if the ball stays in the fingers longer, it's going to be pitched up; if the wrist cocks very quickly, it's going to be a bouncer. People said, 'How the hell can you do that? There's no time.' But of course you could because Michael Holding and Joel Garner, for example, both showed you the ball as they ran up – and that helped.

"Thirdly, I always tried to rotate the strike. The West Indies loved to bowl six balls at you. I was always saying, 'Let's get singles.' Don't get one and let the other guy take a bombardment for the rest of the over.

"The final thing was aggression; take them on. Of course you're not going to hook every ball for six, but don't take a step back. Be positive in your shots and, if you're going to play a big drive, make sure you throw the bat at the ball because it may fly over fourth slip. And if you're getting those singles, fourth slip won't be there any more; the fellow will be at extra cover."

Despite his success that summer, Allan Lamb's technique could not save him at the Oval in the fifth Test. He made 12 and 1. Clive made 60 not out and 36, and at a minute after noon on the final day, England were bowled out. Five-nil to the West Indies.

'Blackwash.'

"When I was out in the second innings I was sitting in the dressing room and this sensation washed over me," recalls Graeme Fowler. "I'd played in all the Tests – ten knocks against those lads. And I was filled with a sense of relief. Not relief that I was out, but that I was still in one piece. I got hit in the head by Winston Davis at Old Trafford, Joel Garner smashed my box to pieces at Lord's. Malcolm had done me earlier in the Oval Test, and now, I suppose I felt that I'd got through it and nothing else could happen."

No side had inflicted such a complete defeat on England in their own country. Since Test cricket began, only four other teams had won all the matches in a five-Test series. The West Indies equalled the world record of eight successive Test match wins, and had not been beaten for 23 matches. Only once in the past 39 games had Clive's side lost.

"We never expected five-nil," he says. "I must be honest and say that we didn't expect to lose, but the margin of victory was a bonus. By now, we were formidable. I think we were largely respected wherever we went, certainly by other cricketers, and people spoke about West Indian cricket with admiration. If this was to be almost the end for me, I could not have asked for much more than that. We were getting near the pinnacle.

"I knew, when I went out to bat in that second innings, I wouldn't be back. But, given the scoreline, it wasn't a bad way for a West Indian captain to leave England. I wasn't too sad. The theatre of cricket is one thing, and that's what the people want to watch but all the players are professionals. I think I remember getting a decent hand after I was out."

And, when he had walked to the wicket, Clive had been cheered by the crowd – and applauded by the England side. He played, said *The Times*, as though he could go on making Test runs for a long time yet.

'Not since Bradman departed has there been, in an Oval Test match, a reception like it,' wrote John Woodcock.

• • •

There would be one final Test tour for Clive. He would lead his side to Australia for a fourth time.

There were big victories for the West Indies in the first two Test matches at Perth and Brisbane. At the Gabba Clive made his 19th and final Test century. He came in at 184 for five and put on 152 with Richie Richardson. With a first-innings lead of 249, the West Indies needed only 23 runs to win on the fourth day. They were 2-0 up in the series, and Kim Hughes stood down from the Australian captaincy at the end of the match, breaking into tears as he read his resignation statement at a news conference.

"I wonder if he got all the help he needed," says Clive. "He was a fine batsman and a decent man. If you are passionate about what you do, inevitably you will have weak moments, and that's what happened to Kim in front of everyone. I felt sorry for him, but I also told him that it was no disgrace to come up against a very strong side. We came up against a very good Australian side in '74/75 and they destroyed us. The difference was that I hung around afterwards and things got a bit better."

With another win at Adelaide, Clive's side completed 11 Test victories in a row. They had also made the series safe. Just once in nine years had his team finished a Test series in defeat. Yet the winning sequence came to an end at Melbourne when Australia managed a draw.

'The West Indies just failed to complete their twelfth consecutive Test victory because of Lloyd's surprising caution in delaying his second innings declaration until quarter of an hour into the final day,' remarked *Wisden*. 'This cost precious time that West Indies could have used as Australia desperately held out at the end of the match.'

"I was very disappointed," says Clive. "Perhaps things should have been handled differently and, for sure, four-nil looks nicer than three-nil. My memory is that it was still a pretty good pitch at the end of the game. But there are many of us who look back at decisions we took which appeared straightforward at the time, only to wonder if we did the right thing."

Clive's final and 175th Test innings of his career was played at Sydney. On a pitch which was enjoyed by Australia's spinners, the West Indies were defeated. It was an anomalous end to Clive Lloyd's time as captain.

"I've always lost the last games," smiles Clive. "I never got the big send-off. We lost the World Cup in 1983; my last one-day final with Lancashire was a defeat and so it was here at Sydney."

Batting first in a helmet and then in a white sunhat, he cut off the back foot against the spin to the point boundary and swept with the turn to the square-leg fence. Then he hit Bob Holland straight and high for six back over the bowler's head. When he reached 50, the electronic scoreboard flashed out, 'Congratulations Big Cat'.

Several more big hits followed but, when Clive had reached 72, his final shot in Test cricket was a drive off Craig McDermott that was caught low at extra cover by the new Australian captain, Allan Border.

It was over.

As he made his way off the pitch back to the dressing room, Clive pushed his sunhat back up his forehead like a man walking home after a long day's labour. The ground stood and applauded. At the non-striker's end, his friend and team-mate, Malcolm Marshall, put down his bat and clapped his skipper away. The Australians did the same.

"I think I was ready to go," says Clive. "Physically I was getting on, but I was OK; Dennis Waight insists he could have kept me going for another two seasons. On the other hand, I think I was running out of options to a certain extent. A man cannot inspire his players forever and a day. Sometimes I would find myself wondering how much more I had to give. There was another element too; I think certain people in West Indies cricket thought it was time for me to go and I bowed to that. But this kind of talk never came from inside the dressing room. I know for a fact that the guys wanted me to stay on, and that Viv, who would succeed me, wanted that too."

There was no great West Indian celebration marking Clive's departure. He recalls that he was given 'a piece of crystal' and, curiously, a table and a set of chairs. "I think they're still wrapped up somewhere," he says with a shrug of the shoulders.

"The West Indies Cricket Board had long memories," says Clive. "I believe that they never quite got over Packer. I think in some way they felt shamed by what happened then, by what the players did. There was a sense that the tables had been turned. They were jealous of what we had done; they were jealous of the money we had begun to earn. I think that there were plenty of people who saw me as a Big Cheese and themselves as underlings, and of course they wanted that position to be the other way around. They let that be the thing that motivated them, rather than looking at what the cricket team had done since they had appointed me. I mean, I got rid of a lot of headaches for them! They didn't even have to think about appointing another captain for the best part of a decade."

In Australia, recognition for Clive's achievements was more forthcoming. In January 1985, with the tour still going on, the Prime Minister, Bob Hawke, awarded him the prestigious Order of Australia for 'service to the sport of cricket, particularly in relation to his outstanding and positive influence on the game in Australia'. It was Hawke, too, who tried to persuade Clive to transfer his allegiance to Australia by offering him a senior position at the Institute of Sport, the country's centre of excellence in Canberra.

"They wanted me to run the cricket," says Clive. "The government would pay for some of it and I think that Kerry Packer was prepared to get involved too. I was interested because I had no clear plan of what I wanted to do when I stopped playing, and this sort of job was very flattering. In the end I turned it down. A few of the Australian players were saying that they didn't want an outsider getting involved so closely in their game. It got very political."

• • •

Clive was now in his 41st year, and a huge part of his life was over. It had been 19 years since he sat in the dressing room at Bombay, wondering if he would be able to cope with the wiles of Bhagwat Chandrasekhar. What a life it had been. The Crown Street Kid had grown up to lead a nation of cricketers to the highest heights; they shone with glory.

Many testimonials were published about Clive in the days after his retirement. In the *Guardian* John Arlott wrote a 'farewell to Clive the colossus'. It ended:

> Lloyd's captaincy has been impressively marked by dignity; firm, unfussy discipline; and cool, realistic strategy … He retires as a well-liked and respected cricketer; a philosophic man who managed to play and conduct his matches in a fashion refreshingly free from the acrimony which has infected the cricket of some of his opponents.

The Trinidad and Tobago Review published a tribute from a Caribbean perspective:

> He has moulded the most successful team in the history of the game. He and his men have expanded the horizons of cricket; they have played before hostile crowds with dignity and Clive Lloyd has been at the helm keeping his cool, loving and being loved by his players and respected in every quarter that the game is played.
>
> He has shown us what courage and self-belief added to self-discipline and talent can achieve. He has warded off eye problems, back problems, knee problems. He has had to fight for his form; has had his battles with administration; successfully led his men in and out of the Packer Affair, always coming out stronger, dignified and victorious – devotion and decency are the qualities that come readily to mind.
>
> His place will not be easy to fill. He has shown us how and has taken us to the mountain top. We salute him.

CHAPTER TWELVE

THE CAPTAIN ALWAYS HAS TO BE
AN HOUR AHEAD

The innings in Sydney had brought Clive a total of 7,515 runs in Test cricket. He had played 110 matches. Only Colin Cowdrey, with whom Clive had sheltered under a table in Jamaica all those years ago, had played more. His batting average of 46.67 placed him among the best Test batsmen of his generation. He had made 19 Test centuries and a further 39 scores of more than 50. He had held 90 catches and had taken ten wickets as a bowler.

No man had led his country in so many Test matches. Of the 74 games in which Clive captained the West Indies, 36 of them ended in victory. There were just 12 defeats, five of them against Australia in his second series. He never lost a game against England.

• • •

Clive had three great cricketing influences in his life, but he only played the game with two of them – Lance Gibbs and Fred Wills. The third was Sir Frank Worrell. When Clive gave the Cowdrey Lecture in 2004, he said this about the man:

> With purposeful astuteness, Sir Frank parlayed his athletic gifts and joined the cricket field and political arena, and effectively eradicated the scourge of plantation-type snobbery that so characterised cricket and Caribbean life.
>
> Sir Frank fiercely disliked the social conditions into which he was born and raised. And selflessly he embraced the daunting challenge of breaking down those fiendish barriers of colour and class. Through education he sought to ameliorate the human condition, and in the spirit of cricket he elevated the level of sportsmanship on playing fields throughout the world.
>
> From Manchester to Melbourne, from Punjab to Port-of-Spain,

Sir Frank enriched the life of millions whom he touched on and off the field.

And I am honoured to acknowledge that it is his informed leadership, his grace and dignity, and his relentless pursuit of equality and fair play, that inspired my captaincy of the West Indies team.

In 1967 Worrell died of leukaemia when he was 42. In 1960/61 he had led the West Indies to Australia, the first time a black man had been given the job full-time. His appointment coincided with a robust movement in the West Indies, which was still a British colony, for political self-determination. The issues of the West Indian people governing themselves and their cricket team being captained by a black man, became intertwined. One of Worrell's most fervent admirers was the writer CLR James, who saw the appointment of a black captain as a successful attempt to dislodge the 'mercantile-planter class' from automatic domination of West Indies cricket.

"Up until the 1950s," reflects Tony Cozier, "the chief of police in most territories was white, the headmasters of the best schools were white. The priests were white. And so cricket simply reflected society. Later on, with the advances of the independence movement, cricket played its part – because the game had such an important place in the psyche of the people. They agitated for Worrell to become captain and they wanted the teams in the territories to be led by the outstanding black players: Clyde Walcott in British Guiana, Everton Weekes in Barbados."

'It was widely felt,' wrote CLR James in *Beyond a Boundary*, 'that for years conscious and indefensible efforts had been made to maintain the exclusion from the West Indies captaincy of men black in skin. It needed a vigorous campaign and a massive exhibition of popular feeling before Frank Worrell, a black man, was appointed captain of the West Indies team to Australia.'

Worrell had one passion, believed James: 'to prove that West Indian cricketers could be as good as other Test players. To put it negatively, nothing was inherently wrong with us.'

"Frank was a tremendous leader," says Clive today. "He brought a team together and should have been captain long before he was. I am sad that he didn't live long enough to chart a course, to give us all a template. But I think we know what he would have liked to do and that was what I tried to do as captain. It's what I try to do today. I want to emphasise that, although we are a developing nation, we can still produce champions. And we have done so in different walks of life: in education, literature, athletics, politics. West Indians have excelled in these important areas of life. I want to do whatever I can to help and that's why, whenever the West Indies asked me to come back, I did so."

Clive and Frank Worrell were a generation apart and spoke only on a couple of occasions, yet they had much in common. They both possessed the virtues of the Caribbean black lower-middle class of which they had been a part: a respect for certain principles that arose from their Christian upbringing; a respect for education and the tradition of the teacher; and a respect for learning which, in different ways, both men saw to be the instrument for their own liberation – and that of the men whom they captained.

"Worrell epitomised a certain tradition that adheres in West Indies cricket," says the academic and cricket writer, Clem Seecharan. "The commitment to style, to professionalism, the notion that, although you didn't boast about it, you knew that you represented your people. That you mattered. And the way that you played, the way you carried yourself and conducted yourself was very important. You were an ambassador. I think that Clive recognised these things too and brought them to the dressing room when he became captain."

"Both Frank Worrell and Clive Lloyd were soft-spoken, so they did not conform with the West Indian characteristics of excitability and passion that can cloud a captain's judgment," says Tony Cozier. "Worrell and Clive were calm on and off the field.

"In addition they both led their sides when there was an age-gap between them and many of the players coming through. Worrell was older than Sobers, Kanhai, Hall, Hunte and Nurse. He was already a great player and they looked up to him. Likewise with Clive. He was well-established by the time Richards, Greenidge, Roberts and Holding played their first series.

"The other similarity was that their players did not consider themselves so much as individual islanders, which can cause problems. Many of those who played for Worrell had played league cricket in England. In the leagues they were West Indian, not Guianese, Barbadian or Jamaican. So Worrell had a team of West Indians. With Clive, it was county cricket. Nobody in England referred to 'Joel Garner the Barbadian' or 'Viv Richards the Antiguan'. They had the experience of playing together and against each other in England, as West Indians."

• • •

"The first thing I should say about my captaincy is that it was thrust upon me," remarks Clive. "When I was appointed, I knew nothing about the way the Board worked, I had no back-up system. If I had a problem, I had no idea of who to ring. I had to sort everything out for myself. Apart from the manager, the Board Secretary was my only point of contact. So I had to learn as I went along. My immediate priority was to get the players to respect me. Once you've got that sort of rapport with your players, you're almost there. I had a group of individually talented men who, to an extent, were jealous of each other's capabilities. This was not a bad thing because it created competition.

"But I thought a lot too about how to create harmony. So, when people roomed together, more often than not I would put a batsman with a bowler and, if possible, they'd be from different territories too. So the bowler does well and says that evening, 'I want to see some runs in this room tomorrow night.' In that way, they built up a competitive spirit and a camaraderie without it becoming too harsh. They became room-mates, not just one player from Barbados and one from Trinidad.

"This was a small thing, but it was part of something much more significant. For respect in me to grow, the players had to be assured that I understood the West Indies psyche. The West Indian comes from a particular set of circumstances, our upbringing and the way we approach life, and I realised what it all boiled down to; I had to get them all to respect one another."

Clive laughs and tells a story to illustrate his point.

"There was a dinner recently in honour of Garry Sobers and, in his speech, Wes Hall said, 'Garry, we love you as a man can love another man – and still be a man!' You see, that's understanding the West Indian psyche!

"Some people may not appreciate this, but in the Caribbean we think differently from other people. We have different backgrounds. We are a people who are free, relaxed and intelligent and at times we can be volatile. We were born in the warmth of the sun, we enjoy ourselves, we can be playful. There are carnivals in nearly all of the islands; that's the sort of people we are. But what I had to do was temper these qualities to create an atmosphere of professionalism. I had to say, 'It's not all beer and skittles, boys. We have something here that we can be the best at – if you hold on to certain things and repress other feelings.'

"That's why we had a curfew. Late nights, even if you're not drinking, are not the best preparation for facing international bowlers. In the past, when I started playing, this didn't always happen. We always had the ability, but what I wanted was the physical fitness to complement that skill. No longer would we be known as cavalier and casual. I didn't like that. I wanted us to reveal other parts of the West Indian psyche: the intelligence, the belief, the fact that we were winners, men of substance. That meant making the fellows aware that they actually had those qualities and saying, 'You've got to restrict some of the other things we like doing, the extra-curricular activities.'

"I didn't have the curfew so I could treat them like little boys; it was all about discipline. Our cricket was our work, it was a living. If you wanted to go out with a girl, you had not to do it at some ungodly hour or you had to wait until the Test match was over. One or two of the guys broke the rules, of course. I remember Des Haynes and Jeff Dujon on their first tour of Australia; both overslept in Sydney. They got a big fine and weren't happy but I told them, 'They do sell alarm clocks in this country,' and they had to run some extra laps after we'd finished. Each time they passed, the guys were shouting, 'These are some of the most expensive laps you'll ever run, boys.'

"But they got the message. I also used to make sure the team bus never waited more than five minutes after the scheduled departure time. If you missed it, you made your own way to the ground or the airport and you got a fine. So all the guys who were there on time would shout, 'Drive on!', 'Time to go, driver', 'Start her up, my man' as soon as they sat down.

"That always made me laugh, but the point was those sort of disciplines meant we played disciplined cricket. And I'm convinced that the guys liked the discipline. Gordon Greenidge, for example. You only had to look at his kit bag and you knew he could only be an opening batsman because he was so organised. If he said, 'There's a spare stud in my bag on the right next to my batting gloves,' you knew it would be right there.

"Recognising the difference between people is another very important quality for the captain to appreciate. I had to treat the players properly, with subtlety, to get the best out of them. Gordon, for example, was a very different sort of guy from Vivian Richards. I always had total respect for Gordon as a great cricketer and as a decent man. But he needed to know that you were very close to him and that he was always part of your team. And then you have Viv – the maverick. The West Indian that everyone should want to be like. With Viv, all you had to do was put the maroon cap on his head and he was a transformed individual.

"Yet it wasn't all about skill. I insisted that anyone who played for the West Indies had the right attitude. I was insistent that they had to fit in to what we created. Now Sylvester Clarke – may he rest in peace – was desperate to get into the side but, when he'd made it, he transgressed and got fined a lot of money. After that, he realised that this was the West Indies he was playing for, and he had to conform to our professional standards. I emphasised to the players who broke the curfew, 'You're disrespecting your room-mate, yourself, the team and the people you represent.' So respect was important. If I had not received that personal respect, we would never have been successful because the fellows would only have done just enough. They're not going to do that little extra. On many occasions I would ask my bowlers, 'Can you carry on?' and, although they were tired, they would give me another spell."

"There is no doubt that Clive Lloyd was a great captain," says Michael Holding. "And he was a great captain because he knew how to reach his individual players. He knew what made a man tick and how that person got to be in his comfort zone. That was his strength, rather than obvious tactical brilliance. He kept these island people together from different places, different social backgrounds, and that is the most important factor in captaining the West Indies, and, if you can't do that, as we have seen, you will never captain the West Indies well. Clive never thought about where a man came from. There was never any political interference with selection. Clive was Guyanese, but he would never favour his own countrymen. He threw all that out of the window. He got to know his players, he knew what we liked and disliked. And so we felt comfortable.

"He was the father-figure in the dressing room, on the field and in the street. We would all go to him to talk about our problems. We had this respect for him and looked up to him. He was laid-back, not a jester, and he made us relaxed. But, as with all fathers, we knew he had authority. Of course he ticked us off. He would take control of us if we messed up. It was him, not the management, who would discipline us first. He always led and just got better as he got older. He didn't just captain the side on reputation and not do his own work. There was never a time when he said, 'Do what I say, not what I do.'"

"Trust was very important," says Clive. "Because the players came from all over the place, they had to know that I was for them and not out for myself. So I said to them, 'Gentlemen, we're sharing everything.' I told them how much I was paid, they knew what my expenses allowance was. Mind you, most of that went on them. These fellows loved Chinese takeaways. I would get a meal for 17 people and there'd be a hundred cartons on the table because they liked their food so much. We ate, laughed and spent the whole night talking cricket. And I didn't mind because these guys gave me their all. None of them wanted to shirk. I was always honest with them and discussed everything. The young guys would ask for financial advice from me, cricketing advice, even personal stuff. There was nothing they couldn't ask. It was because I was honest with them, that I could trust them to be honest with me.

"There were certain things I had to do to galvanise the players. When you're a captain, lots of people look at the way you run the show. When you are a leader, a fellow looks up at you, probably more than you realise. Even people who seem unlikely candidates need guidance on and off the field. A man must be able to come up and discuss things and feel comfortable with his captain.

"I had to make these people feel it was really worth playing this game – because it is a tough game. You're there for five days, the temperature is over a hundred in the shade. You have to train hard, make sure you behave yourself. Those are the things that you must have if you want to be a professional."

"Clive was our best ever captain," says Desmond Haynes. "Even in the later days when we'd see him strapping himself up in the dressing room and we'd say, 'You know the best thing for a lame horse is to be shot, Cappie,' he was still a great batsman then. One of your goals each series was to make more runs than Lloydy – and it didn't happen too often.

"He was so fair to us. He'd say, 'OK, Viv got the hundred today, but who brought him the drinks and the towel?' So the guys who didn't play, sure, they were disappointed they had been left out but they wanted the team to do well because they knew the prize money would be split equally 16 ways."

"When a new player like Dessie or Jeff Dujon came along," says Clive, "I always thought it was important to get things straight right away. Often I'd room them with a senior guy. Education has to filter down. Because I knew that these fellows, Des and Jeff, would one day captain their territories, so, when they went to play in the Shell Shield, they would do the things we did in the West Indies. Then, when their fellows came through to the Test side, they already had a flavour of what to expect – and of what we expected from them. I wanted to create players who were interested all the time. Not ones who are looking at you to give them all the answers, I wanted men who could sort things out for themselves.

"Straightaway with a new player, I would explain the importance of what these men were representing. They had to know that people back home or West Indians in Britain walked tall when we were in the ascendancy. They felt proud about themselves and they could cheer on the best team in the world who could beat anybody. I would say that the status that had given us, the respect it had given us, did not come about simply from being good cricketers. It came from adhering to certain values, no matter who we played. We always had to win and be the best, but there had to be respect. I wanted my players to put all these thoughts in a little bowl, and I hoped they'd consider them before they went out and played each day.

"I have always thought that there's a connection between leadership in sport and leadership in business. To get results, leaders surround themselves with the right people who can achieve their goals. I managed to get my players to perform to certain standards. Likewise, a business leader will take a person's best points and make sure their weaknesses are covered by the attributes of another. The result is a near-perfect balance that enables your team to deliver; now the key word here is 'team'. A leader should always remember that he cannot be all things to all men. But true leadership means you have the ability to guide and focus men for the greater good of the team. And so, when it comes, success is an expectation, rather than a surprise."

Clive sits and thinks for a moment.

"There were stresses too, of course, any leader will tell you that. The captain always has to think: what are my goals? What do I want to achieve in this series? What about the next one? The captain has to help other guys to do well when they're failing, even if he himself is out of nick. If you don't have all these skills and others – doing the TV interviews, speaking to the press – then you're wasting your time. The captain always has to be an hour ahead. Who would be bowling then? When is the new ball due? Who should have it? Being a captain in county cricket helped me tremendously because I had to think about the strengths and weaknesses of 200-odd cricketers. How did they get out last year?

"Having a pretty good memory helped. Something I've done since I was a kid was home in on batsmen all the time, looking for faults. Are his feet moving? What's he doing with his hands? Is his head to one side? How does his bat come down? When we had to win in Australia in '81/82 to share the series, we needed to break the partnership between Rod Marsh and Kim Hughes. Rodney, I recalled from years ago, sometimes played with a stiff bottom hand. So I had a man go in at short extra, and sure enough he jabbed it straight to Desmond Haynes. We won the Test. So, the captain has to be a thinking man. It's like playing cards, or dominoes, you have to know what's gone before. If you can't think, you will run into trouble."

"Very rarely did he show that the job was on top of him," recalls Desmond Haynes. "We knew he was the boss alright, but only once did I see him have a rant in the dressing room. We went to Australia in '79/80 and he had a bit of a problem with Alvin Kallicharran. Different batsmen were being rested so Alvin wasn't batting in the same spot. We were at Perth against Western Australia and I could hear this grumbling. Alvin was saying, 'First I'm three, then I'm four. Now it's five.' And Clive really lost it. There was an explosion: 'That's it – I'm playing ten men this game.' It was the first time I had seen him so angry. 'Why in the name of God am I being provoked?' he shouted. He told the manager, 'That's it, ten men for this game.' He told the opposition. Eventually he relented, but it was a fearsome sight. And there was a funny conclusion to this tale. I opened with Lawrence Rowe and he got out soon. Lloydy came in three and Terry Alderman got one to get big on him and the Cappie gloved it behind so he was out for a few. Back in the dressing room he was even more upset. So, he was human after all! It sent a serious message to me listening to it all, though: 'Just get on with the cricket.' He would pull anyone up if they needed it, even Viv. This occasion though was a one-off. In my time it was never repeated."

"If I got annoyed, then the team would know about it," says Clive. "They would know from my manner and my tone of voice that they had messed up. I didn't have to shout, but I would tell them, 'This has happened. I don't like it, it's not going to happen again.' From time to time I made examples of people.

"I remember Albert Padmore, I think it was. He said once, 'Listen, Skip, you must understand that, when we see you annoyed, we know that we've stepped over the line.' Albert was a very quiet guy, but it showed that he was always there thinking and that he and the other players knew if they did something bad, they were letting me down, because they knew they were playing for their captain.

"You see, as captain, you're not going to have everybody behind you. If you get the majority of the dressing room behind you, you're doing well. You have to be able to impose yourself on the players, you must be a disciplinarian, but it doesn't mean you can't be one of the guys now and again. If you're living with these fellows, playing with them, in the dressing room with them day in day out, you can't help but be one of the boys."

• • •

"The captain of the West Indies has to take some pretty tough decisions. My judgment had to be right. When I made a decision of consequence as the West Indies captain, it was of more importance than any one prime minister in the Caribbean. They were only making decisions for one territory; I was making them for the whole of the West Indies. So the job was an important one. Winning was so important to these people scattered throughout the region and across the world. It was not an easy job. Have a look in the books. How many Test captains lasted more than ten years? Not a lot. It became a stressful occupation because there was an air of expectation that we would never lose. I had to keep getting everyone up for the challenge.

"I don't think even today some people realise what we created. That from a team that got beaten badly in Australia in 1976, we had the best part of twenty years of supremacy. What a group of players. I wouldn't change them for the world. I always appreciated everything that they did. I wouldn't fault any of them; I don't know what they think of me, but to run and bowl fast is hard work; to bat in the hot sun is hard work. I have tremendous respect for all those who played under me.

"You know, *Sports Illustrated*, the American magazine, once had an article about the most dominant sides in world sport. They chose three. The San Francisco 49ers, Liverpool Football Club and the West Indies cricket team. Now, I was proud of that.

"When I left there was a blueprint. Everything was there, but sadly we didn't realise things had gone wrong until it was too late."

In 1985, Mike Brearley's book *The Art of Captaincy* was published. He had been an outstanding and innovative captain of his country and of his county, Middlesex, and had returned to lead England to a magnificent triumph, the 1981 Ashes, when the series had seemed lost. He was acclaimed as one of the game's great tacticians.

'Clive Lloyd is a delightful man,' he wrote, 'but he allowed the West Indies to become cynical in the exercise of power. On the field, he had one quality which he shared with Frank Worrell: his restraint and steadiness were important factors in the growing maturity of the West Indies team. But I never felt he had a cricketing brain, as was shown by his lack of ideas when handling the ordinary Lancashire attack.'

"I was very disappointed when I read that and said so at the time," says Clive. "Surely, it is impossible to do something successfully for so long without putting any thought into it. I captained the West Indies 78 times, bringing a team of unknowns through to something special and, when I packed up, I had a batting average that was not too shabby. When Mike's book first came out, I wondered why one professional would want to devalue another man's accomplishment. I have never really been a man to ask for praise, but I would like people to recognise what we have done."

Today, Mike Brearley wants to revise the judgment which he made in *The Art of Captaincy*.

"I have a great deal of admiration for Clive and, because of that, I would like to put things right with him," he says. "I feel that what I said twenty years ago in that slightly off-the-cuff, informal way, as a caption to a picture, was unfortunate and also hurtful, and it wasn't at all the main thrust of what I felt. I would prefer to speak about the great qualities that Clive has, amongst other things the human qualities of warmth, energy and caring. And humour too. I think these are important leadership qualities as well as personal ones. He is a big man, and he came across as a big man and a wonderful cricketer too. He gained the respect of his players, who looked up to him. I also admire his persistence, the way he held the side together and the way he developed the policy of four fast bowlers at a time when West Indies lacked top-class spinners – but had such an array of wonderful and varied fast bowlers.

"Clive made the West Indians into the team that they were. They were the best team in the world for nearly twenty years, and a very great deal of that success was down to Clive and his leadership. Obviously he had good material, but you have to be able to make those people think they're as good as they are and become as good as they can be."

"Tactically, my experience of Clive on the field is that he was good," says David Gower. "There are so many aspects to captaincy. A lot of people have tried to have a go at Clive. They say all he needed to do was to wear a watch, and on the hour change the bowling. It wasn't deemed particularly stressful. All of us would have liked to have taken charge of that bowling attack. But there was a lot more to Clive. It's too simplistic to say he just changed the bowlers but, even if it had been the case, they'd have still have won a lot of games."

"My experience of Test cricket in England is that the opposition got too involved in the theory," says Desmond Haynes. "They talk a good game but, when it comes to action, they're lacking. Clive played it simple. The majority of our work was done in the team room; we already knew who was going to bowl and, if one fast bowler was struggling, another would take up the slack."

"If I had to mark myself out of ten for tactics? It would be pretty high," says Clive. "Eight and a bit or more, nine, I'd say. Much of our tactical preparation was done before we went on the field. I had no need to gesticulate. Before each innings, we discussed the opposition one to eleven, not one to seven and hope for the best. But there was always room for innovation. Sometimes on the field I did things instinctively and I went with my gut feeling."

Two of Clive's best bowlers, Andy Roberts and Michael Holding, have this to say about Clive's tactical acumen.

"On the field," says Roberts, "Clive allowed us to determine what we wanted up to a point. If it didn't work, he would take over and say, 'This is what I want.' He allowed us to make tactical decisions and that's the hallmark of a good captain. He didn't get enough credit for his own tactical shrewdness. Because we were so good as a unit, people thought that anyone could lead the team. Now any man could have led us onto the pitch, but would he have got the same respect as that which we gave Clive? Of course not. The respect was mutual. It was earned and not demanded."

"Clive had a great team, and tactics weren't as important as for a man who had a lesser team," says Holding. "We have had a lot of great cricketers over the years playing in certain West Indies teams but they never won much. He brought us all together; I will say that for ever. Nothing is more important than getting us to play like a team. That is why Clive is brilliant. Off the field we had different interests and did our own thing. On the field we were one, like a gang of bikers. You touched one of us, you touched us all."

"Clive was gifted with seeing the big picture, not just the detail," says Deryck Murray. "Sometimes others looked after those things, but we all knew that the ultimate decision was his. He would accept things that Holding and Roberts would say, because we'd all had different experiences from playing for the English counties. Clive was the conduit for that information, then he decided how that knowledge should be used. He was respected as *the* leader, and that gave us great team spirit. The one thing you cannot say is that he was a poor tactician. If he had been, we wouldn't have got the results we did."

"There are two main types of captain," is the verdict of Steve Camacho, "the player and the tactician, and then a third type who has the attributes of both. That was Clive. He could get the fellows to play for him. That was of immeasurable value because you can make mistakes and still win if the fellows play for you, but you can't make mistakes and win if they don't. Many captains have had outstanding ability and tactical knowledge, but never owned the dressing room. Clive did, and that makes him one of the great leaders."

. . .

After Clive retired from Test cricket, he was appointed captain of Lancashire for the 1986 season. He had also led his county in 1981 and 1982 and for some games in 1983, when he was not playing in the World Cup.

Lancashire were a very different side now from the one Clive had joined in 1969. The County Championship had still eluded them, and the one-day titles which had made up for that omission had dried up.

"Many of the experienced players from the '70s had come to the end and had been replaced with youngsters," says Clive. "We certainly weren't as strong as we had been. In my first stint as captain, we got to three cup semi-finals. We had some good players coming through, Paul Allott and Graeme Fowler. But this was not a team that was drenched with talent."

Clive could do nothing to change Lancashire's fortunes in the Championship. They finished 16th in 1981, 12th in 1982 and 15th in 1986.

"I think there was a feeling," he says, "that, if they appointed me, we would fly to the top. Well, doing the job for a couple of seasons isn't going to make that happen. I truly believe they should have made me skipper years earlier, then perhaps we would have had a chance to get something going.

"Of course it was very different to captaining the West Indies. I was accustomed to bowlers who could put in four or five spells a day, right on the money. Electric fieldsmen, bowlers who could bat. I'm afraid we had very few of those characters at Old Trafford at the time. A couple of years later, it changed. Wasim Akram was there, Michael Atherton, then Andrew Flintoff, Sadly, they were after my time."

"The thing about Clive is that he wasn't old-school," says Graeme Fowler. "In one of my first matches I went in the dressing room, and I got ordered out, because I hadn't knocked on the door. Can you believe it? Playing first-class cricket and thrown out of the dressing room for not knocking on the door!

"Certainly, Clive was a man who demanded respect. But, if you did the right things and were polite and not presumptuous, he was brilliant with you. He didn't think you should have to knock on the bloody door.

"Clive taught me about the philosophy of the game. He used to say that cricket is an extension of your personality. If you can walk into a pub and talk about sport, religion and politics and you have a great night, then do it again. If you talk about those things and get your head kicked in, then stop.

"'Cricket's the same,' he said. 'If you can hit a ball from outside off stump for four over mid-wicket, and can do it regularly, then keep doing it. If you get out, stop.' He had lots of time for those of us that wanted to listen, but he couldn't do it with everybody because some didn't want to learn and some of them weren't good enough to put the ideas into practice. He really did the best he could."

"It was absolutely fine playing under him," recalls David Lloyd. "We were a poor side, a shocking side, a bloody awful side. He did well to take the job on. He was a magnificent leader of men. A great inspiration to all those around him. And he was tactically flippin' bang on. Ask any of them – if you ain't got the tools, you can't do it."

"Tactically, I think it was a strain to try to wring something out of the players," says Clive. "We were a second-class side in many ways. I even had committee members coming up to me and saying, 'Bloody hell, Clive, the opposition are streets ahead of us here.'"

"To captain the West Indies and then that Lancashire side, I think he did get frustrated at times with the ineptitude of one or two people and one or two attitudes," reflects Jack Bond, who had returned to Lancashire in the 1980s as team manager. "If anything, Clive would worry about that and it would get him down. I'm not saying he expected everybody to be perfect, but he couldn't accept people who weren't as serious about the game on the field as he was."

"My feeling," says Peter Lever, "is that Clive didn't realise that the ordinary player – and I think this stemmed from his own modesty – couldn't do what he could do. If someone got out tamely he couldn't see how it had happened. That possibly was his only flaw as captain. He thought that if he could do it, if Michael Holding could do it, why couldn't others do it? It wouldn't do for Clive that cricketers would sit around getting flabby, just content to earn their wage."

. . .

Despite Lancashire's limitations, they reached the final of the NatWest Trophy in 1986. This was the competition that used to be known as the Gillette Cup, and one in which Clive and his team-mates had had such success in the 1970s. It was the first time they had been to Lord's for such a final in ten years.

Ian Gould, the Sussex captain, won the toss and asked Lancashire to bat first. Clive was about to play one of the last innings of his life, on a ground where he had displayed so much skill.

When he walked through the Long Room, his side were 56 for two.

Brian Johnston was commentating on the radio for the BBC.

Here he comes, Clive Lloyd! Well, I think that's as good a reception as I've seen for any player in all the time I've been watching cricket at Lord's. Everybody standing up. A packed Lord's paying tribute to this gangling figure with the white hat and the spectacles. You'd hardly expect him to be a cricketer but, my goodness, he still moves very quickly in the field, and I expect Sussex are hoping to get him early on before he gets that eye in. But once it's in, their hands are going to get stung.

Clive pushed forward to his first ball from the Sussex bowler, Dermot Reeve. The second ball hit him on the pad outside the line and went down the leg side. Clive left the third ball alone. Then he faced his fourth ball:

Reeve, a funny sort of action, he rather looks like Bill O'Reilly speeded up – all sort of arms going and head … He comes in and bowls … and that one hits him on the pad – and he's out – lbw!! – Clive Lloyd is out lbw to Reeve for nought. A very, very sad moment, but I must say Ken Palmer had no hesitation, put his finger up. And Clive Lloyd is out lbw bowled Reeve for nought, 56 for three and I reckon he'll get as good a reception as he walks back. I hope he will. A sad moment for him and for the crowd and, of course, for Lancashire.

"With the benefit of more than twenty years' hindsight, I'm wondering if I should have played in that game," says Clive. "In those days each county was allowed one overseas player and we had myself and Patrick Patterson, who could bowl very fast. He often played in county games instead of me that season. But there was a lot of pressure to play in the final because it was my last year, and people wanted me to be successful and the team to be successful. But Patrick was the man with the firepower. He should have played."

Lancashire made 242 from their 60 overs but lost by seven wickets. "Watch out, Soho!" warned Ian Gould in his brief victory speech before he led his side on a long night out in central London.

The next day, 7 September 1986, Clive drove to Bristol to play in a Sunday League game against Gloucestershire. A cricketer called Gary Sainsbury got him out for two.

Clive never played for Lancashire again.

"Two people shaped Lancashire in the twenty years I was there," says David Lloyd. "One was Jackie Bond, the other was Clive Lloyd. Clive bought in to Lancashire completely. He was the catalyst in getting people into the ground. Like Flintoff or Pietersen today, people would come just to watch him play. The ground was full, week in, week out, at Old Trafford and Clive was 95 per cent of the reason why. When he came out to bat there was a buzz around the ground. Clearly, he is one of the very best players Lancashire will ever have. He was also everything you'd want your best mate to be. You'd trust him with anything, and he's no different now. He was a great ambassador for his people, and in Lancashire you shouldn't hear a bad word about him from anybody. If you do, they're bloody-well wrong. It was a privilege to be in the dressing room with him."

CHAPTER THIRTEEN

IF YOUR COUNTRY CALLS, YOU WANT TO RESPOND

"The decision to retire was mine alone," says Clive. "From both the West Indies and from Lancashire. I had had enough. I had kept picking up these injuries, and I really felt it was time to do something else. There were other things, nothing to do with cricket, that I wanted to do."

One of the first things Clive did was to travel to Africa.

"I had never been to this continent before. Of course I had never played cricket in South Africa because of apartheid, but this was a place that was always on my mind. I did some work as a United Nations volunteer in The Gambia and Sierra Leone. I was with people in their villages making soap, mixing cement, helping to build houses. One time, the village leader had a ceremony for me and I was told it was a real honour. He brought out all his wives dressed in their ceremonial clothes and they sang and prayed for a quarter of an hour or so because I was there. What struck me was these people spoke like the Guyanese, even a few of their words were the same. They grew the same sort of herbs as we did, they were good with their hands, they were fairly tall like us and I thought that this was probably no coincidence. It was a fascinating time for me because this part of the world, this part of West Africa, was where many of the slaves were kidnapped from three hundred years previously before being shipped to the West Indies."

"The United Nations is a fine, fine organisation," says Clive. "I would love for it to be given more respect, to have more access to places, particularly in Africa, even to be more forceful in what they do. I sometimes wonder if enough is being done by these organisations to prevent famine. I think it's true to say that in the continent of Africa the majority of people are still reliant on the land, and yet these famines happen so often. Are there enough long-term projects? Can the United Nations work there more efficiently? Can it do more to try to prevent these countries in North America and Northern Europe from throwing away millions of tons of food every year?

I think it probably could. I would like the future of Africa to be focused in more people's minds. It has the potential to be a rich continent, there's no doubt about that."

Even though Clive had other interests after he retired from cricket, the game was still in his thoughts. Before too long, and without much hesitation, he was back in the dressing room. His last series had been in Australia in 1984/85, and he returned there as the West Indies team manager for the 1988/89 series, with Vivian Richards the captain.

"I think I should have perhaps been more organised when I finished the game," says Clive. "I wasn't absolutely certain of what I was going to do. But, if your country calls, you want to respond."

Today, Clive wonders if he should have been asked to return even sooner.

"Years after I had retired, I went to lunch with Sir Charles Williams, who's a big property developer in Barbados and another guy who used to be the Minister of Sport. They told me this extraordinary story. Apparently, when I stepped down from captaining the West Indies, 'Cow' Williams had offered to pay my salary for five years so I could be manager of the side, so that the continuity would remain and the standards we had set up could be preserved. But the Board President at the time told them that he didn't think he'd get the proposal past his colleagues. So it never happened. If that post had come to fruition then, I wonder what would have happened to our cricket? When Frank Worrell became manager straight after retiring, no-one asked any questions.

"As it was, when I went back to be the manager, we did well in those first couple of years under Viv. We won in Australia, and most of the team I had played with were still there. I ran the nets, gave Viv the freedom to deal with the press and it was fine. I was a tracksuit manager, not a gin-and-tonic manager with my lounge suit on all day."

After the victory in Australia, there were further series wins at home against India and then England, but in November 1990, when the West Indies went to play a series in Pakistan, Clive was not there. He had been replaced as team manager by his cousin, Lance Gibbs.

"Why did it end?" asks Clive. "The truthful answer is, I don't know! The Board just decided that they needed another manager. There was no discussion, it was simply decided that it was someone else's turn. That's how badly organised things were.

"We were winning and I would have loved to have carried on," says Clive. "The Board believed that anybody could captain and anybody could manage. It was like 'Let's give so-and-so a chance' instead of having something settled which could be improved upon. I never questioned it, I just moved on. I suppose that may have been one of my shortcomings

– that I believe you accept these things in life and you go forward. That way you keep most of your friends. You say, 'That's a part of my life over' and you look to the next stage."

For Clive the next stage involved a variety of tasks. He had already been appointed by the Home Office as a member of the Commission for Racial Equality and had become a senior member of the Co-operative Society. His work with Project Full Employ continued, and he was putting his weight behind setting up a 24-hour soul music station for Piccadilly Radio in Manchester.

In 1992, Clive was appointed a Commander of the British Empire for 'services to cricket and for public service in Lancashire'.

"It's strange how these things happen in life," says Clive. "When I was growing up in British Guiana, the governors of the country all had honours. I remember their names easily: Sir Patrick Muir Renison was one. Sir Alfred Savage was another. Then, years later, I ended up with a CBE. And I suppose you don't often get one of those for being an idiot, so it was something I felt very proud about. I was glad to be recognised for what I had done."

• • •

For the next three and a half years Clive offered his experience as a cricketer to the game's governing body, the ICC. He worked across the world as a referee at Test matches and one-day internationals.

"Some of my time as a referee was enjoyable," reflects Clive, "but I always felt that I wasn't at the heart of the game. It was often a detached role and I was having to lecture players because they were wearing the wrong one-inch logos on their batting gloves. To me, this didn't seem to be moving cricket forward a great deal. The rules are the rules, but I knew I wouldn't be a referee for ever. When I could, I liked to let things go, so that the game could flow. Some of the things, such as the banter that goes on in the middle for example, was technically an offence, but I didn't mind a bit of aggression. This was Test cricket, after all. They say there is a lot of sledging in the game today, but it has never been a problem for me. Some people may be surprised to know this but, when I was captain of the West Indies, there was almost no sledging."

'I faced all the great quick bowlers,' wrote Geoffrey Boycott in 2007, 'and not one of them ever swore at me, sledged me or behaved crudely. That's what made Clive Lloyd's team champion winners and champion men. They just beat you. They didn't have to sledge.'

"We may have said 'you lucky so-and-so' now and again, but my bowlers never said anything particularly crass on the pitch," says Clive. "Neither did other players really sledge us. I can't remember anyone sledging Joel Garner or Andy Roberts. The guys just got on with what they did. Once, though, the Australian fast bowler Geoff Lawson gave Gordon Greenidge the big send-off in Sydney. In the dressing room later Gordon came up to me and said, 'Excuse me captain, would you mind if I went and had a word with Geoff?' and I said, 'No problem, why not?' Now, the dressing rooms at Sydney are all in a long line along a corridor and, as Gordon set off, such a mild man, we were all peeking out like schoolboys, wondering what on earth would happen.

"Gordon went and knocked on the Australian door and asked for the captain. 'Excuse me,' he said to Allan Border, 'may I have a word with Geoff?' 'Sure,' said Border. Lawson came out and Gordon said, 'Geoff – I've been playing the game for a long time and I wasn't very happy with what you did there …' then he paused and leaned right up close, '… and if you ever, *ever* do that again, I'll break every bone in your body.' By this time, every doorway had about four heads peeping out like in a cartoon with guys crying with laughter and, as Gordon turned back, they all shot back in."

• • •

In 1996, the World Cup was held in India, Pakistan and Sri Lanka. It was Clive who refereed the semi-final in Calcutta between India and Sri Lanka.

"I had spoken to the President of the Indian Board, Jagmohan Dalmiya, the day before," says Clive, "and suggested that there should be police around the ground, even among the crowd, to stop trouble very quickly if there was going to be any. I was told it was all in hand and there weren't going to be any problems."

But there were, and the police were not there to stop them. Having won the toss but deciding to bat second, India all but lost the game when seven of their players were dismissed while scoring just 22 runs between them.

"It was a big mistake to field first," says Clive. "If you tapped the pitch, it had a hollow sound to it; I think it was badly under-prepared, and so it was always going to deteriorate. Very difficult to chase runs on."

As India's defeat became inevitable, people in the crowd started throwing stones onto the pitch, near the Sri Lankan fielders.

"It was pretty serious," recalls Clive. "I had to bear in mind the safety of the players. So I spoke to the umpires and brought everyone off for a quarter of an hour. We agreed a plan that, once things had calmed down, the game would resume, but I wanted to make it plain that, if there were any further incidents, the game would be abandoned. And with the position it was in, that meant Sri Lanka would be the winners. I wanted this message broadcasted over the loud-speakers but, when they did, it only reached part of the ground, away from the trouble makers."

The game resumed but so did the stone-throwing.

"It was terrible," says Clive. "The Sri Lankan bowler, Chaminda Vaas, was near the fence and this piece of concrete the size of a small football landed at his feet. Had it hit him, it would have been the end. It would have killed him. I ruled that the game was over and it had to be awarded to Sri Lanka."

It was a decision that was widely accepted and Clive was asked to referee the final, in which Sri Lanka defeated Australia. It would be his last duty as a referee for more than six years.

The West Indies had reached the semi-final of the 1996 World Cup, but they lost to Kenya in the group stages, a huge upset. This result, together with their capitulation from a winning position in their semi-final against Australia, made the Board determined to get rid of the manager, Wes Hall, and the coach, Andy Roberts, who had been given the job less than a year previously. The Board turned to Clive. Would he return to coach the side? Clive accepted.

"I was ready to give it another go," he says, "but very soon afterwards I was kicked upstairs to become manager and Malcolm Marshall became coach. So in effect I had been given an administrative role, rather than a hands-on job. I was told by an official that they had done this because they wanted to stop another individual, who was insisting that he should be the manager, from getting the job. This was wrong. What should have happened is that I should have stayed as coach and Malcolm should have been my assistant, learned the ropes and then gone on. But the notion of continuity is something that the Board has sometimes found very difficult to comprehend."

Clive's return to the dressing room was mixed. There were defeats by Australia and Pakistan, but victories over India, Sri Lanka and England.

. . .

The near-invincibility of the team in the past twenty years was clearly over, and in November 1998 Clive had to wrestle with what he describes as 'the most shameful incident in my whole career.'

The West Indian side were due to tour South Africa. They had never played Test matches in the country before, and the occasion was pregnant with symbolism. Apartheid had been dismantled; Nelson Mandela was President.

"What a man," says Clive. "He is *so* excellent. I had met him once, in 1991. I was in the country because once or twice I had done some coaching in the townships, and Ali Bacher, from the South African Board, said to me, 'You must meet the big man.' So a trip was organised, and – I will never forget this for all my days – as we approached Nelson Mandela in the party office he saw us and he said, 'Here's a sportsman I know!' I was blown away because here was a great man who had been incarcerated for 27 years, but he knew who I was. Well, I couldn't believe it. It was the best hour and a half I have spent with any man in my life. I asked him if he felt bitter about what has happened to him, all those years in prison. He replied, 'No, because if I was, it would cloud my judgment.' I took that to heart very strongly. It had a profound effect on me because it taught me that, however strong the temptation is, you always have to look beyond the setbacks to see the greater good."

Unfortunately the greater good was not on the minds of many of the West Indian players. The tour was almost cancelled because of a strike about pay.

After a one-day tournament in Dhaka, the squad for the tour were due to fly to South Africa, yet the captain, Brian Lara, and his vice-captain, Carl Hooper, flew instead to London, where they met other players who were en route from the Caribbean. The group went no further than the Excelsior Hotel. They were unhappy, they said, with their pay and conditions and wanted a rise in the current tour fee of £32,000 for senior players and about £23,000 for junior members of the side.

"I had to fly back to London from South Africa," says Clive. "Boy, I was so angry. At two or three in the morning I was running around hotel corridors trying to find these players who Nelson Mandela, no less, had asked to come to his country. He had even signed 16 letters to the players personally. I mean, it was humiliating. When we had arrived in South Africa, they had dancing and this great big reception and there were about eight of us there. Half the team were still holed up at Heathrow.

"I pleaded with the players," recalls Clive. "I said to them, 'Go to Nelson Mandela's country, then sort out your difficulties afterwards – because the people there really need to be able to see you at your best.' You see, the West Indies had something to give there; black people in South Africa deserved the chance to progress. But many of the players didn't see it that way. I was so disappointed that they couldn't grasp the importance of the occasion, that this evil of apartheid had finally been smashed forever."

When members of the West Indies Board arrived in London, 19 hours of talks followed. Lara and Hooper, whom the Board had sacked earlier in the dispute, were re-instated and there was an agreement about adjusting the players' salary structure.

"When at last we got to South Africa," says Clive, "we were in Soweto and Nelson Mandela, not surprisingly given what had happened, didn't turn up. And some of the guys were saying, 'Where is he?' I told them, 'Do you really think that he'd be here after having to beg you to come?'

"We should have swum to South Africa, such was the importance of the tour. This man was an international icon. He has done so much for his people, for our people, for all people. We were humiliated; it was my worst moment in the game. I will never forget what happened, and I told the players so. 'I will forgive you this, but I will never forget it.' Boy, that was the worst period in my whole career.

"It was all about money. And they never got anything from it. The father of one of the players who'd gone on strike said, 'Why is my boy asking for more money? He hasn't even played a Test match yet.' But the fellow obviously felt he had to go with the crowd. I think many of the team were unhappy with what had happened, but they felt they had to stick it out.

"This was a golden opportunity for the Board to kill off a lot of festering problems, but it was not strong enough. I told them they should have cancelled the tour and had a two-week period to ask players to come forward who wanted to play Test cricket in South Africa under the conditions that had been set. That was the big chance the Board had to pull in the reins on our cricketers. That was the time the West Indies needed to be strong. But they said they would have lost out financially, so yet again money was the thing rather than the principle. We lost out there big time. It was the chance to wipe the slate clean and start again. I believe that this was the defining moment for modern West Indian cricket.

"Now I know what some people will be thinking. 'How can the man who led the Packer side say these things?' But it's obvious that there are big differences between the two episodes. Not least that in 1977 the Test cricket went on. The Board picked another team and we didn't know if we would ever play again. The players in 1998 went about it the wrong way. It's not as if these guys were paupers in the first place. 'Go to Nelson Mandela's country,' I said to them again and again. '*Then* we can have a discussion about it afterwards.'"

When the Test series started, the West Indies were overwhelmed. They lost all five matches; it was only the seventh whitewash in the history of the game. The previous three had been inflicted by the West Indies.

"Up to 1999 I still believed in the players," says Clive, "but some of them, such as Curtly Ambrose and Courtney Walsh, were reaching the end of their careers, and we should have been grooming new cricketers – and we didn't. Where was the academy which would bring players through? It didn't even exist. I had been calling for one since I retired. But people would say things like, 'Garry Sobers never had a coach.' Players need guidance. Tiger Woods has a coach. Look at the Australians, they have coaches. I really felt that towards the end of that second stint as manager there was very little I could achieve. The years of complacency were beginning to hurt us. After all that trouble in South Africa and the poor play there, the Board told Malcolm Marshall and me that they wanted to see an improvement in our leadership skills and they were going to set us targets. Let me tell you, it was the Board at that time that needed an improvement in leadership skills. What was I supposed to do? I can only talk to the players; I can't play for them. Other countries had the technology to improve the technique of their players. We were too far behind and had no financial backing.

"The players at that time were still learning. We had a struggling side, not a settled one. Brian Lara was the captain, and he really had a lot on his plate. There had been the bad defeat in South Africa. Senior players such as Jimmy Adams had been missing. We had tried our best in South Africa but, after such a bad start to the tour, what followed was not really surprising."

"I think that Clive was best as a coach rather than a manager because the West Indies needed him as close to the cricket as they could get him," says Steve Camacho. "At the time, I would say that the cricket administration in the region was not very cohesive, and there was a lot of in-fighting. Men were representing a territory and not the West Indies. So the question is, Did Clive get enough support? People were doing things their own way without consultation. Clive liked doing things his own way too, of course, but his great skill was that he got people to go with him – the hallmark of leadership."

• • •

By the end of 1999, after a poor World Cup in England and a tour of New Zealand which ended 1-1, Clive stood down from his post. "The tour was a disaster. We were properly trounced and humiliated," he says. 'These are very traumatic times for us,' he told a newspaper. 'There are a lot of things wrong at the moment.'

In amongst the professional unhappiness, Clive had also been dealt a substantial personal loss. His friend and colleague Malcolm Marshall had died from cancer in November.

"I was devastated by his death. When I heard, I sat down in my armchair and drank half a bottle of brandy. He had these pains in his side and didn't know what they were. And it got worse. Then it was too late. I didn't take his death very well. We were very close and I respected him so much."

CHAPTER FOURTEEN

TO BE HAPPY, A MAN HAS TO FREE HIS HEART FROM HATRED

When he was captain of the West Indies in the late 1970s, Clive was asked to speak to the United Nations on the subject of Apartheid and the international sporting ban on South Africa. The sentiment of his speech was unequivocal.

> Whenever men don their sporting apparel to contest on the field of sport, where men choose freely to replace the violence of man with the healthy organisation of athletic competition, and where the only true victors are the human spirit and human brotherhood, that is where I'll stand firmly committed.

Today, when he speaks about racism, his views are just as strong.

"I will sit down and talk to anybody over a drink, on any subject. If someone is a racist, I see it as the triumph of the unintelligent. One thing I do know: I don't have a racist bone in my body. And I will not compromise when it comes to racism. I dislike it intensely and will fight against it any time for a white guy or a black guy. That's how I am. Cricket has done this to me because I've played when I've been the only black guy in the team; I've captained sides and been the only black man there. So it has taught me a lot and I *cannot* be racist. I respect every colour, every class, every creed, every religion. I make no apology for that. The white guy, the black guy, the Asian guy. We all have a right to feel proud of who we are.

"I can't change who I am. I am a person who has never seen colour; I see human beings. Cut me and my blood will be the same colour as yours. I am a citizen of the world.

"When I was captain of the West Indies, the assistant manager, Frankie Thomas, used to read all of my mail before I did. He would divide it into two piles and say, 'These are for you; these ones you don't need to see.' It was abusive mail. Not in keeping with the standards of correspondence I was used to, I might add."

Clive does not see his opinions on race as being one separate compartment in his life. They are informed by the principles he holds at his core.

"I think, to be happy, a man has to free his heart from hatred; he has to free his mind from worries; he has to live simply, give more and expect less.

"I believe in togetherness. And that is how I believe the fortunes of people in the West Indies will be improved. I am a federalist, I always have been. We should play as one. We need one flag, one airline which is properly run and flies overseas as well as throughout the Caribbean. The great brains of the West Indies who studied politics and economics should be working towards this. Never mind if they're Trinidadian, Jamaican or Guyanese. You see, in the West Indies, we don't have an anthem. We need one with drum rolls, you know, a piece of music that makes the hair on the back of your neck stand up. Something to make us feel proud.

"When I was manager on the '96/97 tour we played a Test on Australia Day. They wanted to play my anthem, the Guyanese one. But I said, "Courtney Walsh is the captain, play the Jamaican anthem. At the beginning of play an opera singer sang the anthem, and it was so powerful that a Jamaican guy there who had married an Australian had tears rolling down his cheeks. I said to Courtney, 'If you don't do well in this Test after something like that, then there's a problem.' That's what we need for the West Indies, a great rolling inspirational anthem that can bring you to tears and inspire you to great feats. It must have all the ingredients that make a man want to fight until he's given his last drop of blood.

"I recognise that a lot of people want to do their own thing, but let me tell you, they all want the West Indies cricket team to do well – so you can't have your cake and eat it. You must say that working together is better for everybody. My team achieved that one-ness. If a guy from Trinidad is in the final of the Olympic 100 metres, will I be watching it hoping he wins? You bet your bottom dollar I will, willing him on. That is what I want to see.

"And part of that vision inevitably means people sharing. Until we get away from this mind-set of individual territories going their own way, we will never enjoy anything profound together. Is it not time to have the type of unity in the Caribbean that is now being accepted in Europe?

"We have to stop thinking, 'Am I Trinidadian? Am I Jamaican? Am I Guyanese?' and think instead of what we can do for the region. That is what we have to achieve, and that is the thing I would love to preach to the people here. Barbados has blue seas and in Guyana we have brown water, but we'd still like to go there for the Easter weekend and feel welcome. When I go to Barbados, I need an immigration card. We have to open up our ideas and stop trying to decry one another. It's a serious situation.

"Like most countries in the West Indies, Guyana has its problems in some areas. But my greatest hope is that our people will in time ascend because of the amount of wealth from minerals and other resources that exist. It is my fervent hope that my beloved country realises its full potential. That is my dream, and I hope it comes true.

"Guyana has a lot going for it. It is such a beautiful country. I think we can be the finest country in South America because we have everything we need. Look at the produce at the markets in Georgetown every day, beautiful fresh stuff and all grown in Guyana. What we need is investment from overseas to supplement what we already have."

Just as when Clive was a teenager in Georgetown in the 1960s, Guyana is still divided politically today between the black Guyanese and the Indo-Guyanese. About half the population has Indian roots, and more than a third African.

"For Guyana to progress we have to stop seeing blacks or Indians and just see Guyanese working together," says Clive. "The government should reflect the nation. So let's have less of the two parties and more of a shared government; then the blacks wouldn't be able to say to the Indians, 'You're acting in your own interests' or vice versa. You presume I'm thinking of a perfect world, but I'm just thinking of a better Guyana, not a perfect one."

. . .

"A person's environment is so important. I think one of the best things I ever did after I retired was to work for the Housing Action Trust in Brent in north-west London. It was started by the Conservative government, who had this plan to go into run-down areas. The idea was to get the backing of a majority of the local people and, if that happened, the government would give them a hundred million pounds to regenerate the area. We would take people to see where their new flats were going to be, they had a hand in designing their own place, and it was so satisfying. In the past, people never had that sort of say about how their houses should be built. It has always been my way of thinking that if you have a decent home, for the majority of the time you have a decent citizen.

"Many of the things I have done away from cricket get me thinking, yet still I return to the example of my own mother and father who kept me on the right path. My mother was an extraordinary woman. She had so many children to look after. Her own, her nieces and nephews, and then later, their children. She would wash clothes with a board, she cooked not with a stove but with fire. There wasn't much time to worry about the state of her fingernails! It was a hard life for us all, but a happy one. Food was there, maybe late some nights, but there was this love that always resided in the house. That was daily life.

"She knew her cricket too, did my mother. In later life she went to a game when she lived in the USA, and there were quite a few people there. One player got fifty, and they all stood up to applaud. My mother's friends turned to her and said, 'Are you not standing to join in, Sylvia?' and she replied from her chair. 'I've seen my son play cricket. I only stand for centuries!'

"My mother's life was one of service, and I think I've learned that true happiness comes through service. I felt so strongly about her. She was the sort of person you could imagine dying for. When we went to collect my CBE, and she came with me, she said, 'Never in my dreams did I think you would be taking me to Buckingham Palace.' I always wanted to give things back to her because of what she did for me. When she moved to the United States, I bought her the biggest house on the street. She said, 'Thank you so much, Clive, I can now invite my friends for tea and be proud of the house.' I'm so glad that, when she died, she was happy. That was very important to me. Like a lot of people, I have asked myself the question for much of my life, 'Did I do enough for my mother?'

"She knew that all her children were the future, that it is the children who are the integral part of any country's success story. It's so important that we give them something to strive for, either through the work they do or through education. Then they will understand what success means. For some of them, that confidence may mean that one day they can scale Mount Everest, or run a big company; for others there are smaller but no less important goals to achieve. The point is that kids have to know that success is possible, and the people who run sport, who run cricket, need to know this too.

"Of course we are responsible for helping them towards that success. What are we teaching them? What is our legacy to them? We have to be certain that what we do has a lasting effect for the better on our children. How do we get their attention when there are distractions such as crime or drugs or even computer games? What will become of these kids for whom education is a chore rather than a way of life?

"Yet it saddens me that there are parts of the world where children cannot go to school because of corruption, war, hunger or poverty. There are places where kids haven't got the energy or the nutrition to last a day in the classroom. Learning is not even a blip on their daily chart. You know, people of my generation grew up thinking that, after the Second World War, things would be different, that all of these huge obstacles for children would disappear, or at least be less difficult to overcome. But if you look at the Middle East, parts of Africa, even parts of Europe in the 1990s, it's not so. We must educate the children and leave them a legacy we can be proud of."

CHAPTER FIFTEEN

WE HAVE TO CHANGE THE WAY WE THINK ABOUT EVERYTHING

The Trinidad Hilton Hotel, Port-of Spain. 15 November 2006

Clive is in his room, wearing his vest, slacks and polished shoes. He is ironing his shirt for this evening. He will be the guest speaker at the dinner to celebrate the 50th anniversary of the Trinidad and Tobago Cricket Board. From his window, he can see down to the famous Queen's Park Savannah, the large open space where local people have played games for generations. Half a dozen football matches are in progress.

"You know," says Clive wistfully while working on the collar of the white shirt, "fifteen years ago, even ten years ago, I reckon those boys down there would have been playing cricket. Not today."

Later that evening he taps his fingers at the top table in the Joao Havelange Centre of Excellence in Tunapuna. Gold beads shimmer around the cutlery and the glasses. In the middle of the table stands a large vase full of flowers. A pair of goldfish dart around the stems. The guests are being entertained by the tenor, Raymond Edwards.

"He was pretty good," quips Clive, at the beginning of his address when the singing is over. "He must be from Guyana."

"The stakes are high," he says, referring to the 2007 World Cup which the West Indies will host in a little under five months. "The journey seemed so far away a few years ago, but it is almost complete. Are we ready to rumble? It is our challenge to transform a logistical nightmare into a dream. Failure is not an option. If the short-term gain of a successful Cricket World Cup will be a massive financial windfall for the Caribbean, then the long-term benefits for the region and West Indies cricket take on even greater proportions."

The contrast between Clive's hopes for the future of West Indies cricket and the reality of the present, could not be more stark. At the time of Clive's speech, the West Indies side had won two Test matches in the previous three years; a serious state of affairs. Yet the decline in the region's cricketing excellence had been apparent for much longer.

• • •

After Packer and World Series Cricket, Clive returned to captain the West Indies in 1979. From that time until his retirement, the team were beaten in only three of the 47 Test matches in which they played, a loss rate of 6.4 per cent. In the next six years, when Vivian Richards was captain, that figure rose to 18.9 per cent, and under successive captains it has risen and risen till the wins and losses are almost a mirror image of what they were in Clive's years.

Period	Principal captain(s)	P	W	D	L	% Lost
Dec 79 – Jan 85	C. Lloyd	47	23	21	3	6.4
Mar 85 – Aug 91	V. Richards	53	28	15	10	18.9
Apr 92 – Aug 95	R. Richardson	27	12	9	6	22.2
April 96 – Dec 99	C. Walsh, B. Lara	34	10	8	16	47.1
Mar 00 – Dec 02	J. Adams, C. Hooper	39	10	10	19	48.7
Apr 03 – Jun 06	B. Lara, S. Chanderpaul, R. Sarwan	47	5	13	29	61.7

"The greatest reason for the decline of West Indian cricket is that we became thoughtless," says Clive. "Too many people assumed that we had a right to go on being great for ever. It was as if they believed that West Indians would always produce great cricket in the way that France is famed for its fine wine – a never-ending national institution. But life has changed for people in the West Indies, cricket has changed in the rest of the world, and we failed to appreciate those substantial changes.

"To put it simply, the West Indies have lost for so long because there are not enough great players. That's obvious. Great players don't just turn up, they have to be shaped. Yet what very few people seem to realise is that the Test team I had in 1975/76 was really no different from the one that there is today in terms of its potential. Fidel Edwards and Daren Powell can both bowl at 90 miles per hour. Chanderpaul and Sarwan are both world-class batsmen. Our cricketers are free-flowing men. Early on, Viv Richards was a free-flowing guy, he got forties and never made big scores. But you knew once he had harnessed his talent and got the mental side of his game right, then he was going to be a class player. Gordon Greenidge took some time to get going, same with Michael Holding. All those guys came in and worked at their game.

"The great West Indies sides were shaped, just as this one could be. The problems we are having now are the consequence of a decade of letting the fruit wither on the vine. There have been big cultural changes in the West Indies. The regional cricket competition is not what it was. Our cricketers no longer play county cricket. The Board has not used its authority wisely. The players' expectations, what they want from the game, what they want from life, have changed. Above all, we neglected to plan for the future."

• • •

"When people speak about the demise of West Indian cricket," says Clive, "the influence of America is never very far from their lips. I disagree. I think the real sporting distraction has not come from basketball or the other American sports, but from football. There are the Reggae Boys in Jamaica, the Soca Warriors in Trinidad, Barbados has a side. You can make a good living from these games and, if young boys are looking at the West Indies cricket team nowadays, there's little to inspire them because we're getting beaten; we're really up against it. It's true that in some of the islands, the first thing that a politician does is put up a basketball court; it's much smaller and cheaper than a cricket ground, but I don't believe that a lot of kids go on to play professionally."

Clive is right. The 2006/07 roster for international players contracted to the NBA (the National Basketball Association) in the United States shows that there are four players registered from the Caribbean. Two are from the island of Hispaniola – a region not known for its cricket – one is from Guyana and one from Saint Vincent.

In the summer of 2007, Garry Sobers was in England and spoke to an audience about the problems facing cricket in the Caribbean:

"If someone said to me that soccer is the reason for West Indian cricket falling so low, I might think about it. But the real problem, ladies and gentlemen, and it is a problem for sport around the world, is television."

Sir Garry mentioned his own boys, both fine sports players, whom he believed had suffered because of the distractions of modern life.

"When they got home from school they would not go outside and play, they would sit in front of a video. That's your real culprit. Kids do not organise games of cricket by themselves, playing outside morning, noon and night. Today, if it is not organised, nobody leaves home. They wait for you to pick them up, take them to the ground, give them the best cricket attire. The natural flow of the game has gone."

"It's true that kids have many more things to do with their time," says Clive. "If you want to improve at your sport, you have to be dedicated, do little else, train hard and that's less likely to happen when there are so many distractions. And if they have a job that pays a decent wage, they'll be saying, 'Why the hell should I go through all this?' In my time there wasn't much to do. Now you can fill your day doing all sorts. You can watch DVDs all day long if you want. That is why it is so important to catch them early. We must inculcate the right things in these children before they go down the wrong lane. We must get the structure to life there early enough."

Clive had seen the challenges facing modern Caribbean cricket at first hand. By October 2006, he was back with the West Indies side. "Third time lucky," he grins. Once again, the West Indies had called on him and he had answered.

"It was about this time that some people were saying that it was a conflict of interest for me to be back, because I was connected to the Board through the cricket committee. What sort of conflict were they talking about? One that involved me wanting to bring the glory days back to West Indies cricket? That was, and has always been, my only aim. I will do anything, join anything, for that to happen. How can people say that is a conflict of interest? Only the rancorous."

"I wanted him with us in 2006 and 2007," says the former West Indies captain, Brian Lara. "I was never given much choice in West Indies cricket, but any time the opportunity came to involve great players such as Clive, I welcomed it. Clive was there during my favourite time as captain, the 1998/99 series against Australia in the West Indies. He was the manager and Malcolm Marshall was the coach, and we worked so well together. We'd had a disastrous time in South Africa, and I was surprised to be named as captain. They gave it to me for a probationary period, something which hadn't happened for years in West Indies cricket, but I took up the challenge and, because Clive was there, at least I had a small semblance of support. He created a very good environment, even though we had an unsettled side. There were experienced players missing, other players were still learning, and we took on the best side in the world and drew the series two-all. Clive had a great ability to listen, to impart knowledge without imposing himself on me. It was Clive who allowed me to grow and to learn from my mistakes. He is a very gifted man.

"Clive will be remembered as a great leader. We are products of the previous generation, and Clive is the product of Sir Frank Worrell. I am a product of the guys who left the stage in the early 1990s. I think he was able to bring to West Indies cricket that genesis feeling when the Caribbean was looking for independence. He understood the state of mind of the black West Indian and the state of mind of the descendants of the indentured labourers. I will always see him carrying that torch and taking the game to a different level. He made us invincible. It was the pinnacle of our sport, and he was the leader."

Clive would be with the squad for the 2007 World Cup and, before that, the ICC Champions' Trophy in India, a competition that the West Indies had won in England two years previously. The West Indies Cricket Board stated that Clive would 'make himself accessible to captain, coach and manager to assist in any way which will build morale, strengthen the team's performance and encourage a stronger culture of professionalism and discipline'.

The West Indies played very well in India, only losing in the final to Australia, the best side in the world. Clive was encouraged. The tournament was a rehearsal for the 2007 World Cup, but he also knew that, behind this short-term success, profound difficulties lurked.

"The first thing that struck me being back in the dressing room was the physique of the players themselves," he says. "These guys were a different body shape to the fellows I played with. You know the players wear these skin-tight things under their whites nowadays? Well, the West Indies players looked like middle-distance runners in theirs. Athletic, sure, but slim rather than being powerfully built. If you ever saw Andy Roberts with his shirt off, or Wayne Daniel, they were built like middleweight boxers with huge shoulders and big chests. These were strong men.

"For one-day cricket it's OK, I suppose, because two spells is fine. But for Test matches it's four spells a day, or even more, and you have to be very strong. It will take some time because a lot of these players have come through so quickly. They still have a lot to learn in Test cricket. They haven't yet scaled the heights but they must always, always, be encouraged to do so. If they have the right guidance, it will happen."

• • •

The West Indies played Pakistan in the opening game of the 2007 World Cup at Sabina Park in Jamaica. Before the game began, Clive led out some of his own World Cup winners onto the pitch. The 'strong men' walked behind him one more time. Vivian and Andy. Mikey and Joel. Rohan, Lance and Deryck. Vanburn and Alvin. Gordon, Collis, Colin and Faoud. Maurice, Larry and Bernard.

Clive was presented with the original big-eared cup, the Prudential Trophy, and for the third time lifted it to induce ecstatic delight in thousands of West Indian cricket fans. Afterwards Clive took the cup and some of his old team-mates into the Sabina Park dressing room.

The scene must have inspired the players, for they beat Pakistan by 54 runs. But there was to be no meaningful renaissance for the West Indies. Over the next 38 days, they would play another eight games of cricket (the whole 1975 tournament was over in a fortnight), losing five of them. The only victories were against Zimbabwe, Ireland and Bangladesh. In the second phase of the competition, they finished sixth out of eight.

"I really thought we would do well in the World Cup," reflects Clive "because we can play one-day cricket with some competence. I genuinely believed that we could have made the semi-finals if we had put our minds to it. Look at how we did in the ICC trophy in India against the same sides. We played well against Pakistan in that opening World Cup game.

We got our disciplines right and showed that we can be a pretty good side. But for this team the discipline is there, and then the next moment it goes. Do you know why that is? Fitness. Their fitness didn't carry them through.

"When I was captain, our fielding sessions were two hours long, and we enjoyed what we did. Running five miles, doing our exercises. When we trained before a match, people would come just to watch and applaud when it was over. Our training was very intense. With these players today, I would like to see them work a little bit harder because when they're at peak fitness they can compete with the rest of the world. I saw it in India. They probably need another Dennis Waight to get the best out them.

"I want these young men to be enthusiastic, diving all over the place; they should be able to catch pigeons. They should have good arms to throw the ball at any angle. They should take the advice of my mother who said, 'Young people never get tired, they only get hungry!'"

In Clive's opinion, there was a significant happening between the end of the Champions' Trophy and the start of the World Cup. The side got rid of their trainer, an Australian called Bryce Cavanagh.

"He was good," says Clive, "but I believe the players thought Bryce was being too tough with them. I saw how he worked and I never minded because I knew there would be benefits. What the players seemingly don't realise is that, if you are at the peak of physical fitness, it's that stamina that can see you through in a desperate situation, late in the day when it really matters. It was no coincidence that we got to the final of the Champions' Trophy when Bryce was there."

Clive thinks for a moment.

"To be unfit in your mid-twenties as an international cricketer shows that there is something wrong. Have we lost the work ethic somewhere along the way, I wonder? Do today's cricketers realise that the good things require sacrifice? In the 1970s, I studied for an economics degree at the University of Salford at night. I used to come out of my class at eight o'clock in the evening and stand in the winter air waiting for a bus, hopping up and down to keep myself warm. I was playing for Lancashire, I was an international cricketer who had scored Test match hundreds and I was taking the damn bus back to my flat in Didsbury. You know how I got to Old Trafford for much of my early career? Carrying my kit on the X23 bus from Great Harwood into Manchester city centre and then a cab to the ground. I travelled like that for years.

"Fitness and discipline were the two mainstays of the team I played in. But sadly, when I was back for the World Cup, both those qualities had diminished. It takes time to instil the rules, and that is one of the responsibilities of the coach. If a player stays out late at night and doesn't play well the next day, he is letting his team-mates down.

"This was a particular problem for this World Cup. Discipline is important in everything cricketers do, but the schedule included far too much free time. Look at the headlines England made, and the same with the South Africans. These things happened because of the long intervals between games. People got bored and wanted to let their hair down and enjoy the hospitality of the islands. Apart from that, a shorter tournament would have left the West Indies Board better off financially. How much did it cost to keep all those players and officials out there for so long?"

Clive's concerns about how the West Indies and West Indians have changed in the past quarter of a century have been clearly articulated by the academic and cricket lover, Professor Hilary Beckles. In 2004, in an essay entitled *The Caribbean, Cricket and CLR James*, he wrote this:

> The new post-nationalist paradigm has its own distinctive moral features, ideological trajectory and social culture. An important feature is that cricket heroes have rejected the popular perception of themselves as role models, ambassadors and representatives of social idealism. They see this as limiting and socially bankrupt.
>
> Today's cricket hero, therefore, now wishes to be identified as a professional craftsman with only a secondary responsibility to the wider socio-political agenda carried out by his predecessors. He does not wish to carry the burden of responsibility for nationalist pride, regional integration and the viability of the nation-state. He sees himself as an apolitical, trans-national, global professional, aiming to maximize financial earnings within an attractive market, and is principally motivated and guided by these considerations.
>
> The logical implication of this self-perception is that the cricket hero wishes to distance his performance and psychological state from the considerations of the 1950s and 1960s, from the political project of nation-building. These post-nationalist players want to function as 'pure' entrepreneurs within the market economy of sport, and with a minimum emotional or ideological bond to the psychological needs of nation-states. Their commitment is to the cash nexus that recognizes none of the sentiment of the political agendas of the nationalist paradigm. Sport, they suggest, is an economic activity that transcends political boundaries and ideological sensibilities.

"I just don't think the boys understand the gravity of what they've been chosen to do," says Clive sadly. "All I have is my own experience, but

I recall so clearly seeing Charlie Griffith, Wes, Garry, Conrad Hunte. I watched them come through the gate at Bourda when I was a little boy. Never did I think I would play with them. I would watch in awe as they played in the nets. I'm not so sure we have the same thing here now. These guys are missing quite a lot. They are very unfortunate that they will never know what it was like to be part of a group of people who ruled the cricketing world."

"People have said that today's players don't have a sense of history, but who is that down to?" asks Brian Lara. "It is down to the people who put them there. It's like my parents have instilled in me the legacy of our family name, telling me about the things that are important. I feel it is down to the employer to lay the foundation for what he wants coming forth from the employees. These men are 21st-century cricketers. There are a lot of things that are important to these men today that weren't even relevant forty years ago. The side that was built on the legacy of Frank Worrell had a very different motivation from today's side.

"What is West Indies cricket all about now?" continues Lara. "It's about the commercial side. You will find a lot of young players moving away from the history and knowing about great players. They're more interested in the money side of the game, but I don't think it's the players who are at fault.

"My own view is that it's important to know who you are and what you represent. It is an important part of making a successful team. And I think you can see that with the Australians today and the way Steve Waugh made them aware of certain things."

• • •

Clive was happy to be back serving the West Indies during the World Cup, but he was frustrated by the limitations of his role. He helped with the nets, with the batsmen and the bowlers. He hit catches to the wicket-keeper.

"I suppose I was a co-ordinator and advisor," says Clive, "ironing out the odd fault here and there. But I wouldn't want to do this job again because I didn't have any power. I had no vote in team selection and so at times I felt a little bit like a nodding donkey, and that was very distressing. I think that a cricketer of my experience, in that situation, should have been given a voice in who played in the side. I would like to see a selection committee make the decision about the side, not just the captain and the coach. In a tournament as important as the World Cup, such a decision should be reached through consensus. When a side is at home, this is what must happen; it's the way it's done in other countries. When we're away, we can have conference calls. If you are a selector, it should be a full-time job. Home and away. It's all about seizing responsibility. If the side is selected properly, and then does badly, everyone is responsible. It's transparent."

All the players in the West Indian side that won the 1975 World Cup had played county cricket in England; the eleven that lost to England in their final game of the World Cup in 2007 had played 51 first-class county games between them; 30 of those games had been played by Brian Lara.

"A player learns so much from county cricket," says Clive. "It almost goes without saying that my cricket improved greatly because I played with Lancashire. I got used to playing on different sorts of wickets; I faced different sorts of bowlers. I also played with and against some of the best players in the world, so you stored up the things you experienced against them, things that can come in handy in a Test match. I think overseas players also learn new disciplines in county cricket. We were batting or bowling four or five times a week, we were very fit. We were mentally strong and physically strong too because we had to do our own training. You had to look after yourself and not indulge too much away from the game, simply because of the amount of cricket you played.

"The dressing-room experience was invaluable too. As an outsider, you learned how to conduct yourself, to be proud of what you were and what you could do. You also had to play pretty well most of the time to get the respect of your team-mates and the supporters."

"When Clive and other West Indians played the county game," says Clem Seecharan, "they were provided with a framework for the development of that generation of great Caribbean cricketers. They obviously had skills, probably no better than those of some of today's guys, but they got into a professional frame of mind and the responsibility that went with it. Many of them also needed the county game to earn a living. Today, the cricketers in the West Indies are doing better financially and don't need the county job. But they're missing the kind of discipline that the overseas professional had to demonstrate."

"I don't think we have the qualities that the English counties want any longer, but this may change as the players gather experience," says Clive. "We have all-rounders, but so do other countries. What they want, we don't have at the moment. Spinners, seriously quick bowlers. We have some talented guys, but they will only be wanted once their talent comes to fruition.

"Our young players are coming through the ranks so quickly that, when their form dips in international cricket, they have nothing to fall back on. There's no first principle to return to. Now that we have the academy set up and university teams playing in our domestic cricket and the under-19s playing in our one-day tournament, this could be the turning point that we're all hoping for. This in turn can improve the standard of our inter-island cricket.

"The standard has dropped tremendously. For a start the players need to be better paid. And to do that we need a huge sponsor to make it worth the while of the top players to play there. We need development sides in the tournament to expose as many players as we can to first-class cricket. By that I mean the University of the West Indies sides playing in the competition. I want these young men to know about cricket and education hand in hand like they do at Oxford, Cambridge, Durham and Loughborough. We should extend the invitation to the international sides from the USA, Canada, and Bermuda. It should be a tournament that is the envy of the world with an overseas player for each side. That is my vision, but for the past few years the cricket here has gone into steep decline.

"Look at the example of Fidel Edwards. He was picked for the West Indies pretty much by being spotted bowling fast in the nets. He started well and then, when it all went wrong for him, he didn't know why. He had nowhere to go. We need to harness the talent in a uniform and transparent way; this is why the academies are so important. We need to stick with the talent once we've found it, and then make sure there's enough money to sustain it. We can't muddle along thinking we'll just pick up another Brian Lara or four Malcolm Marshalls. Kids are doing different things nowadays. We want a different sort of kid, the one who wants to get up early in the morning and do the training because he wants to make a name for himself."

• • •

One of Ken Gordon's final tasks before he stood down as President of the West Indies Cricket Board in August 2007 was to commission an investigation into the state of West Indian cricket. Many such papers had been published in the past, with little effect. The investigators this time were led by PJ Patterson, the former Prime Minister of Jamaica, and they asked for the views of administrators, former players, politicians and ordinary people. Clive's views were also sought, and their interim report appeared in July 2007. Its opening statement was: *West Indies cricket does not belong to the WICB. West Indies cricket belongs to the people of the West Indies.* The report also noted that future West Indian cricketers should possess certain 'non-negotiable' qualities which would include education and training, fitness, discipline, team spirit, West Indian identity. The document lingered on the state of the relationship between the Board and the players. It pointed out that 'few West Indian cricketers, past or present, have expressed satisfaction with how they have been treated by the Board.'

"I've had a long and interesting relationship with the Board," smiles Clive. "And nowadays I'm connected to it directly because I'm the chairman of the cricket committee. The Board has had a lot of criticism over the years, and much of it the Board has brought upon itself. What is so important, crucial I would say, is that, from now on, it must have a better relationship with the players. The two have been at loggerheads for too long, and it has hampered West Indian cricket.

"The tendency has been to tinker, change things unnecessarily, because we have not been winning. There's been little rhythm, and I think this is down to the fact that there have been many presidents of the WICB in the past ten years. The Board has looked fragmented, and of course that feeling has been picked up very quickly by the players.

"In the past the Board was often made up of former players. I would like to see that again; men who are determined to bring the game on; men of good repute, who have West Indies cricket at heart; men who want to see the game bloom again and return to its halcyon days.

"The cricket committee now has myself, Andy Roberts, Desmond Haynes, Deryck Murray, Courtney Walsh and Ian Bishop on it. That's important. When we left for Packer, it was the cricketers on the Board who said to us, 'We understand what you're doing.' The Board should have a formal arrangement that half of its members be cricketers. Businessmen have their place, of course they do. Modern cricket is a business. But you still have to think of the game's best interests.

"I can't tell you what war is like because I've never fought in a battle. But I know about cricket because I've been in those trenches and seen everything there is to see, the good, the bad and the indifferent. We must have people looking after our cricket who can say the same. I don't want to see people on the Board whose main aim is self-aggrandisement. "

• • •

During his time as team manager, coach and co-ordinator of the West Indies team, Clive spent much time talking to and watching one of cricket's greatest batsmen, Brian Lara. No man has scored more Test runs than him. Twice, Lara has scored the highest Test innings in cricket history; 375 against England in 1993/94 and 400 not out against the same opposition in 2003/04. Clive was lucky enough to watch as Lara made 153 not out in Barbados in 1999 when the West Indies beat Australia by one wicket. It was one of the great innings of modern cricket. In its match report, *Wisden* recorded that 'irrefutably, Lara's undefeated 153 was the hand of a genius. He guided his men to victory as though leading the infirm through a maze.'

"That batting was so special," recalls Clive. "You could see from his batting that day that here was a man in a different class, one who had oodles of talent and played the game as a thinking man.

"I have a great deal of respect for Brian," he says with affection. "You know what I wish? I wish that he could have played in a different time.

Brian played in the wrong era; he would have been the greatest asset to us. Never mind his great skill as a batsman, his determination was so obvious. And so I feel very aggrieved for this guy. As a batsman he led by example, of course, and as a captain he had some excellent tactical ideas. But, because he wanted to do well, he would experiment. His problem was he was trying things with a side that didn't have that much experience."

"I like my time," laughs Brian Lara warmly. "Sure, it's nowhere near as successful. I played for the West Indies for 17 years, and one of the things I was unable to fulfil was getting them back on track. I mean, how great must it have been to turn up knowing you were the favourites and you were almost certain to win? But if I had my career back in my hands, I would have loved to have worked my period a little bit better, to have got more out of that time."

"I wish a player of Brian's quality had had a few more happy moments as captain," says Clive. "He took a lot of criticism, particularly from ex-players."

He shakes his head and tuts.

"This is a man who scored nearly 600 runs in a three-Test series against Sri Lanka in 2001 – and lost. All the Tests ended in defeat. This is the man who scored well over 500 runs against Australia a year later, and the same thing happened. How much more can a man give? I know just how much he wanted to do well as a player and as a captain but, with the teams he had around him, he couldn't really go forward."

. . .

Clive's vision for the future of the West Indies is as earnest as it is simple: that one day the side will be great again. Players with the gifts given to Brian Lara will need to be part of such a team, and Clive knows that such men are born, not manufactured. But, he says, many other things can be done to give the West Indies a chance to be world-beaters once more.

"We have to change the way we think about everything, from the bottom to the very top. We have to use the Caribbean education system; after all, we have four universities now. We have to get cricket back into the schools. We have to use technology, we have to get people's brains working. Above all, the regional academy must be a success.

"The academy must be the root for our growth. It must educate the players with some cricketing nous. We must employ people who can pass on the knowledge they have built up by playing the game themselves to the highest standard. And the people who get the jobs must be rigorously examined. They must be asked to display their cricketing strengths. Don't just give somebody a job because they have the right paperwork.

"The kids at the academies must be taught by the very best. If you can't work out how to bat against leg spin for example, you have to be told by someone who can. You have to know how to drop your hands and you have to know that you can't drive through the line. Now, coaching qualifications are important but a guy who's got all the badges in the world but has never made a Test fifty on a turning wicket can't tell a kid about these little intricacies. You have to have learned them from experience.

"The main thing is to get the talent, get the people who can impart the knowledge and bring the players to fruition. I know it is an uphill task, but cricket is so important to people here; it's one of the main ingredients of the glue that keeps us together."

He pauses for a moment.

"I'm thinking about the past and the future but especially today," he says. "I think about today's players, and my overwhelming emotion towards them is not anger that they have been unsuccessful but concern. We did so well that everybody expects the West Indies teams to be like those of the 1970s and 1980s, but it cannot happen without hard work, attention to detail and respect for the game. I would like the players to know that, if they put in the greatest effort yet lose, the people won't mind.

"These players have been burdened with what the West Indies have done in the past, and I think that's probably wrong. This is a new era, it's their time and it's up to them to go out and show people what they're capable of. A lot of people are backing them to do well, including myself. They have a lot of support."

CHAPTER SIXTEEN

I'VE NEVER HEARD THESE GUYS SAY THESE SORTS OF THINGS BEFORE

St John's Wood Road, 17 May 2007

Lord's on a damp and threatening Thursday. By twenty past eight in the morning two queues of MCC members, fifty yards long, bookend the Grace Gates. Macs are on, pipes are already lit, shooting sticks have been splayed and voices are raised. A Test series is starting. The West Indies are coming.

A mile away, near Primrose Hill, Clive is in another hotel bedroom. He is soon to be speaking at a breakfast put on by the Professional Cricketers' Association. On the little stage he will sit on his bar stool next to Devon Malcolm, tell a couple of nice jokes, speak softly and sincerely, and put a questioner right about Andy Roberts. People will listen.

. . .

Alistair Cook drives Corey Collymore through extra cover. "That's four," says Clive. He is not at the Test match, but back in his hotel room in a chair with his feet up on the bed. His ICC blazer and the West Indies tie that he wore to breakfast have been hung up by the door. Clive has retired as a referee: "The travelling was getting too much," he says. His time with the West Indies in the dressing room ended after the World Cup. The coach, Bennett King, has gone. The captain, Brian Lara, has retired.

The Test match is on the telly, and Clive is picking at the *Daily Mail*.

"Look at this fellow here," he says pointing to the paper with a chuckle. A motor cyclist is pictured giving a V-sign to a speed camera. "He thought he wouldn't get caught because he had no number plates," reads Clive, "but what he didn't know was that there were only three bikes of the type he was riding in the country."

He looks over the top of the paper at the television and watches a bit more of the cricket.

"It's funny, isn't it," he says quietly after five minutes or so. "All those

201

times I captained the West Indies, you'd have thought the Board might have invited me to watch a bit of the game today."

The room is warm, and Clive's eyes are heavy. They close for a second.

Collymore comes in to bowl. A mile away, out on the square, Alistair Cook drives another boundary.

Clive does not see it. He has fallen asleep.

His hands are folded on his lap on top of the newspaper. They are huge. Earlier, in the lobby of the hotel, he laid his palms flat on the reception desk while chatting to the concierge. His fingers seemed to stretch on without end. His hands were as broad as a pair of paperback books. The diamond-and-gold rings he wears could hold a furled napkin but sat firmly on his fingers.

I take a good long look at the man in front of me.

Who is Clive Lloyd? Where does he come from? What does he believe?

Clive is breathing quietly.

All my life I've had to prove something. I suppose that's what's made me a determined person. I hope that my children have got that sort of thing instilled in them. Go out there to do your best, I tell them, and always try your best. You must always try your best, and you must give that 100 per cent all of the time. Sometimes you can't, but you must feel that you have. And, if you fail, you must feel that you have given it your all.

I have always been a fighter. As a boy in hospital, then not being able to continue my scholarship, my family not being able to pay for my school fees. Later, there were times when I couldn't get a run. Then I was paralysed after the accident in Australia. But I was always fighting, showing I was good enough, showing I was a leader. I think I did all the things that people called for. And I think it made me a better person because I can look back and say, 'Well, hey, you know, I made things happen.' I think you are judged on the obstacles you overcome. That's me. I always think that I have another obstacle to overcome and even now I don't think I'll change.

There were always these challenges, you know? And there was my style – people didn't like my style, but I always remember what Bradman said: that people thought he wasn't as stylish as Ponsford, but what Bradman knew was that cricket is the only game where they talk about style. In golf it's the lowest score. In tennis it's who gets to six games first. No. It's not style, it's what you do while you're there. So it doesn't matter how you look, Bradman said, and I always remember that.

*Then there were the people who called me a 'glorified slogger'.
I heard once that Cyril Washbrook said that. Well, I must be a
pretty good slogger for 30-odd thousand first-class runs. I used
to leave people behind. Why should a guy with my height not
put people off their stride? I was an entertainer. I pulled people
over midwicket for six, and other batsmen couldn't do that.
Was Botham a slogger? Was Viv a slogger? They hit it in the
air as much as anybody. I think you can distinguish the good
from the better and the better from the best because the best
do extraordinary things. I wanted to hit it somewhere. People
didn't come to see me block. They came to be entertained.*

*Not many fellows play Test cricket until they are 40 and are still
successful. That shows that a man has been thinking, working
things out. All these challenges, I met them, I overcame them
and I think it has done me the world of good.*

*Yes, I know that, when they come to write the Book of Cricket,
my name will be called.*

Clive's eyes open. He looks at the television screen and then checks his
watch.

"You hungry?" he asks. "Shall we get something to eat?"

• • •

Clive's house. June 2007

Clive is sitting on the sofa and is on fine form. At the recent Test at
Old Trafford he was asked to present Darren Sammy, St Lucia's first
international cricketer, with his debut cap. As he walked down the pavilion
steps with the West Indies side to make the presentation, Clive was given
a rousing cheer by the locals. On the outfield he stood in a circle with the
players and gave Sammy the maroon cap, and his blessing. The words
of inspiration must have worked. Sammy took seven for 66 in England's
second innings, including three wickets in one over. On the way back up
the pavilion steps, Clive shakes hands with someone on the benches. "Get
yer pads on, Clive!" shouts a wag.

Clive is about to watch a recording of the tribute to him made by Sky
TV from its *Pioneers of Cricket* series. Clive has yet to see it, but friends
who watched it during Sky's coverage of the Test series have told him it is
very complimentary.

The programme features West Indian players from the past talking
about Clive's attributes as a captain, how the Packer years shaped the side
and the consequent dominance of West Indian Test cricket.

The programme starts. When Garry Sobers speaks of Clive's leadership
skills, he calls him 'Clyde'.

"He's always done that," chuckles Clive. "Always called me Clyde for some reason."

Michael Holding speaks: 'Clive will go down as one of the greatest captains the world has ever seen and someone who has done a great deal of good for West Indies cricket.'

Vivian Richards: 'We didn't start as superstars; we gradually grew. It took someone who you trusted as a leader to accomplish that. Clive did a magnificent job.'

Wes Hall: 'He was the one who was responsible for the West Indies becoming the embodiment of world cricket supremacy.'

Joel Garner: 'He was a father, brother and friend. He was everything. He understood us.'

When the programme finishes, Clive is clearly touched by what he has seen.

"You know, I've never heard these guys say these sorts of things before. These icons, these legends of West Indies cricket, were talking about what I did. For the first time that I can remember, it was people saying that it wasn't all down to four fast bowlers, that perhaps there was something I did that was significant. People have kept ringing me from the West Indies to say 'well done'. I think maybe the show meant something to them."

• • •

The Kensington Hilton Hotel. August 2007

We are back where we began. On a sofa in the foyer of the hotel near Shepherd's Bush where, eighteen months ago, Clive talked about his hopes for this book.

He is enjoying a bacon sandwich and a cup of tea. He is full of ideas.

"I've written to the ICC," he says. "I have a plan to reform cricket in the United States. They're in a bit of trouble over there. Different factions, sanctions thrown at them by the ICC. I would like to be part of the development of the game there. I know the place, I've visited the country for thirty years, I think the people respect me. I want to get my teeth into something like that."

Clive puts down his cup of tea. The gold bangle he always wears on his right wrist, the one that used to belong to his grandmother in British Guiana before he was born, chimes on the saucer.

"I tell you what else we should do. We should do a lot more for players who played the game and have fallen on hard times. Some of these guys are almost destitute. From the first game of every one-day series, some of the money should be put into a fund. That would bring in a lot of cash – and the interest, a couple of million dollars, we could use it to help players. There are former players in the West Indies who are struggling to pay for their own medical bills. There are old players who need help all over the world. My old team-mate from Lancashire, John Sullivan, he died in a nursing home. We have a lot of guys who gave yeoman service to their club who end up with very little. Not everyone has been able to enjoy cricket like I have."

Clive sits right back and stretches his arms almost the full length of the sofa.

"A friend wrote to me the other day and said, 'Today is a gift, that's why it's called the present.' I like that phrase. I still want to seize the moment. You know, even now, after everything, I am still in love with cricket and I always will be. It has given me so much. It's such a beautiful game because it shapes people's lives. It teaches its players honesty, integrity and fair play, and what is life if it is not about integrity, honesty and fair play? A game of cricket is life played out in front of you. There is victory, that's the goal, but it is not one that can be claimed easily. The game may bring tough times and there will be obstacles to overcome so, when the day is done and you reflect on a match that you have won, you feel like a fulfilled person. Now, what other game gives you that?

"You know, when I walk into Lord's, I still get a little tingle. I love to be in these special places, where the turf has offered up so much over the years. The throng in the concourse. And best of all, if a young person comes up to me and respectfully says 'hello', it makes my day. I think, 'Yes, I must have done something right.'"

Clive Hubert Lloyd C.B.E.

Born: 31 August 1944

TEST CRICKET
Batting and Fielding

Matches	Innings	Not Outs	Runs	Highest	Average	100s	50s	Cts
110	175	14	7,515	242*	46.67	19	39	90

Bowling

Overs	Maidens	Runs	Wickets	Average	Best
286	75	622	10	62.20	2-13

ALL FIRST-CLASS CRICKET
Batting and Fielding

Matches	Innings	Not Outs	Runs	Highest	Average	100s	50s	Cts
490	730	96	31,232	242*	49.26	79	172	377

Bowling

Overs	Maidens	Runs	Wickets	Average	Best
1,616.3	378	4,104	114	36.00	4-48

ONE-DAY INTERNATIONAL CRICKET
Batting and Fielding

Matches	Innings	Not Outs	Runs	Highest	Average	100s	50s	Cts
87	69	19	1,977	102	39.54	1	11	39

Bowling

Overs	Maidens	Runs	Wickets	Average	Best
59.4	7	210	8	26.25	2-4

ALL LIMITED-OVER CRICKET
Batting and Fielding

Matches	Innings	Not Outs	Runs	Highest	Average	100s	50s	Cts
378	343	72	10,915	134*	40.27	12	69	146

Bowling

Overs	Maidens	Runs	Wickets	Average	Best
487.4	57	1,958	71	27.57	4-33

TEST BATTING AT DIFFERENT STAGES OF CAREER

	Matches	Innings	NOs	Runs	Average	100s
Pre-captaincy, 66/7–73/4	36	64	5	2,282	38.67	5
Captaincy, pre-Packer, 74/5–77/8	29	49	3	2,312	50.26	6
Captaincy, post-Packer,79/80–84/5	45	62	6	2,921	52.16	8

CLIVE LLOYD AS TEST MATCH CAPTAIN

Tests: Played 74   Won 36   Drawn 26   Lost 12
Series: Played 18   Won 14   Drawn 2   Lost 2

Year	H/A	Opponents	Won	Drawn	Lost	Series result
1974/75	Away	India	3	–	2	Won
1974/75	Away	Pakistan	–	2	–	Drawn
1975/76	Away	Australia	1	–	5	Lost
1975/76	Home	India	2	1	1	Won
1976	Away	England	3	2	–	Won
1976/77	Home	Pakistan	2	2	1	Won
1977/78	Home	Australia	2	–	–	Won *
1979/80	Away	Australia	2	–	–	Won *
1979/80	Away	New Zealand	–	2	1	Lost
1980	Away	England	1	3	–	Won *
1980/81	Away	Pakistan	1	3	–	Won
1980/81	Home	England	2	2	–	Won
1981/82	Away	Australia	1	1	1	Drawn
1982/83	Home	India	2	3	–	Won
1983/84	Away	India	3	3	–	Won
1983/84	Home	Australia	3	1	–	Won
1984	Away	England	5	–	–	Won
1984/85	Away	Australia	3	1	1	Won

* Other Tests were played in the series

CLIVE LLOYD AS ONE-DAY INTERNATIONAL CAPTAIN

Played 82   Won 62   Tied 1   Lost 19

He captained West Indies in seven major tournaments, as follows:

World Cup

Year	Venue	
1975	England	Winners
1979	England	Winners
1983	England	Runners-up

Benson & Hedges World Series Cup in Australia

Year	Opponents	
1979/80	Australia, England	Winners
1981/82	Australia, Pakistan	Winners
1983/84	Australia, Pakistan	Winners
1984/85	Australia, Sri Lanka	Winners

Series (of more than one match) against individual countries

He captained West Indies in nine such series, winning all nine.

Benson and Hedges World Championship in 1984/85 in Australia

He captained West Indies in two matches, losing in the semi-finals.

CENTURIES

TEST MATCHES

118	England	Port-of-Spain	1967/68
113*	England	Bridgetown	1967/68
129	Australia	Brisbane	1968/69
178	Australia	Georgetown	1972/73
132	England	The Oval, London	1973
163	India	Bangalore	1974/75
242*	India	Bombay	1974/75
149	Australia	Perth	1975/76
102	Australia	Melbourne	1975/76
102	India	Bridgetown	1975/76
157	Pakistan	Bridgetown	1976/77
121	Australia	Adelaide	1979/80
101	England	Manchester	1980
100	England	Bridgetown	1980/81
143	India	Port-of-Spain	1982/83
196	India	St John's	1982/83
103	India	Delhi	1983/84
161*	India	Calcutta	1983/84
114	Australia	Brisbane	1984/85

ONE-DAY INTERNATIONALS

102	Australia	Lord's, London	1975

ACKNOWLEDGEMENTS

I am very grateful to these people who have talked to me about Clive Lloyd:
Jeffrey Archer, Mike Atherton, Ronald Austin, Jack Bond, Keith Booker, Mike
Brearley, Chris Broad, Steve Camacho, Don Cameron, Ian Chappell, Tony Cozier,
Colin Croft, Johnny Dennis, Duncan Fearnley, Graeme Fowler, Joel Garner, Lance
Gibbs, Ian Gould, David Gower, Tony Greig, Desmond Haynes, Michael Holding,
Geoff Howarth, David Hughes, Allan Lamb, Brian Lara, Peter Lever, David Lloyd,
Jacklyn Lloyd, Waveney Lloyd, Vince Miller, Mushtaq Mohammad, Deryck
Murray, Harry Pilling, Vivian Richards, Andy Roberts, Gordon Rohlehr, Clem
Seecharan, Jack Simmons, Garry Sobers, Dennis Waight, John Winter.

I have read and occasionally quoted from the following books:
Brian Bearshaw, *From the Stretford End* (Partridge Press, 1990)
Brian Bearshaw, *The Big Hitters* (Macdonald, 1986)
Hilary Beckles, *A Spirit of Dominance: Cricket and Nationalism in the West Indies*
    (Canoe Press, 1999)
Hilary Beckles, *The Development of West Indies Cricket: The Age of Nationalism*
    (Pluto Press, 1999)
Hilary Beckles, *The Development of West Indies Cricket: The Age of Globalisation*
    (Pluto Press, 1999)
Richie Benaud, *On Reflection* (Collins Willow, 1984)
Derek Birley, *A Social History of English Cricket* (Aurum, 2000)
Mike Brearley, *The Art of Captaincy* (Hodder and Stoughton, 1985)
Emilia Viotti da Costa, *Crowns of Glory, Tears of Blood: The Demerara Slave
    Rebellion of 1823* (Oxford University Press, 1997)
Tony Cozier (ed), *The Wisden History of the Cricket World Cup* (Wisden, 2006)
Joel Garner, *Big Bird: Flying High* (Arthur Barker, 1988)
Ray Goble & Keith Sandiford, *75 Years of West Indies Cricket, 1928-2003*
    (Hansib, 2004)
Gordon Greenidge, *The Man in the Middle* (David & Charles, 1980)
Gideon Haigh, *The Cricket War* (Text Publishing, 1993)
Gideon Haigh, *The Summer Game* (Text Publishing, 1997)
Michael Holding, *Whispering Death* (Andre Deutsch, 1993)
Simon Hughes, *A Lot of Hard Yakka* (Headline, 1997)
CLR James, *Beyond a Boundary* (Hutchinson, 1963)
CLR James, *Cricket* (Allison & Busby, 1986)
Frank Keating, *Another Bloody Day in Paradise* (Andre Deutsch, 1981)
Alan Knott, *A Stumper's View* (Stanley Paul, 1973)
Clive Lloyd, *Living for Cricket* (Hutchinson, 1980)
Michael Manley, *A History of West Indies Cricket* (Andre Deutsch, 1988)
Rod Marsh, *Gloves, Sweat and Tears: The Final Shout* (Penguin, 1984)
Malcolm Marshall, *Marshall Arts* (Queen Anne Press, 1987)
Trevor McDonald, *Clive Lloyd* (Granada, 1985)
Trevor McDonald, *Viv Richards* (Pelham, 1984)
Alan Ross (ed), *The Penguin Cricketer's Companion* (Penguin, 1979)

Clem Seecharan, *Muscular Learning: Cricket and Education in the Making of the British West Indies at the end of the 19th Century* (Ian Randle, 2006)

Clem Seecharan, *Sweetening Bitter Sugar: Jock Campbell, the Booker Reformer in British Guiana 1934-1966* (Ian Randle, 2004)

Jack Simmons, *Flat Jack* (Macdonald, 1986)

Garry Sobers, *My Autobiography* (Headline, 2002)

Rob Steen, *Desmond Haynes: the Lion of Barbados* (Weidenfeld Nicolson, 1993)

Jeff Stollmeyer, *Everything Under the Sun* (Stanley Paul, 1983)

Ivo Tennant, *Frank Worrell, A Biography* (Lutterworth Press, 1987)

David Tossell, *Grovel!* (Know the Score, 2007)

Clyde Walcott, *Sixty Years on the Back Foot* (Orion, 2000)

Graeme Wright, *Betrayal: the Struggle for Cricket's Soul* (Witherby, 1993)

A number of the photographs in this book are reproduced by kind permission of their copyright owners, and I would like to thank the following:

PA Photos for Clive batting in the World Cup final and Clive with Brian Lara; Getty Images for Clive batting and bowling; the Marylebone Cricket Club for the portrait of Clive with Sir Richard Hadlee and Barry Richards; Lancashire County Cricket Club for the Lancashire team photo and Clive with Harry Pilling. Other photographs are from Clive's own collection but, if any photographic source believes that any of the remaining photographs are theirs, they should contact Fairfield Books to rectify the matter.

The *Wisden Cricketers' Almanack* has been a valuable resource, as have these magazines: *The Cricketer, Playfair Cricket Monthly, Wisden Cricket Monthly, The Wisden Cricketer.* Articles in these newspapers have helped a great deal too: *The Times, Guardian, Manchester Evening News, Daily Chronicle* (Guyana), *Stabroek News* (Guyana), *Jamaica Gleaner.*

CricketArchive, Cricinfo and the Wisden internet sites have reassured and corrected me on numerous occasions.

I want to thank Singing Francine for the calypso *Tribute to Clive Lloyd* which appeared on her 1976 album *Yours Truly.* I am also grateful to the BBC for its archive and to Sky for its *Pioneers of Cricket* profile of Clive.

I owe five people in particular special thanks:
Frank Keating, Simon Kuper, Stephen Chalke, Peter Mitchell and John Stern.

I would also like to thank:
Jason Lloyd, Chris Aspin, James Motley, Melanie Etherington, Steven Lynch, Gideon Haigh, Ray Funk, Matthew Engel, Scyld Berry, Charbel Mattar, Sinéad Garrigan Mattar, Rupert Lister, Catharine Lister, Jane Durie, Susanna Kendall, Lucy Lethbridge, John Wilkins, Rob Steen, Simon Hardy, John Barnett, Andy Searle, Frances Underwood-Cooke, Kevin Young, Ollie Upton, Tony Godwin, John Skermer, Michael Croton, Malcolm Lorimer, Keith Hayhurst.

To Madeleine, for everything you've done, a million ovations.
And to Clive. Thanks for everything, boss. It's been a real pleasure.

Simon Lister, Chesham, September 2007

THE COWDREY 'SPIRIT OF CRICKET' LECTURE

Delivered by Clive Lloyd at Lord's, 19 July 2004

Mr President, Ladies and Gentlemen, I am honoured to have been asked to speak to you this evening.

First, because you, who are my audience, are such distinguished supporters and servants of the game of cricket.

Second, because the venue is Lord's, so steeped in history and, as I shall explain, with a special place in my own history.

And third, because the lecture is named after a man who so reflected all that is special about it.

Of you, the audience, I would say simply this:

Many of you are involved in cricket administration. And I know what an under-valued role that is. Players – driven as they are, understandably, by the single-minded realisation of their individual and collective talents – will probably always see administrators in an unsympathetic light.

But what you do, what I also now do, has to be done. It will never achieve public acclaim; we will probably always have to be satisfied with knowing that the young and shining stars walk out upon a stage we helped to build. It may be the beginning of a Test for them, but it is also the fulfilment of a longer and more complicated organisational journey that we have shared on their behalf.

Their prize is success and fame; ours the knowledge that we have helped cricket to live on from one generation to the next.

Of this ground, Lord's, what can one say? Its beauty, its history and traditions, its rightful claim to be the home of the game, all these things speak for themselves. I greatly admire the way MCC and its leadership have so well preserved not just the ground physically, but its symbolic role as the guardian of cricket tradition: of excellence, of collective contribution (teamwork), of discipline and, above all, of integrity and fair play. And I applaud MCC's leadership of the Spirit of Cricket campaign.

In my professional career of over twenty years, with the West Indies and with Lancashire, I have experienced many magical moments at Lord's, the most special being at nine in the evening on June 21st in 1975 when, on the balcony, with my team-mates around me, and in front of thousands of jubilant spectators, I held aloft the World Cup. A special moment.

But not just special to me, or to West Indies cricket. That inaugural World Cup was special for the game itself, because I believe it was at that point that all lovers of the game, free spirits and purists alike, accepted that it had changed, that there was now a fresh element that had come to stay, that one-day cricket could, and was, adding a significant dimension to cricket without detracting from it.

And speaking of purists, let me for a moment reflect on that special purist – the pure stroke maker, the pure gentleman – who was Colin Cowdrey. You were right to name this Spirit of Cricket lecture after him, for he embodied all that was best in the game. As a young cricketer, and ultimately an opponent on the field, I was a great admirer of Colin, my liking and respect for him unaffected by the fact that he was the opposing captain in my first Test series with England and led his team to a one-nil victory – one that owed as much to his inspiration of this team as to the many runs he scored. It is noteworthy that, three decades on, he remains England's most prolific batsman against the West Indies, scoring six centuries and over 1,700 runs in 21 Tests.

But rather than lamenting the fact that he was our nemesis, I prefer to acknowledge with gratitude the many qualities he brought to the game. Some saw him as a gentle man, and in a way he was. But I remember, too the dedication, determination and mental toughness that under-pinned his batting, and the calm astuteness, the character and discipline he manifested as a leader. He may have been a generous man off the field, but I can assure you he gave nothing away on it.

He was an equally significant contributor off the field. As a past chairman of the ICC he initiated the ICC Code of Conduct and the move to independent officials in Test and one-day internationals. Without his work, my work as an international referee probably would not exist. He never promoted change for its own sake, but always with the aim of making the game better. And that he did.

As a player and captain, I was greatly influenced by two men: Frank Worrell and Colin Cowdrey. Alas, Frank passed from time to eternity far too young; Colin, too, ended his innings too early. But their inspiration remains. And for me, it was more than just cricket. I was particularly honoured to succeed Colin as chairman of the Heavy Rollers, a vibrant organisation that provides disadvantaged kids in this country with the opportunity to enrich their lives by playing cricket, a point I will return to later.

Mr President, in the essays of Montaigne it is written that "the value of life lies not in the length of days, but in the use we make of them; a man may live long yet live very little." Indeed, much to our chagrin, Sir Frank Worrell left us prematurely at age 42. But it is our good fortune that this reluctant hero lived his life in deeds and not years.

In his brief sojourn, Sir Frank used his gift of the game to transform a society in disrepair and left the world a better place. With purposeful astuteness, he parlayed his athletic gifts and joined the cricket field and political arena, and effectively eradicated the scourge of plantation-type snobbery that had so characterised cricket and Caribbean life.

Sir Frank fiercely disliked the social conditions into which he was born and raised, and selflessly he embraced the daunting challenge of breaking down those fiendish barriers of colour and class. Through education he sought to ameliorate the human condition, and in the spirit of cricket he elevated the level of sportsmanship on playing fields throughout the world.

From Manchester to Melbourne, from Punjab to Port-of-Spain, Sir Frank enriched the life of millions whom he touched on and off the field. And I am honoured, Mr President, to acknowledge that it is his informed leadership, his grace and dignity, and his relentless pursuit of equality and fair play, that inspired my captaincy of the West Indies team and fuelled my goals as a professional.

I aspired to continue the legacy of this legend as defined particularly by the epic 1960-61 West Indies tour of Australia, which epitomised the spirit of cricket and spawned the Frank Worrell Trophy, the symbol of cricket's supremacy between West Indies and Australia.

The late John Arlott – perhaps cricket's greatest, undoubtedly its most revered commentator and scribe – wrote that "cricket is a game of many facets. If it is not all things to all men, at least it is different things to different men. They may see it as violent or pastoral, profound or shallow, romantic or pragmatic, graceful or harsh, dramatic or soporific, compelling or boring."

Were he alive today, he could in current circumstances have added "pure or political, alluring or discouraging" – for these are challenging times for our game.

It is customary to talk about living in changing times, but when you think about it we are ALWAYS living in changing times. What matters, as someone said, is that we "adjust to changing times while holding to unchanging principles." It is in protecting those principles that we face so much challenge today.

In discussing it, I will – perhaps not surprisingly – reflect a little of the concerns of my two predecessors as Cowdrey Lecturer, Barry Richards and Suny Gavaskar.

Barry talked of the growing inequalities between cricket-playing nations.

Suny talked of the growing problems of behaviour on the field.

I, too, will touch on these challenges – and others.

First there is the challenge of growth – and the danger of international inequality within the game.

From my vantage point, I have rejoiced in the growth of cricket across the globe while becoming increasingly concerned at some of the ramifications of both the proliferation of the game and its inevitable commercialisation.

I feel strongly that, as more countries become involved in cricket, and young countries – in cricketing terms – come to the international Test arena, there has to be greater fairness not just on the field but in the administrative and financial arrangements too.

Fairness on the field has little meaning if the teams are unfairly matched because of economic and social variances between their countries.

The ICC has performed miracles in broadening the scope of the game throughout the world. It is now vital that this vibrant organisation gives leadership to ensure the viability of the more economically challenged cricketing nations within its membership.

To that end, the ICC should effect and oversee the equitable distribution of funds – TV revenue, sponsorship, and other monies – between developed and under-developed countries. Currently countries such as my own West Indies are seriously disadvantaged and, as a result, infrastructural development and player development are falling behind. Despite individual exceptions, for sometimes great human character or talent overcomes all obstacles, there is a correlation between national economies and the performance of their sportsmen and women; it is inevitable. Year after year of disproportionate investment in players and facilities must ultimately lead to disproportionate levels of success. This cannot be good for a game that thrives on healthy competition and close contests between countries.

World cricket must decide whether it is to consist of occasional riveting battles between three or four super cricket nations – Australia, England and South Africa, obviously – and one-sided, poorly-attended intervening series between the strong and the weak, or whether it is prepared to do what is necessary to build up the number of competitive Test-playing countries. One way is by spreading the money within the game in order to help develop the facilities and talents of the newer competitors. The other is to create a sensible second tier of international cricket, perhaps built around regional competitions, so that they can slowly, but hopefully steadily, move up to senior Test status.

We should remember too the players. Yes, they get much from the game, but they also give the best years of their lives to it. As an international referee responsible for helping to maintain discipline and fair play within the game, I may seem to players from time to time to be an unsympathetic figure, but I have in fact much sympathy with the concerns they sometimes express. These are the stars of our game, the role models, the few upon whom so many in the game depend for its popularity and success. They should be treated well. They should be communicated with as adults. They should be consulted on matters that affect them. They should be paid fairly to reflect their importance to the game and the brevity of their careers. They should travel in comfort; there have to be better ways to save money than to ask them to travel across the world in economy class. And thoughtful arrangements should be made for players' wives, families and special guests attending international matches. The more we give to them, the more we can expect from them – and, I believe, the more we will get.

But, as I say, we have a right to expect something in return. Not only the expression of their playing talent but behaviour that makes them effective role models for the young and aspiring. Frankly, there is too much unnecessary posturing on the field, and I regret to say not enough honesty in acknowledging dismissals – or boundaries – and thus helping the umpires whom they too easily criticise if they believe they have suffered from a bad decision.

That leads me to the second big challenge facing cricket. It's to do with the laws and their enforcement.

As an international referee I myself represent one of the changes that has taken place in the game. Few know exactly what we do, so let me take a moment to explain, then raise some questions from my experience so far.

The ICC referee is the representative of the ICC at all Test matches and one-day internationals.

It is assumed he is concerned about behaviour on the field. In fact, he is responsible for maintaining an overview on many aspects of the staging of the games: player safety, pitch and out-field preparations, facilities for umpires and officials, the standard of practice facilities, the adequacy of sightscreens, and so on.

But it is true that his primary responsibility is to ensure a fair and sportsmanlike game. Above all, he is there to ensure that the ICC code of conduct is upheld, to investigate and adjudicate upon alleged breaches of the rules and, if necessary, apply appropriate sanctions to anyone found to be in breach.

He makes judgements on the basis of four levels of defined behaviour: from showing dissent or using offensive language to overt racism, gambling or attempted intimidation of officials.

A key role, and an area of special concern to me, is to contribute to the standard of umpiring.

The referee is not there to umpire and has no right to interfere with the role of the umpires under the laws of cricket. But he is there to help the umpires by maintaining an overview of how the game is being played that they, with their concentration ball by ball, cannot be expected to do.

It is also his role to assess and report on the performance of umpires. It is not only the TV commentators and audience who look closely at every decision; every appeal for a dismissal is recorded and viewed, and detailed notes on the quality of the umpiring are kept so that the ICC is always working with umpires to improve performance.

Let me say that I have the utmost sympathy for these gentlemen. How many people have their minute-by-minute performance monitored by cameras and considered and reported upon, not by annual performance reviews, but on a daily basis? And that's after they have already been reviewed and commented upon on television in front of millions. There are times when one wonders why anyone would do it!

What I do believe is this: if technology is going increasingly to be used to reflect on the performance of the umpires – both by television and by officialdom – surely umpires should also have the opportunity to use it, to improve upon or supplement their performance.

How can it be right to ask an umpire to take a split-second decision based on his own eyesight and hearing while everyone else then judges and, if justified, and sometimes when unjustified, criticises that decision, having made use of technology designed for the purpose?

It is time to use technology to the full extent. Umpires should be able to defer to the precision of Hawkeye, particularly in determining whether a batsman is lbw, whether there has been a bat-pad catch, and whether a batsman is caught behind the wicket where there is dispute over whether the ball has or has not been played.

I know there are problems about the time this will take, especially if a team is inclined to excessive appealing. But it should be possible to design restrictions on appealing, of the use of technology, monitored by the referee.

We should not delay any longer in acting on this. I believe there is overwhelming support for it. And it is in the interests of everyone, not just the umpires, but the players and public too.

Although we have some outstanding umpires on the international panel, the challenge of umpiring in today's conditions is greater than it has ever been and, speaking frankly, too many mistakes are being made. They are made not just because it is almost beyond human beings to make faultless decisions when things happen so fast.

There is a lot at stake in international cricket these days; what matters is that we get it right. And if the technology will help, the technology should be used.

Another challenge arises from the need to maintain standards of behaviour on the field of play.

This varies. There have been recent series that have been a joy to referee, such has been the good-natured spirit in which they've been played.

There have been some that have been less satisfactory.

I know that last year Suny Gavaskar expressed his concern about sledging and behaviour on the field. Before each match I talk to the captains and make it clear the ICC's view about how the game should be played. Once it begins, I keep the closest eye on this.

What I would say is that there has always been a bit of banter out there, and sometimes the frustration of a bowler whose appeal has been disallowed leads to a momentary lapse, and the players and the game are big enough to live with this.

But I agree with Suny that there is no need for nastiness, it is not necessary, it is not within the spirit of the game, and is best stamped out before 'the level of the bar' drops and we find ourselves tolerating as 'business as usual' behaviour that is foreign to the best traditions of the game.

In taking a firm line, referees are not being unnecessarily prissy. They are, I believe, reflecting what the game's players and supporters want.

Nor are they there to make cricket less competitive. It should be hard-fought out there. There's a lot at stake.

I learned as captain of the West Indies the importance of winning. It is by winning that Test teams rally their countries behind them, win sponsorship and encourage the young to the game.

Some say to me that they find it surprising that I am a referee when I myself led the West Indies in an uncompromising way. But I did not believe then, and I do not believe now, that playing cricket in the right spirit means not playing it hard. It simply means playing it within the laws of the game and playing it honestly. I believe we always did.

I would like to touch on just one other area where reform is necessary. Over the past 15 years or so, one of the more revolutionary developments has been the day-night game. Undoubtedly, it has colour and commercial appeal. As a referee, however, I have to say that it does present the teams with starkly contrasting conditions, providing one with a considerable advantage – frankly: the difference between day and night. I believe, therefore, that such fixtures should not be scheduled for quarter-finals, semi-finals or finals. Once more, there's a lot at stake; at this level, fairness between teams must be paramount. It cannot be right that the game is settled with the toss.

Mr President, in recent years through the prism of our sport, we have seen the good, the bad and the ugly. As we contemplate the world today, we wonder whether cricket is not in fact a reflection of life. I referred earlier to John Arlott. He also wrote, "No sport runs deeper into life than cricket."

As such, cricket has from time to time found itself on the cutting edge of progress, the very fact that it is being played becoming a reflection of peace between peoples.

Nowhere was this more so than in recent weeks when we saw the very best of cricket as India toured Pakistan for the first time in fourteen years. As the tour got under way, the Pakistan President expressed the hope that it would improve relations between the South Asian neighbours.

It was indeed a memorable moment in recent cricket history, although we should note that it was caused by the improved political relations between the two countries and only possible because the politicians decided to allow it. Still, it added to the improvement in relations between the two countries, and we should be proud of that.

The issue of the cancellation of tours is, thank heavens, not one for referees, but it is one that has once more been placed firmly on cricket's agenda. I do not intend to take sides tonight, other perhaps than to say that those who believe cricket tours can be influential for good – as they are perceived in Pakistan and India – must surely accept that, if they can have that influence, it must follow that there can occasionally be a converse side, too. It is tricky territory.

I do believe, however, that whatever one's view about the imposition of moral judgements into decision-making on tours, cricket should not isolate itself from the needs of the communities that live beyond its boundaries for it can do so much good.

Lord's is a leader in this respect, for who can but admire the outstanding charitable work of the Lord's Taverners?

I strongly recommend that the ICC and the entire international cricket fraternity become more involved in community outreach ventures and make their own contribution to improving the human condition whenever and wherever possible.

As cricket generates new wealth from increased commercialisation and the proliferation of the international game, so it can afford to share with those impoverished souls in our community, many of whom live vicariously through their super-heroes in white.

I know you will join me in commending the Indian cricketers for arranging for a ten-year-old Pakistani girl suffering from cancer to received free treatment in India from three leading hospitals in Vellore, Bangalore and Bombay. Such a humanitarian gesture speaks volumes about the wider spirit of cricket and what it can do for the world.

In past days, it was taken for granted that touring sports teams would visit hospitals and schools and disadvantaged communities, bringing a brief moment of attention and hope into their lives. Cricket, as well as our countries, would be better off it we could firmly re-establish that tradition.

Mr President, these are, as I have said, challenging days. But there is much to say that is good. As I have mentioned there has been the return to the cricket fields of the teams of India and Pakistan. In this country, there's been the fresh success of a young England team, and the success of Twenty20, a development that will without doubt find its place on the international stage.

And, around the world, big crowds continue to come, provided they believe they will see genuine competition.

And it is in the creation of genuine competition that the biggest challenge lies.

That will not happen by accident.

It means the strong helping the weak.

If they do, they will strengthen the whole international game.

If they do not, three or four countries will end up endlessly playing themselves – and everyone will lose patience with that.

This is a genuine case of helping the few being for the greater good.

In the meantime, let us at every level of the game embrace MCC's ideal of the spirit of cricket.

Let us exorcise the bad and the ugly.

Let us encourage honesty and integrity.

Cricket came to assume the connotation of propriety. Hence the phrase, "It's just not cricket!"

We can be proud of that.

We must protect it.

And with your continued leadership, we will.

INDEX

Clive Lloyd and his family are not included.

Acfield, David 67
Adams, Jimmy 183,189
Alderman, Terry 168
Aldridge, Brian 136
Alexander, Gerry 84,85
Alley, Bill 108,135
Allott, Paul 160,172
Ambrose, Curtly 182
Amiss, Dennis 19,107
Amsterdam, Leslie 37
Andrews, Eamonn 136
Andrews, Gordon 89,90
Archer, Jeffrey 23
Arlott, John 76,92,93,160
Ashe, Arthur 116
Asif Iqbal 68,89
Atherton, Mike 172
Austin, Richard 121,122,139
Austin, Ronald 22,36,40

Bacchus, Faoud 130,142,192
Bacher, Ali 180
Bailey, David 82
Baptiste, Eldine 141,144,147,150
Barker, Keith 52
Barlow, Eddie 64
Barrington, Ken 54,108
Bearshaw, Brian 99
Beckles, Hilary 194
Beckles, Lennox 58
Bedi, Bishan 104,106,110
Bedser, Alec 108
Bell, Ian 13,14,80
Benaud, Richie 113
Bird, Dickie 92,110
Bishop, Ian 198
Bland, Colin 20,68
Blofeld, Henry 100
Bond, Florence 61
Bond, Jack 20,57,60,61,63,65, 67-9,76,80-2,99,173,175
Border, Allan 138,159,179
Botham, Ian 7,137,144,153,156,203
Boyce, Keith 79,87,88,94
Boycott, Geoff 43,69,76, 131,178

Bradman, Don 51,72,73,103, 136,145,150,153,158,202
Brancker, Rawle 43
Brearley, Mike 15,109,110,131,148,170
Brind, Harry 100
Brown, David 76,77
Burnham, Forbes 78,79,81,111,139
Busby, Matt 20
Butcher, Basil 22,35,38,40,41, 43,46,51,55,56,65
Butts, Clive 141
Bynoe, Robin 42

Camacho, Steve 28,39,40,138,172,183
Cameron, Don 134
Carew, Joey 122
Carr, Donald 17
Cavanagh, Bryce 193
Chanderpaul, Shivnarine 99,189
Chandrasekhar, Bhagwat 46,47,104,110,160
Chapman, Brian 67
Chappell, Greg 94,101,127
Chappell, Ian 70,94,96,101,119,126,127
Charlton, Bobby 20
Chichester, Charles 42
Christiani, Ernest 25
Christiani, Harry 25
Christiani, Robert 25,27,45
Clarke, Sylvester 139,147,150,165
Close, Brian 70,105,106,108
Collingwood, Paul 12,80
Collymore, Corey 201,202
Collymore, Rex 38,39
Compton, Denis 27
Constantine, Learie 51,60,68,77,116
Cook, Alistair 201,202
Cook, Lily 50
Cowdrey, Colin 27,54,55,161
Cozier, Tony 55,75,111,162,163

Croft, Colin 117,120-2,127,130, 134, 135,138,139,150,151,192
Cross, Mervyn 132
Curtis, Tony 29

Dalmiya, Jagmohan 179
Dalrymple, Jamie 15,17
Daniel, Wayne 104,107, 108,127,141,147,192
Davis, Charlie 49,75
Davis, Winston 157
De Beer, Arrie 11,12
Dennis, Johnny 9,10,13
D'Oliveira, Basil 43
Dubois, William 29
Dujon, Jeff 165,167
Durani, Salim 46

Edrich, John 108
Edwards, Fidel 189,197
Edwards, Raymond 188
Edwards, Ross 91
Elliott, Charlie 108
Engineer, Farokh 60,61,65,84

Fearnley, Duncan 16
Fernandes, Maurice 30
Fernando, Dilhara 17
Flack, Bert 107
Fletcher, Duncan 7,15
Flintoff, Andrew 172,175
Foster, Maurice 87,192
Fowler, Graeme 144-6,148,149, 153,154,156,157,172,173
Fredericks, Roy 19,38,79,87, 90,91,95,101,102,104,123,141

Gaekwad, Aunshuman 104
Garner, Joel 115,117,120, 122 124,127,130,138,144-6,149-51, 156,157,163,178,192,204
Gaskin, Berkeley 21,40-3
Gaskin, Winifred 41
Gavaskar, Sunil 12,73
Gibbs, Lance 23,25,26,28,30,36,38, 77,87,102,104,161,177,192

Gibbs, Oscar 66
Gilchrist, Roy 51
Gilmour, Gary 90,92,93,108
Goddard, John 42,43
Gomes, Larry 130,142,144,154-6,192
Gomez, Gerry 42
Gooch, Graham 131
Goodall, Fred 134,135
Gordon, Ken 197
Gould, Ian 8-18,174
Gower, David 7,144,148,153-5,170,171
Grant, Bernie 23
Graveney, Tom 27,54,55
Greenidge, Gordon 12,84,87, 90,91,122,141,142,146,149, 153,154,163,165,179,189,192
Greig, Tony 71,104-11,115,117,118,120
Griffith, Charlie 40,41,48,51,58,64,80,108,195
Griffith, Teddy 38,49

Hadlee, Richard 7,134
Haigh, Gideon 127
Hair, Darrell 8,9,18
Hall, Wes 29,47,49,51,58,64, 80,108,163,164,180,195,204
Harmison, Steve 9,10,13
Harper, Roger 141,144,156
Hartley, Peter 17,18
Hawke, Bob 159
Hawke, Neil 51
Hayes, Frank 76
Haynes, Desmond 12,23,118,120-2,141,142, 149,154-6,165,167,168,171
Headley, George 45,50,51,56
Hector, Richard 26
Henry, Omar 10
Higgs, Ken 61
Holder, Vanburn 87,88,94,95, 102,104,107,130,151,192
Holding, Michael 8,19,102-4, 106-11,118,120,124,125, 127,130,134,138,139,144, 146,150-2,156,163,166, 171,173,189,192,204
Holland, Bob 159
Hooper, Carl 181,189
Hopwood, Len 60

Howarth, Geoff 133
Hughes, David 67,68,81,98,99,102
Hughes, Kim 144,158,168
Hughes, Simon 15,16
Hunte, Conrad 43,46,47,51,163,195
Hutton, Len 26

Ibadulla, Billy 68
Illingworth, Raymond 82
Imtiaz Ali 103,104

Jackman, Robin 99,100,139
Jackson, Michael 143
Jacobs, Bill 72
James, CLR 162,194
James, Mr 31
Javed Miandad 88
Jayasuriya, Sanath 10
Jayawardene, Mahela 8,10,14
Jessop, Gilbert 110
Johnston, Brian 67,174
Jones, Jeff 55
Julien, Bernard 68,79,83, 86-9,102,103,107,130,192
Jumadeen, Raphick 103,104,107

Kallicharran, Alvin 75,77,82,87,91,118, 122,139,149,168,192
Kallicharran, Derek 141
Kanhai, Rohan 22,35,38-41, 43, 46,71,77,82,83, 87,88,91-3,163,192
Kapil Dev 141
King, Bennett 201
King, Collis 87,130,131,139,192
King, Lester 38
Knight, Roger 10
Knott, Alan 19

Laird, Bruce 120
Laker, Jim 91,119
Lamb, Allan 149,153,156,157
Lambert, Leslaine 141
Lara, Brian 99,181,183,189, 191,195,197-9,201
Larkins, Wayne 131
Lawry, Bill 133

Lawson, Geoff 179
Lee, Peter 81
Lehmann, Darren 12,13
Lever, Peter 59,60,62,65,68,69,81,173
Lillee, Dennis 71,90,91,93-5, 100,102,105,108,147,148,152
Lindwall, Ray 28
Livingstone, Danny 57
Llong, Nigel 8-10,16,18
Lloyd, Andy 144,146-8
Lloyd, David 60,66-8,70, 76,77,80,82,98-100,173,175
L'Ouverture, Toussaint 29

McCosker, Rick 94
McDermott, Craig 159
McMorris, Easton 42
Madray, Ivan 23
Majid Khan 89
Malcolm, Devon 201
Malinga, Lasith 17,18
Mallett, Ashley 71,117
Mandela, Nelson 107,180-2
Mankad, Vinoo 53
Manley, Michael 120,139
Marley, Cecil 77,78
Marsh, Rod 93,96,127,168
Marshall, Malcolm 130,141, 142,144,146,149-51,154, 155,157,159,180,183,191,197
Marshall, Roy 57
Martindale, Manny 51,116
May, Peter 38,154
Mayers, Vince 40
Mendis, Gehan 155
Mendonca, Ivor 23
Milburn, Colin 43
Miller, Carlyle 38
Miller, Keith 28
Misson, Frank 51
Monty 34
Mortimore, John 67
Moseley, Ezra 147
Muralitharan, Muttiah 7,8,14,15,17,18,148
Murray, David 139
Murray, Deryck 77,84,87-90, 95,96,102,106,111,114,121, 122,124,125,128,132,134, 151,152,171,172,192,198
Murray, Geoff 38

222

Murray, John 108
Mushtaq Mohammad 64,115

Nadkarni, 'Bapu' 46
Nicholas, Mark 7
Nurse, Seymour
43,45,46,51,163

Oakman, Alan 77
Obama, Barack 29
O'Reilly, Bill 174
Owens, Jesse 140

Packer, Kerry 113-132,160,198
Padgett, Doug 69,70
Padmore, Albert
103,104,107,108,169
Palmer, Ken 174
Parker, John 134
Parks, Jim 55
Pascoe, Len 125
Patel, Brijesh 104
Patterson, Patrick 147,174
Patterson, PJ 197
Pearce, Tom 150
Persaud, Indal 38
Pervez Mir 88
Philpott, Peter 39
Pietersen, Kevin 14,175
Pilling, Harry 59-63,65,76
Pinnock, Renford 49
Plunkett, Liam 12
Pocock, Pat 148,149
Poitier, Sidney 29
Pollock, Graeme 64,73
Ponsford, Bill 202
Powell, Daren 189
Prince Charles 16
Prince Philip 96
Pringle, Derek 145
Procter, Mike 64,67,96

Ramadhin, Sonny 27
Reeve, Dermot 174
Renison, Patrick Muir 178
Rhoades, Cedric 82
Richards, Barry 7,64
Richards, Vivian 19,21,84,87,
88,94,102,103,107,110,122,
125,130,131,137-9,141,142,
145-7,149,154,159,163,165,
167,168,177,189,192,203,204

Richardson, Richie 141,158,189
Roberts, Andy 84,86-90,
98,102,103,105,107,108,
118,120,122,125,127,132,
138,141,150-3,155,163,
171,178,180,192,198,201
Rohlehr, Gordon 34
Robertson, Austin 115
Roopnarine, Rupert 34
Rowe, Lawrence
75,104,132,139,168
Rutnagur, Dickie 47,142

Sainsbury, Gary 175
Sajid Mahmood 12
Sammy, Darren 203
Sangakkara, Kumar 12,18
Sarwan, Ramnaresh 99,189
Savage, Alfred 178
Seecharan, Clem 23,163,196
Sharpe, Phil 69
Shepherd, John 63
Short, Peter 75
Shuttleworth, Ken 81
Simmons, Jack
15,16,20,57,61,62,65,81,139
Simpson, Bobby 19
Singh, Dr 26
Smith, Mike 77
Snow, John 120
Sobers, Garry 27-9,39-48,
55,56,58,64,65,70,75,83,
84,103,111,119,153,163,
164,182,190,195,203,204
Solomon, Joe
22,35,38,40,41,44,45
Speed, Malcolm 13
Spencer, Lady Diana 16
Spencer, Tom 95,100
Statham, Brian 61
Steele, David 19
Stollmeyer, Jeff 42,79,120,126
Strauss, Andrew 7,8,13,14
Sullivan, John 62,65,205

Taylor, Brian 66
Tharanga, Upul 12,13
Thomas, 'Bruiser' 36
Thomas, Frankie 184
Thomson, Jeff 90,94,95,100,
102,105,108,125,147,148
Todd, Eric 67

Trescothick, Marcus 14
Turner, Alan 94
Turner, Glenn 68
Turner, Stuart 66,67

Underwood, Derek 63,107

Vaas, Chaminda 180
Venkataraghavan, Srini 46
Viswanath, Gundappa 104

Waight, Dennis
125,126,137,138,159,193
Walcott, Clyde 23,27,38,51,
80,109,131,136,162
Walker, Max 90-2,94,108
Walsh, Courtney
150,182,185,189,198
Wardle, Johnny 51
Warne, Shane 104,148
Washbrook, Cyril 59,60,203
Wasim Bari 88,90
Wasim Raja 89
Watson, Chester 51
Weekes, Everton
27,28,45,51,72,162
West, Peter 94
Whitlam, Gough 78
Wight, Norman 35
Wilberforce, William 29
Williams, Charles 177
Williams, Eric 111
Willis, Bob 76,77,120,144
Wills, Fred 21,34-6,38,40,161
Wiltshire, Cedric 42
Wiltshire, Colin 26
Winter, John 50,51,53,54
Wishart, Ken 39
Woodcock, John
76,93,98,107,145,158
Woods, Tiger 182
Worrell, Frank 21,27,38,39,
42,43,45,46,48,49,55,84,
101,148,161-3,170,177,191

Yardley, Norman 153

FAIRFIELD BOOKS

The following is a full list of published titles.
Those with an asterisk are out of print – but it may be possible to track down copies.

Runs in the Memory
County Cricket in the 1950s
by **Stephen Chalke**

* Caught in the Memory
County Cricket in the 1960s
by **Stephen Chalke**

One More Run
by **Stephen Chalke**
talking with Bryan 'Bomber' Wells

Fragments of Idolatry
by **David Foot**

* At the Heart of English Cricket
The Life and Memories of Geoffrey Howard
by **Stephen Chalke**

* The Appeal of the Championship
Sussex in the Summer of 1981
by **John Barclay**

Harold Gimblett
Tormented Genius of Cricket
by **David Foot**

Guess My Story
The Life and Opinions of Keith Andrew
by **Stephen Chalke**

* No Coward Soul
The Remarkable Story of Bob Appleyard
by **Stephen Chalke** and **Derek Hodgson**

Born To Bowl
The Life and Times of Don Shepherd
by **Douglas Miller**

Charles Palmer
More Than Just a Gentleman
by **Douglas Miller**

Ken Taylor – Drawn to Sport
by **Stephen Chalke**

* Sixty Summers
Somerset Cricket since the War
by **David Foot** and **Ivan Ponting**

It's Not Just Cricket
by **Peter Walker**

* A Summer of Plenty
George Herbert Hirst in 1906
by **Stephen Chalke**

Tom Cartwright
The Flame Still Burns
by **Stephen Chalke**

Five Five Five
Holmes and Sutcliffe in 1932
by **Stephen Chalke**

Supercat
The Authorised Biography of Clive Lloyd
by **Simon Lister**

For full details of prices and availability,
or to join the mailing list for news of future titles, please contact
Fairfield Books, 17 George's Road, Bath BA1 6EY
telephone 01225-335813